DIFFERENT DRUMMERS

A STUDY OF CULTURAL ALTERNATIVES IN FICTION

by Meredith Cary

The Scarecrow Press, Inc.
Metuchen, N.J., & London 1984

Library of Congress Cataloging in Publication Data

Cary, Meredith.
 Different drummers.

 Bibliography: p.
 Includes index.
 1. English fiction--Women authors--History and criticism. 2. American fiction--Women authors--History and criticism. 3. Individuality in literature. 4. Deviant behavior in literature. 5. Social norms in literature. 6. Idealism in literature. I. Title.
 PR111.C37 1984   823'.009'9287   84-1346
 ISBN 0-8108-1689-X

Copyright © 1984 by Meredith Cary
Manufactured in the United States of America

TABLE OF CONTENTS

Foreword	vii
1. Introduction	1
2. Alternative Groups	13
3. International Options	59
4. Ethnic Alternatives	92
5. New Roles in Old Societies	134
6. The Eccentric Role	181
7. Escapes	212
8. The Sum Greater Than the Parts	241
Bibliography of Recommended Works	283
Chronology of Recommended Works	286
Index	291

ACKNOWLEDGEMENTS

As is true of so many of us who work in this field, my most basic gratitude must go to Florence Howe for her disinterested support and perfectly timed encouragement. I am deeply indebted to my dean, James Davis, who has fostered like an administrator and encouraged like a friend. Among the many individuals who deserve my thanks for helping, encouraging, advising or discussing in the areas of their own skills, interests and specialties, I would like to mention, particularly: Phyllis Bultmann, William Bultmann, Evelyn Darrow, Carol Diers, Golden Larsen, Lawrence Lee, Natalie Sally Mackler, Rita Oleyar, Kathleen Orange, Sara Stamey, Dal Symes, Ken Symes, Herbert Taylor. In addition, there are those whose generous belief does not submit to categories--Deborah Larsen, Susan Cary, R. D. Brown.

FOREWORD

People who do not fit in have fascinated writers since the first novel was written in English. The fiction this idea has produced presents a remarkable world view. It assumes there are people who wish to live up to their best selves without feeling the need to tell the rest of the world that it should do so, too.

Characters governed by this principle are disconcerting. They do their duty cheerfully, but what they think of as their duty turns out to be surprising. They want to lead an ethical life, but they do not force their values on everyone else, as moral innovators usually do. Even as parents, they do not dictate. They trust to learning, instead.

The result is charm. These people are cheerful, affectionate, resourceful, optimistic, compassionate, sensitive, generous, tolerant, reasonable, often funny, and always "good." They are gallant, rather than heroic, because they never wish to dominate. They are seductively sure that everyone is already doing the best they can. This conviction helps them bear with people who try to make them over into something normal. It also strengthens their belief that variety in value systems, attitudes and manners is a basic social need.

Fiction which presents such individuals may take any form. It may be philosophical, or funny, or both. It may use anything from war to the kitchen for its plot. It may tell the story of one man or one woman, or it may have a cast large enough to require a chart. It may be told in letters, or a monologue, or have a narrator, or use an omniscient point of view. The ending may be happy, or wistful, or merely brave. All these enormous differences turn into secondary detail in comparison to the idea the novels share.

The people who write such fiction are as different

from each other as the individual novels are. Some of them were charismatic, but some were recluses. Some were privileged, but some were in prison for debt. Some were remarkably free, but others had as many as a dozen children. Some led such conventional lives that they are always referred to by their husband's name. Others were involved in anything available, working as a spy, serving in a war zone, getting a Ph.D. Some were intellectual and worked out a theory to support their ideas. Others were devout and simply believed. Some knew what they were talking about because they were themselves remarkable, either frankly, in public, or as a kind of secret life. Others were clearly not the kind of person they wrote about--sometimes once, in an almost puzzled way, and sometimes over and over, as if trying to understand, or hoping to settle a score.

Diversity in source and form is appropriate to fiction about living differently. It documents how widespread and durable the idea is. Examples of this kind of novel have cropped up continuously and have been loved by their contemporaries for three hundred years. Such survival outside the support of literary history and its critical norms is evidence of an abiding dream.

1. INTRODUCTION

When Virginia Woolf called for a new kind of novel which would not provoke "the usual feelings" in "the usual places," she was invoking the future and did not mention that such a literature had been flourishing for centuries. Since the novel's beginning, women have been creating fictional worlds in which unusual people are accepted casually and allowed to get on with their nontypical lives in an open way, without defensiveness. In such novels, social variety makes room for women as individuals and offers relief from the uniformity of social norms silently assumed as universal in more traditional works with larger reputations.

It is inevitable that the major reputations go to works which arouse "the usual feelings," since traditional literary history embraces the "usual" values and enforces them under the banner of verisimilitude. We cannot expect traditional literary historians to describe a novel of social alternatives when traditional criticism does not recognize that such a novel exists.

Silence about variety is not willful neglect. Footnotes to standard discussions include scattered praise for many of these undervalued works. They are sometimes mentioned as brilliantly written, and a critical aside may even point them out as interesting "despite their faults." This kind of uneasy reference demonstrates the power of novels which depart from the usual attitudes in so many ways that they turn into puzzles, for traditional critics. The difficulty comes from the obviously talented writing, which should make them "masterpieces." But their assumptions about people and behavior are so unusual that their plots, themes and characterizations cannot be fitted into the usual pigeonholes of criticism. These characteristics seem like mixed signals to standard critics, who solve the problem by deciding that such works are "flawed masterpieces" or "brilliant failures," instead.

When the "flaw" is analyzed, traditional judgment usually mentions the sad lack of some basic element of fiction. Elizabeth Gaskell's <u>Cranford</u> turns into a collection of sketches, or an idyll, for example. Its events and outcomes do not match standard views of what is probable, and therefore they are not recognized as a plot.

Similarly, the characters in Charlotte Smith's <u>The Old Manor House</u> are not developed according to the usual concept of male and female response to maturation and other stresses. Her unusual results are not considered innovative --they are used to show that characterization has been omitted from an otherwise interesting work.

Nonstandard themes also cause trouble. When a novel's point is too unusual to be dealt with in a routine way, the work may be made manageable through downgrading to an unreliable form of journalism, as is done traditionally to Aphra Behn's <u>Oroonoko</u>.

Whatever is singled out as the root of the problem, the result in traditional literary terms is the same. These novels do not fit smoothly into standard overviews of fiction. Inevitably, they sink into a critical silence as soon as their contemporary audience has been satisfied.

The loss to future readers is unfortunate--Woolf may not have known that the experimentation she called for was already going on. But a failure to give appropriate credit is by no means the most serious result. Far more important than courtesy to the dead is the damage to future writers, who are cut off from an enduring strand in the fiction of the past. Intellectual isolation wastefully confronts each generation with the task of discovering alternatives and options all over again, as if from the beginning.

This unfortunate silence does have one good effect in that it helps demonstrate the importance of such socially and psychologically innovative works. A less vital impulse would die out in the face of persistent neglect, but there is an astonishing durability to fiction which creates a world where the "usual" roles are no more than neutral possibilities in a wide range of social options offered without ranking or preference.

It is a vision which has continued to flourish almost underground, generation after generation, to the relief of the writers who work in the field and to the delight of readers who accept the reality of such a view. Contemporary readers avidly enjoy such fiction. And when novels of this type are unearthed, they maintain their enormous appeal, even after hundreds of years.

What is the source of their power? Sylvia Townsend Warner's Lolly Willowes demonstrates an answer. In Warner's reuse of the Faustus legend, it is a woman who sells her soul. The reason for her bargain is the traditional one --she can find no other way to satisfy the desire which has gripped her life, and she considers her goal so crucial to her existence as to make it worth any sacrifice.

It is the subject of the bargain that makes Lolly Willowes different from the usual Faustus. Warner's heroine sells her soul to escape from the standard female role. She considers the arrangement worth every penny of the price.

The extravagance of this woman's eagerness to escape the "usual" symbolizes the importance of the idea, even though less drastic measures normally suffice. Warner's novel goes on to demonstrate a number of the other elements common to fiction of this sort.

Typically, escape from normality comes only after standard society has been allowed to display itself in its most favorable light. This plot feature shows that atrocious violations are not the point. Instead, the true difficulty comes from applying any social standard uniformly. Since it is the uniformity and not the particular standard which is at fault, fictional demonstrations need to present conventional people sympathetically, respecting them as tolerant within their norms. Average ways of life must be recognized as working out well for people who fit into their roles. Only when problems come from the principle of "normality," and not from the fact that people sometimes misapply the rules, can fiction show how uniform assumptions afflict unique individuals who move beyond the norms.

Another representative element is the recognition that a new "normality" cannot be substituted for standard attitudes. Doing so would only shift the outsider's role, leaving people who are now conventional without a social niche. Accordingly, the right to be traditional is carefully maintained as one possibility in a behavioral smorgasbord.

Routinely, no explanation is given by individuals who need a different value system. For one thing, self-justification is not necessary when choice is genuinely free. To the contrary, an effective description of one person's choice might turn out to be repressive if it accidentally put pressure on family and friends who would otherwise be content with a socially usual life.

A frequent drawback to the lack of publicity about alternatives is that characters face their dilemma without knowing others have gone before them. Their struggle is prolonged by the conviction that they must be the only person alive who does not fit into normal society. But they seem to benefit from this pressure, since it tests the strength of their conviction before they commit themselves.

Once free, they sometimes discover a new social group, as is the case in Lolly Willowes. But the alternative community may not strike them as a source for peers. Warner's heroine decides not to join any group, for example, since even the damned are left alone by Lolly Willowes' tactful devil, when that is what they prefer.

If they do decide to join a new group, they are welcomed automatically, on the basis of their choice. Yet they are committed to nothing, since participation remains voluntary. Both old and new community members are entirely free to come and go at their own option, without judgment or comment from others in the group.

These elements in common emphasize the silent links among novels organized around the idea that individuality is freely available to those who want it. Individual examples tend to be as varied as their central assumption about variety would imply. Nevertheless, any literary form will develop into types. Patterns in this fiction have emerged as writers struggle to protect the social and personal growth of the intensely individual personalities for whom their unusual worlds exist. It is the categories established by its writers which offer the most helpful approach to this fiction of social alternatives.

Alternative Groups

Refugees from the usual world may deliberately construct a society of their own, since solitude is not their goal.

Sometimes, new social groups are organized around elaborately worked-out definitions which guarantee respect for individuals. For example, Sarah Fielding's David Simple justifies a careful redefinition of friendship and then uses it as the basis for a community which will be utopian for the people who are comfortable in its unusual value system.

Equally effective works may avoid even the appearance of rule setting by refusing to launch into definitions or to identify commonly held principles in any overt way. Instead, they may establish a kind of neighborhood and allow its assumptions to emerge informally in social gatherings. In this way, Elizabeth Gaskell's Cranford depicts unflagging tolerance without adding official perorations on the principle and practice of caritas.

International Options

Variety does not always depend upon a unique and separate social design. Some authors are satisfied that cultural discrepancies among nations provide sufficient opportunity for individual development. The resulting novels are crucially different from the typical international novel, where one culture is finally preferred as "better" in some universal way. Instead of a hierarchy of nations, novels of variety work out a multinational point of view which allows characters to find the value system most appropriate to their particular needs without downgrading the nations not chosen as deficient or cruel.

Culture shopping takes more than one form. In American fiction, choice may be presented as relatively absolute. Edith Wharton's Age of Innocence, for example, shows New York society forcing young women into one or the other of only two available social roles. One of the heroines is comfortable with this situation, but the second heroine does not fit into either possibility. Searching for a social view which will make room for her, she turns to Washington, D.C., but she is not accepted as herself until she finds Paris.

English fiction does not need to rest upon such final choices since European cultures offer different standards. Such convenience lets people seek their freedom stage by stage, instead of all at once. Geraldine Jewsbury's Zoe points out how nations allow freedom to their citizens for different reasons and in different ways. A culture which is tolerant of young people may be very limited in its views of maturity, for example. On the other hand, a nation determined to maintain the purity of its young may be refreshingly detached in confronting adult eccentricity. Jewsbury uses such patterns of difference to show that cultures should be chosen on a temporary basis and set aside again by individuals as they grow into new stages. The individual options are pre-existing and are accepted by the social structures which include them. Therefore, they are a route to non-confrontational and guilt-free lives for individuals who bother to choose.

Ethnic Alternatives

International variety takes on a particular form when ethnic considerations are added. Novels in this category tend to be less optimistic than are their all-white parallels, since their characters consider themselves to be less free to move around in search of suitable environments. Nevertheless, choices crossing ethnic divisions in various societies remain a possibility which has been explored in several ways.

A politically fostered cultural exchange is the basis of Nina Bawden's Under the Skin. The growing astonishment of an originally eager African visitor to London shows how differently cultures may view correct behavior. Social reactions which are too inevitable to provoke comment in one society may be weirdly unjustifiable in a different context. Citizens may trample each other's sensitivities in the most well-intentioned way through observing irrelevant rules. Since Bawden's novel ends with an exchange visit by the Black man's London host family, the work maintains a dispassionate refusal to choose between cultures on any basis other than suitability to particular individuals.

In American fiction, a tangled ancestry is the usual access to social variety. Nella Larsen's Quicksand is a particularly interesting example, since a first glance suggests that it intends to compare femaleness and Blackness as influences on personal growth. By the time the reader has decided that each role has its own area, the novel has compared the very different value systems of the Black community and the white community in the United States. It goes on to examine ethnic identity in contrasting American and European norms.

A trip abroad is not always required. Margaret Walker's Jubilee looks at three value systems within American society. In the beginning, Jubilee's heroine is exposed to discrepancies between the values held by free Blacks and those embraced by slaves. After the war, she is accepted without comment by whites, since she resembles her slave-owning father in physical appearance. As a result, she is able to explore "white" values with an insider's view. Her discovery of this third social system impels her to reexamine her own privately assembled rules about behavior.

New Roles in Old Societies

Alternative ways of life are sometimes chosen on an intensely private basis. There may be no optional society available, and even sympathy may not emerge. In such circumstances, unique individuals who will not accept social isolation must be resourceful even beyond the courage routinely shown by the extraordinary people who populate these fictional worlds. Forced to be overt, they may describe their needs, when they realize normal options will not provide for them. Talking about themselves allows some kind of contact with the uncomprehending world which would be mutilating to them if they failed to resist the normal mold. Communication is the central issue here, since they do not want to be completely isolated, and self-doubt is not a problem, once they have accepted their own uniqueness.

How to survive unmaimed without social or intellectual support is a basic problem in Toni Morrison's Sula. This novel traces the experiences of a woman who "has sung all the songs there are," as she says. Moving beyond all the existing possibilities, she develops a unique role for herself and to a certain extent, she explains it. Yet the communication problems which surround uniqueness produce an utter bewilderment in the longtime friend upon whom the heroine focuses her emotions.

The central character in Elizabeth Stuart Phelps Ward's The Silent Partner is more successful, because she frames her explanation in terms which can be understood in her conventional surroundings, no matter how uneasily. Rejecting both marriage and lonely idleness, Ward's heroine designs a new role which allows her to foster intellectual development when it is wanted by people who do not have conventional access to self-cultivation. Since her new mission brings her into contact almost exclusively with the socially disadvantaged, her wealthy family and friends vigorously disapprove. Nevertheless, some of them keep in touch with her since they are able to accept her theory, even while they remain astonished at her choice of how to live.

To question social standards without going into exile is not strictly the behavior of women, or of Americans. English fiction occasionally features men who feel invaded by the heroic model usually held up as correct for males. The problem for non-heroic men is parallel to the alienation felt by women who reject the passivity and subordination of the matching female role, and their responses are often similar.

Charlotte Smith's The Old Manor House illustrates this concern by developing a male personality which avoids both the heroic and the anti-heroic extremes. Smith's hero is humane rather than judgmental and conventionally triumphing. His determination to stand by his own values withstands pressure from all the traditional challenges, including war and love and brotherhood.

The Eccentric Role

Some novels feature the existence of little used patterns within society where eccentricity may be at least tolerated and sometimes even valued, in a distant way. In George Eliot's Daniel Deronda, for example, three of the characters would be treated as socially hopeless outcasts if they were not musicians. Fortunately for them, "the artist" is a role in English society which justifies almost any amount of abnormal behavior. In Daniel Deronda, being an artist constitutes a socially assumed way of life with rules so different and so clear that it can be seen to have a value system all its own. The role allows remarkable people to be themselves without having to give up contact with the conventional world.

In her Wives and Daughters, Elizabeth Gaskell uses the opposite approach to the same pattern. She replaces the traditional idea of eccentricity by describing a new development in nineteenth-century English life--the scientist. As a neighbor, Gaskell's young hero remains largely unvalued for his kindliness and sensitivity, partly because these traits are not really expected in a man and also because they take an unusual form in his personality. Eventually, though, his patient dedication to research makes him notable in the international scientific community. When London intellectuals begin to fuss over him, the local people finally offer a puzzled acceptance.

Escapes

The twentieth century seems to have developed two categories which are not present in earlier forms. Both types assume current society already offers many options. In this situation, central characters need to find the most comfortable possibility in a sometimes daunting array of roles.

The more tentative of these twentieth-century forms focuses on an individual who has decided no particular social role really fits, though tact and a resourcefulness with camouflage will keep this discovery from becoming socially awkward. Works of this sort seem to leave their individuals mentally free while expecting them to adapt their behavior enough to gain an indulgent companionship from conventional society.

These novels use an often hilarious tone which allows their unique individuals to maintain their integrity while immersing themselves in a society which finds them baffling. Equally amusing is the persistence with which the central personalities perceive normal value systems as conglomerations of utter chaos.

An unusually wide-ranging treatment of this idea is Diane Johnson's "California novel," The Shadow Knows. Johnson's heroine explores a dismaying array of political, legal, social, institutional, emotional, moral, economic, intellectual, professional, sexual and ethnic stereotypes in contemporary American society. Only after she comes to terms with everything else can she privately accept her own identity in a realistic way.

A less personal quest occurs in Barbara Pym's A Few Green Leaves, which examines role stereotypes in contemporary English society. In this highly entertaining novel, roles hamper, limit and entangle everyone, including normal people, but only the rare, determined individual does anything about it.

The Sum Greater Than the Parts

A more aggressive approach suggests that cultures in the throes of change may be ineffective at enforcing their traditions and norms. While this loss of control is deplored as a "breakdown" by people who fit into the conventional roles of the past, it offers a lifesaving freedom to individuals whose value systems place them outside the old norms. Unique individuals need not be content with falling between the cracks developing in the old social fabric. Instead, they are able to pick and choose in a perfectly open and visible way, developing a new context, to please themselves, out of the shards of the old.

English writers seem particularly at ease with this idea, and the fiction they write in illustration offers a considerable range. A relatively traditional example is Dorothy L. Sayers' academic novel, Gaudy Night. Sayers establishes the college as a microcosm. And then, in good scholastic fashion, she classifies the women who live there as well as those who pass through. This method allows her to organize a taxonomy of women which reveals the almost infinite variety already available to anyone who takes the trouble to look beyond the simplest, most automatic choices.

A less comforting view occurs in Doris Lessing's The Golden Notebook. Echoing the social fragmentation which accompanies change, this work offers a heroine who is "two women"--one of whom is several people, including an artist who discovers herself to be made up of "bits and pieces" from "everywhere." The heroine's self-restructuring is not presented as a joyous outcome, though it is finally a route to self-acceptance in a world composed of breakdowns.

More energetically optimistic is Margaret Drabble's responding novel, The Realms of Gold. Describing herself as "greedy," Drabble's heroine reaches out for everything. She gets what she reaches for and is not overwhelmed by diversity since she keeps only what interests her beyond the moment.

Drabble's gathering is the affirmative face of Lessing's "bits and pieces," an association which emphasizes the underlying assumption of these works. Social change may shatter the old rules and cause the old ideas to apply in so partial and haphazard a way as to be irrelevant, except for the people who cling to the past. Such a situation may not produce true tolerance, but it will create enough uncertainty to make room for even genuinely individual people to thrive, if they wish to take the trouble.

The idea that individuals may benefit from situations which would usually be considered a loss is a modern echo of Elizabeth Gaskell's nineteenth-century theory about motherless girls. A thread running through Gaskell's novels is the assumption that children will not be acculturated in the usual way if their mother dies while they are young. The loss of cultural "leading strings" may cause problems, as it does in Ruth. But Wives and Daughters establishes the opposite point by showing the advantage a motherless girl has over her more normally controlled and indoctrinated contemporaries. Unguided in matters of conventional female behavior, a motherless girl is left free to develop herself as a unique individual without bowing unnecessarily to social norms. For girls whose potential includes uniqueness, this is an invaluable escape.

Few writers rationalize the development of individuality in their characters so carefully as Gaskell did. More typically, readers are simply confronted with a personality which cannot survive as "normal," and the background which permitted or fostered uniqueness is not defined.

In either case, the major focus is on a world where nonstandard individuals are not rejected. They do not defend themselves and are not expected to do so. They are not loners, or misfits, or victims. Nor do they respond to their difference by attacking, hating or victimizing the normal majority. Instead, in these works, unusual people flourish beside the usual in the amiable self-confidence of varied individuals who are well suited to their individual lives.

All the works dealt with here have in common this conviction that remarkable people are likely to live uncommon lives. Despite this shared purpose, the individual novels on this list seem very different from each other. Each has its own type of plot, setting, characterization, tone, literary method and secondary theme.

It is appropirate that novels about extraordinary individuals should be even more diverse than a three-hundred-year time span would otherwise guarantee. The books, as well as their characters, seem to listen to their own drummers. Therefore, it is necessary to approach each novel as a highly separate work--no other method makes it possible to respond to the individual music which each author and each free character seems to hear.

2. ALTERNATIVE GROUPS

Sarah Fielding, <u>David Simple</u>
Frances Trollope, <u>Michael Armstrong</u>
Elizabeth Gaskell, <u>Cranford</u>
Judith Rossner, <u>Any Minute I Can Split</u>

others:
Geraldine Jewsbury, <u>Constant Herbert</u>
George Eliot, <u>Felix Holt</u>
Dorothy L. Sayers, <u>Gaudy Night</u>
Jane Rule, <u>The Young in One Another's Arms</u>

When people withdraw from the world in order to establish a small society of their own, fiction about their lives is routinely called utopian, and analysis focuses on two basic elements. In utopia, a perfected population is cheerfully submissive. Laws also are ideal.

Fiction accepting these guidelines has its defects built in. Any society which depends upon people being perfect will be a vacant world. And even if a remarkable enough population could be assembled, legal uniformity would drive people mad from boredom. These conventional limitations are assumed so automatically that authors and critics joke about them as inevitable. Therefore, works which manage to avoid them are routinely set aside as being nonutopian in essence.

Replacement societies can sometimes resolve the issues which defeat conventional utopias, however. When variety is accommodated in the group design, laws enforcing similarity are not needed. Instead, members voluntarily adapt to each other because they have not been able to find what they are looking for in the standard world. They want to be themselves and still have access to a sympathetic society. Their own needs commit them to the idea that individual personalities must be left intact, and so each of them expects other members to bring their histories with them. Since recruits are not made over when they join, the fears and drives which come from their responses to personal pasts prevent the usual utopian monotony.

Fiction concerned with such social groups divides itself into two types. Earlier examples tend to emphasize recruitment by following refugees as they struggle to live according to their own values in the normal world. Only when they have given up do they turn to an alternative group. Novels of this sort highlight and define the problems in the usual world which make options essential.

A second type of these utopias casually sets "the world" aside and focuses on life within an already functioning group of individuals in retreat from the world. This literary structure makes it possible to show in detail how alternative societies work. Recruits have withstood pressures to conform to the world, and so they are prepared to defend themselves in the alternative society, as well. At the same time, they must develop some means of handling the tensions differing self-images produce, if they are to function as a community. And, like any utopia, they must find some way to keep their values intact while protecting themselves from assaults and invasions by "the world."

Novels which describe individuals gathering in practical and satisfying groups produce sometimes surprising reader reactions. In the eyes of her major contemporaries, for example, Sarah Fielding was better than her famous brother at understanding the human heart.[1] Still, literary history has used two hundred years of additional thought to set aside the judgment of Samuel Richardson, Samuel Johnson and Henry Fielding. In the assessment of our own contemporaries, David Simple is not "a person" because Sarah Fielding "has no people" in her work.[2]

This response to David makes sense only in the context of "Fielding scholarship." Fielding scholars focus on Henry, rather than on Sarah--the first item listed on Sarah's standard chronology, for example, is the birth of her brother[3]--and anyone would agree that David certainly is not Tom Jones.

However, readers who look at David for himself notice that he does have a personality--a remarkable one. He is so charismatic that he accumulates around himself a group of refugees who find him a blessed relief from families who misunderstand them and acquaintances determined to set them straight.

Because David and his friends are such unusual individuals, Sarah Fielding devoted most of David Simple to the individual self-discoveries which bring the refugees together and maintain them as a stable group in the face of every pressure conventional society and nature can supply. The novel is a series of life histories of people who do not uphold standard views in any relationship. Their attitudes get them into trouble with parents, brothers, aunts, in-laws and friends. Their behavior also conflicts with standard rules about abstractions. Normal attitudes toward marriage, femininity, manliness and dependency amaze and startle them and sometimes make them laugh.

Simply having trouble in the world is not enough to qualify a person for David's group, however, since membership involves more than mere escape. To make this idea clear, Fielding allows some of David Simple's characters to tell their stories and then move on. Modern critics are occasionally dissatisfied with this structure, evaluating it in terms of Henry Fielding's frank digressions. In Sarah Fielding's hands, however, such a plot feature is part of a coherent procedure since its function is to integrate personal pasts into an overall framework which limits her group and defines her population's goals. Personalities who are bent only on withdrawal will withdraw from David, as well as from the world. But their readiness to turn away from David's personal charm must seem merely random unless their reaction to their own past is included. Only when they are allowed to tell their stories can they be established as serious individuals whose difference highlights the active commitment which characterizes individuals who become one of the friends.

Friendship is officially the basis of the group in David Simple. The first statement of principle comes from David's need to survive a series of changes in his life. Betrayed by the brother he has always trusted and loved, David is too demoralized to risk other attachments. An uncle takes pity on him and saves him from total reclusiveness, but the uncle dies. Utterly alone, David discovers how ill suited he is to solitude. His "darling passion" is "doing good," a need which cannot be indulged in isolation.

He rescues himself by defining "friendship" in his own way. He decides that "friends" enjoy a "union of minds" which leaves no room for either selfishness or separation of interests. Once he knows what he needs, his problems are solved. He will search for a friend, and while he looks, he will have his travels to keep him in touch with other people, for some of whom he may "do good."

The novel follows David's exploration of society in order to reveal his personality as a basis for the group which is to come. Conversations with new and temporary friends mark the stages of his developing understanding. He is attractive, agreeable and rich, and so he easily gains entry into every kind of group. Most people accept him as a leisured idler, and their lack of curiosity allows him to observe unhampered and shock himself in silence at the selfishness and coldness of people in every social class. When finally he is asked what he is doing, David's description of the friend he is looking for provokes the amused answer that he will no doubt set out next to find the philosopher's stone, that being no more impractical a quest.

This taunt calls attention to the absoluteness of David's refusal to be educated by the world. When people treat him cordially but turn out to be unfeeling, or neglectful, or tolerant of cruelty, he questions them in order to be sure he has not misjudged. When they answer by explaining the world to him, he does not try to convince them they should live a different way, since that might bring guilt and regret upon them. Nor does he exchange his own view for their sophisticated attitude, since doing so would lead him into behavior he rejects. He does not even explain his feelings, since they are irrelevant to people who accept a conventional life. Regardless of whether he has been affronted by foppery or disgusted by depravity, his response is simply to withdraw.

One thing David does change his mind about is his brother's nature. After exploring society from the titled to the servant class, David becomes uneasily aware that his brother Daniel has treated him in a way which is more normal than not. In the context of the world, Daniel's readiness to serve David ill turns out to be almost ordinary. The discovery makes David even more ready than before to sympathize with others who share his dismal fate.

One of the charms of David's travels is his responsiveness to the griefs of people whom he meets. He is quick to weep over other people's lives. But through his tears, he watches their reactions for evidence of the shortcomings he never will forgive. Since his experience has forced him to become intensely aware of the difference between sympathy and trust, he can visualize no worse torture than to spend his life with people who behave in a way he must despise. Even wild with love, he never tries to persuade anyone to share his values. To be real company for him, friends must spontaneously generate views similar to his, out of their own interpretation of experience.

People who succeed as David's friends qualify in two essential ways. They have been driven from the world through betrayal by a person who should have protected them. And they react to social wretchedness by insisting on the rightness of sympathy and trust even while admitting that these character traits have brought them only grief. They are very ready to explain their views to David. The result is that each individual who joins the group adds to the combined understanding of what it means to be a friend.

The first recruit, Cynthia, brings a history of betrayal which is both personal and abstract. Her father insists she marry a stranger who explains himself in a way which forces her to think he is looking for a kind of "upper servant." She has been raised conventionally, which means she has been taught not to ask questions unsuitable for girls. Nevertheless, she has educated herself well enough on the sly to be convinced it is prostitution for an intelligent woman to marry a "clown" for her keep. She laughs at her father's insistence, believing he cannot be serious. As a result, she finds herself without a family. Frightened and helpless, she gratefully accepts the protection of a wealthy friend, only to discover that normal people think financial dependency takes precedence over a lifetime of affection. Poverty has turned her into a "ladies companion" who can no longer be a "friend."

People destined for David's group are always slow to take offense, and so Cynthia bears neglect and scorn as best she can. However, she is less ready to forgive her friend's teenage nephew when he approaches her without any of the courtesies due to ladies from gentlemen who admire them. The nephew is sure his rank entitles him to her favor automatically. Trustingly, she explains the problem to her friend. The reaction is so predictably abusive that she leaves her friend's house in horror and despair.

Cynthia explains that her life has taught her that friendship which is used for self-interest or gain is really a substitute for slavery in a society which apparently regrets having outlawed the legal form of that abuse. David is intrigued by this addition to his view and offers himself to

Cynthia out of admiration. It is easy for her to refuse him, since her emotions are preengaged. She would not marry him anyway, however, because the world has taught her to be wary of dependence on a friend.

Camilla is a gentler soul than Cynthia, and her more emotional nature twice almost costs her David's esteem while he is silently evaluating her past. She measures up well as a sister, since her only use of the indulgences she gains as the favorite child is to get favors for her brother, Valentine. However, when her father falls violently in love and marries a young woman who turns out to be a vicious stepmother and manipulative wife, Camilla occasionally feels almost pleased that her father suffers a little, while she and Valentine suffer to the point of despair.

David is shocked at what looks like vindictiveness to him. However, he wants to hear the rest of Camilla's story, and before he can withdraw his heart from her, he realizes her nature is so loving, overall, that perhaps an occasional fault might be allowed.

This forbearance of David's is rewarded immediately, since Camilla's next reactions are pure, even by David's exquisitely sensitive standards. Goaded beyond endurance by his new wife, Camilla's father finally strikes Camilla. Dissolved in tears, she tells her brother she must leave so that she will not accidentally expose their father to the realization of what a dupe he is.

Camilla and Valentine become eligible for membership in David's group when they run away together. They started by assuming they could find a friend among other family members, but their stepmother has denounced them for incest, and she is believed. Their innocent love for each other has always been remarkable, and the normal world is quick to see perversity in anything unusual. Refused shelter everywhere, they are beggared and hopeless, and Valentine is ill when David finds them.

Harrowed by her own experience and helpless to indulge her brother any longer, Camilla has invented some rules about the emotions which govern her life. She is convinced that her father is a fine man, yet he has behaved very badly to his children. She explains to David that this means even good people can judge rightly only when their own passions are not involved.

As if to prove her own point, Camilla feels jealous the first time she sees Cynthia in David's presence. Fortunately, Cynthia is involved with friendship and not at all with love, and so Camilla's brief lapse is noticed by no one but herself. The reunion of these women who are longstanding friends therefore offers immediate proof of the rightness of Camilla's insight into the relations of passion and friendship. Camilla's behavior also shows that occasional lapses can be controlled, when value is placed upon doing so.

Since Valentine's story has already been told as part of Camilla's experience, he completes the group by facing the conflicting claims of genuine love and helpless dependency. His situation is complicated by the fact that he adores Cynthia, who is understandably touchy on this combination of topics. He cannot offer marriage, since it would increase his dependency on David. And he will not explain himself to Cynthia since he has nothing but emotion to offer her.

By demonstration, Valentine adds his conviction that a passion which cannot lead to good must be controlled. The importance of this idea emerges in the four-way courtship which follows. Valentine cannot explain himself to Cynthia since he is as helpless as she is. David cannot offer himself to Camilla since she is dependent upon him. The difference in economic rank also makes it impossible for Valentine to discuss his sister's feelings with David, since his doing so would seem like using her for barter. And Cynthia is too much a woman of the world even to consider interfering in other people's feelings.

This mesh of praiseworthy refusals to encroach on the feelings of others is an active value in the group, rather than a set of hesitancies. Because such tact is crucial to each of them, the four lovers might have languished in a perpetual stalemate if Camilla's father had not finally reappeared, restored to his senses by the death of his wife. Since Camilla is now protected by a man of funds, David feels he may ask for permission to court her. Camilla responds frankly, as is considered right in their honest, small world. And as soon as their own happiness is agreed upon, they confront Valentine and Cynthia with the necessity of overcoming their sensitivities for the greater happiness of the group. Finally equipped with both male and female friends, David's travels are over.

The meaning of this outcome is partially defined by

contrast with other people whose personalities make them possible candidates for David's group. Isabelle is invited to spend time with the group in the hope they may be able to relieve her obviously overwhelming grief. The story she tells includes three "friends" whose goal sounds similar to David's. There is the same readiness to value friendship above everything. In both cases, financial dependency does not take precedence over trust. Money is automatically shared by anyone who has some, and help is accepted without groveling by those in need. In addition, both groups regulate themselves without reference to the conventions of the outside world.

These principles turn out to be not enough, however, just in themselves. In Isabelle's story, Dumont sounds like a man who would do well with David's friends. Too poor to claim the woman he loves, he watches Isabelle being courted by a wealthy rival and never utters so much as a sigh. When his friend's wife yields herself to a destructive passion for him, Dumont goes only so far as to beg the unworthy wife to conquer her feelings. Both his dependability in friendship and his trustfulness are displayed when he does his begging on his knees without considering what such a posture might suggest to accidental witnesses.

Dumont's story shows that "friendship" cannot survive alone. He and the Marquis de Stainville have been companions from boyhood, and though they both think of themselves as friends, Stainville's view of the term turns out to be tainted by the world. In school he is easily duped by a troublemaker who convinces him Dumont is interested only in his money. Dumont's response is to clear up the misunderstanding and then cut off Stainville's apologies by pointing out that a "true friend" bears with another's "frailties."

The description certainly applies to Dumont's behavior, but neither of them thinks to measure Stainville by the same rule. It is an omission which reveals a crucial problem. If frailties are equally distributed, mutual kindness will strengthen emotional bonds. But if one person always forgives and the other must always be forgiven, "friendship" no longer applies. The difference becomes a life-and-death matter when Stainville finds his long-suffering friend on his knees, trying to reason with Stainville's shameless wife. Forgetting friendship as usual, Stainville automatically makes the conventional assumption and stabs Dumont in the heart without a word of explanation. However, true friendship cannot be defeated, even by death as Dumont's reaction proves.

With his last breath, he declares himself "well pleased" and begs Stainville to forgive himself as heartily as Dumont forgives him.

This tale adds three elements to the definition of friendship for David and his group. Stainville's role in the story shows that wishing to be a friend is not enough, since a lack of trust overrides otherwise good feelings. Dumont's death shows that one-sided friendship must fail, no matter how faultlessly it is lived by the one who understands it. And these ideas amplify and modify Dumont's gentle insistence that constant perfection should not be required of friends.

Isabelle's story about herself casts additional light on the problems created when conventional people come in contact with truly selfless friendship. When her father urges her to marry a man she does not know and has no interest in, Isabelle resists on principle. Then she discovers her best friend, Julie, is helplessly in love with Le Buisson, her unwanted suitor. She does everything she can to push Le Buisson toward returning Julie's feeling. She is glad that the attachment would relieve her of unwanted attention, but her primary goal is to indulge her friend. When they marry, Julie unwisely tells her story to prove the depth of her love, but what Le Buisson hears is that he has been manipulated out of his own satisfaction. Hatred quickly replaces his infatuation, and Julie dies of it.

To Isabelle, the message is that friends must not gratify each other "to their ruin." Doing so constitutes self-indulgence, rather than friendship, since giving pleasure to friends is more intense than any other form of personal satisfaction.

Overall, Isabelle's story adds to the novel's definition of friendship by showing that it must be shared between equals. Dumont's flawless generosity of spirit cannot supply the deficiencies in those who collect around him. Self-indulgent love causes Stainville's wife to take poison and follow Dumont into death. Stainville realizes his lack of trust has kept him from being the friend he would like to be, and so he retires to a monastery where he hopes to do no more damage. And Isabelle insists that a convent is what she needs, as well. She has destroyed a friend, a brother, a sister-in-law and a lover because she has failed to understand the difference between indulgence and friendship. So crucial a defect in her character convinces her that withdrawal is the only way she can avoid adding to her list of victims.

In establishing simple withdrawal as equal to defeat, Isabelle's story underlines the active intention to do good which is as crucial to David's group as friendship is. David and his friends admit that Isabelle is probably right to withdraw, even though doing so would be wrong for them. They depend entirely on each other for companionship and love, but they must stay in contact with the world so they can relieve suffering wherever they discover it.

Contemporary readers were so intrigued by David that Sarah Fielding added a sequel which shows friendship as a functioning way of life rather than as an innocent and idealistic goal. The emotional structure of Volume the Last reverses the order of the original book by following David's group into poverty and death. This plot material at first seems very different from the adventures of hopeful energy and commitment which filled the earlier work, but a careful look at implications shows that only the form of trouble differs. The ideas which organize the group endure.

Destructive pressures in Volume the Last come from several sources. The group's kind of friendship makes it vulnerable to outside friends who hide their falseness for a time. Financial security disappears when an inheritance is questioned and false friends lead David on against his better judgment to pursue a lawsuit which eventually fails, with costs. Group members lose each other's company when false friends get Valentine appointed as governor of Jamaica, hoping the devastating climate will have its usual effect. Since their only child is sickly, Valentine and Cynthia leave her with David and Camilla when they go. The child's death during their absence tests the mutual trust among the adults. David and Camilla want their five children to grow up in the principles of friendship and goodness, but realistic views of survival in the world force them to wonder if at least the sons ought to be sent away to school, where worldly preferment is a possibility.

Unlike the group in Isabelle's story, David's group does not falter in the face of disaster and death. Poor, they cheerfully move to the country. Beggared, they calmly move again and take up subsistence gardening. Burned out, they rejoice at losing their shelter to fire rather than to the usurer who claims their tiny cottage against an unpayable debt--they know that the accidental loss will provoke their neighbors' kindliness, instead of scorn. When their oldest son dies, they are relieved that he has been spared the shock of a public school. When all but one of the other children die, they are reconciled because abject poverty would have made pleasant lives impossible for them, had they lived. When Valentine dies in Jamaica as predicted, and Camilla dies in childbirth and resignation, David instructs his only remaining child that it is better to mourn a friend's miseries than to mourn their loss. David must convince her, since he is on his way to his own death of the "complicated disorders" he can yield to now that most of his family is safely dead. The little girl shows every sign of being a genuine member of the group. She understands David's reasoning that anyone who can endure to watch friends live is certainly tough enough to bear seeing them relieved of life.

Since these values are participated in equally by all its members, the group does not come to an end when David dies. David entrusts his only living child to Cynthia as a matter of course, and Cynthia is equally casual about accepting the charge. Little Camilla and Cynthia agree to a future of mutual trust and the calmly shared commitment to do good which guarantees that the group will reach beyond David's deathbed.

When a group can outlast the death of its charismatic central figure, the ideas it operates on are reaffirmed. Individuals in David Simple's group enjoy trusting each other in the face of anything, and they are free to indulge themselves this way since the trust is mutual. All of them "do good" because it gives them pleasure, and to them that feeling is a sufficient reward. There is no possibility that such individuals will be understood or even gently dealt with by "the world," and so they are well advised to involve their emotions with individuals who independently share their views. Focusing on their own group without fully withdrawing from the rest of society gives them a way of resisting pressure to conform to what other people call reality without giving up the pleasures of companionship.

Novels which depict such gatherings of individuals are often more negative about normal society than is usually the case in fiction which absorbs itself with remarkable individuals. For example, the world which forces David to go in search of friends is unremittingly cruel. This comparative heavy-handedness may spring from a novelistic need to make unusual distinctions dramatically clear. But it also suggests that writers who work in this fictional form find it easier to visualize a different kind of utopia than it would be to show

how an unusual individual might be able to survive undamaged in the conventional world.

The changes Frances Trollope made in her plans for The Life and Adventures of Michael Armstrong suggest that designing utopia taught her the same lesson concerning the world which Sarah Fielding learned. Michael Armstrong was originally planned as a two-part work. First, Trollope would convince her readers that reform of the factory system was everybody's business. Then she would show how change should come about.[4] She intended to recommend two methods. There were to be constitutional reforms. In addition, private individuals were to "raise their voices" in their "own little circle" in order to bring public opinion into the fray.[5]

These extremely well-behaved techniques are appropriate, because her fictional reformers are uniformly mild. But before Trollope could finish her work, factory hands decided to correct some difficulties on their own, by violence. Sadly, Trollope gave up the idea of turning Michael into a reformer, since doing so would be asking public sympathy for a cause that in itself was righteous but now was stained by violent acts.[6]

Trollope's change of plans shifts the emphasis of Michael Armstrong. A theme of the sort she first visualized would have implied that social horrors of any magnitude could be solved by being mentioned. In fact, Michael Armstrong argues the opposite idea. The novel ends in the establishment of a happy group of congenial friends who must exile themselves from England in order to lead decent lives. Early realism about the lives of the poor routinely seemed overdone to contemporaries, but Trollope was willing to be vivid, nevertheless, in order to justify the social restructuring which is the only satisfactory outcome Michael Armstrong can suggest. The novel as it stands shows that "outrages" in the actual world made a utopian alternative necessary by validating a theme Trollope would have set aside if she could have believed that a man like Michael might be able to change the world.

In contrast to David Simple, which designs a group and then assembles it, Michael Armstrong offers an alternative society only informally at the end of the novel. In the earlier stages of the book, every effort is made to avoid so definitive a withdrawal. Mary Brotherton sells her estate and moves to Europe because all her other struggles have proved to be in vain. The factory boy and girl she adopts and educates are to be the companions most likely to make her happy and allow her to "do good," but her decision to limit herself to so small a group comes only as a last resort. When Michael finds his way to Europe, Mary pleads with him to treat her as an equal in order to cooperate with the kind of life she seeks. And in a letter to a sympathetic friend, she explains that she and her "family" must live permanently abroad since English society as a whole refuses to think of factory children as fellow humans without reference to their pasts.

These casual and private explanations are in keeping with the story they bring to a close, since the point of Trollope's novel is the impact of the factories on individual lives. Workers are mutilated by the machines and beaten by the overseers, and owners are enough enthralled by the "triumphant perfection" of "British mechanism" to forget that the human part of the machinery was made by the "Great Artificer" rather than by man. These results are so widespread that most people look on them as a natural side effect of progress, despite the inevitably demoralizing effect on workers and owners alike.

No matter how universal a situation may be, however, it remains personal in the details of its presence in actual lives. With this in mind, Trollope concentrates on the particular experiences of families caught up in the system in a way which individualizes both the social problem and its result. She studies the circumstances of conventional people in order to show how the system works when no one thinks to question it. She also adds unusual characters to demonstrate that behavior is not necessarily inevitable simply because it is typical, and that conduct which is routine in one context may seem very unnatural when looked at from a different point of view.

The normal result of factory ownership is embodied in the Dowlings. At Dowling Lodge, only money and rank are honored, while any feeling which does not have self-interest at its center is held up to ridicule and blame. With the partial exception of Martha, the unattractive daughter who escapes socialization because she does not look sufficiently "genteel," family members have been "seared and hardened" by "opulent self-indulgence." When financial failure finally comes, it is no more than the outward form of the moral bankruptcy which the rest of the family is too selfish to resist.

The Drake family illustrates a parallel decline in the characters of factory workers who fail to hold themselves separate from the system within their own minds. The teenage Drake daughters cannot make decent clothing for themselves, even when given cloth for the purpose, since they have never learned to sew. The younger children sleep instead of learn at the Sunday school. And Mr. Drake deepens the family's trouble by using what little money the children make in order to turn himself into a drunk because he cannot bear to see how desperately they must fight to live.

In general, such reactions are taken for granted by workers and owners alike, but Trollope does not suggest that their being submitted to as normal means they cannot be helped. She uses a concerned minister to suggest a way out. Mr. Bell believes character depends on education and social situation. He insists that anyone will respond to improvements in mental, physical and social surroundings.

Conventional do-gooders usually ignore problems among the owners. They believe they have done enough if they force workers to learn to count their wages and sign their names. However, this is not the kind of education Mr. Bell has in mind, since he sees illiteracy as merely the symptom of a more crucial ignorance. Elementary instruction in penmanship cannot help workers who are no more than "operatives" in the minds of instructors and employers alike. The factory poor are deprived of even their humanity when they are treated like "vermin," "toads," and "hedgehogs."

The underlying and usually unmentioned problem is that factory owners and their families are as much in need of education as are the factory poor. When owners harden themselves against the "things which crawl out of" their factories, their emotions and morals become so blunted that they do not even wonder what a worker's life is like. Martha Dowling, for example, is kind to Michael when he is brought to Dowling Lodge, but she never thinks to ask the questions about his situation which would be almost automatic if he were anyone other than a factory boy.

When members of the idle class occasionally get curious, they are dismissed as troublemakers. Mary Brotherton summons a doctor to help the Drakes, for example, but he shows little concern for the deathbed which has roused her sympathy and concern. Instead, his interest is in diagnosing Mary's "very unnatural conduct" which he is convinced must spring from a "religious mania" likely to bring on her own early death.

In such a society, Mr. Bell's concept of education takes on special meaning. His commentary on the factory system provides an analysis which expands Mary Brotherton's exploration of this underworld beyond the simple plot level of her search for Michael. Mary is determined to understand the human system as well as see the factory machines. It is a combination which turns her investigations into the kind of education Mr. Bell is recommending.

When first seen, Mary does not have the look of especially promising material, but that is part of Trollope's point, since factory hands do not look immediately prepossessing either. Before her education begins, Mary is entirely too comfortable on visits to Dowling Lodge, where she accepts as a matter of course the precedence she enjoys as the "richest young lady" in the room. She even presumes upon her status to behave in a way which is insensitive as well as unappealing--she stuffs her handkerchief into her mouth to keep from laughing out loud at other guests.

This rudeness turns out to be a sign that she can be redeemed. Her automatic response to conventional society is satiric--she sketches a caricature of the highest ranking member of local society and writes a satirizing account of the most active gossip in the neighborhood. Even when she seems to behave in a conventionally correct way, she makes her responses in a "childish and silly" voice which would "make the fortune" of a "comic actress." In other words, whether she is behaving badly or well, according to the people she must accept as her peers, she never sees herself as one of them.

Mary was raised to think herself special, but she has been only "half-spoiled" by her upbringing since she actually is remarkable. In defiance of the convictions of all her social peers, she believes she and factory workers are made of the "same sort of materials." Fortunately, her father died without discovering this abnormality, and so she remains uncontradicted until she is old enough to insist on her own views.

As long as her neighbors can explain her behavior as the perfectly normal eccentricity of a rich and beautiful woman, no trouble occurs. But when Mary refuses to mind her own business--in other words, to fall in love with a factory heir--her unusual qualities meet with far less tolerance. Told she cannot get out of her carriage in the slum where factory hands live, she answers that nothing she chooses to do is impossible to her. Commanded not to enter the hovel of a dying woman, she not only goes inside but calls for pillows to make the death easier since she remembers that her own mother gained some relief from being propped up.

Mary is perfectly willing to negotiate with the conventional world when she feels she can. She does not want people to think she cares nothing for propriety, and when she is told a wealthy orphan girl must have a companion, she gets one. Yet her method of obeying turns out to be almost worse than flouting the rules would be. She dresses her old nurse up in black silk and drills her in elegant mannerisms until she can pass as a gentlewoman.

This transformation of Mrs. Tremlett into outward gentility is an important turning point in Mary's education. For one thing, it makes use of the more attractive side of her personality--she thoroughly enjoys changing her nurse's life since she sincerely loves her and delights in her company. In addition, her experiment with Tremlett proves that social training and different clothing can change the way people are treated by the world.

In order to show this kind of outward change as a realistic possibility, Trollope does not suggest that Mrs. Tremlett's attitudes change along with her clothes. Tremlett continues to insist that looking into factory conditions cannot "do good." She knows this on the best authority--everyone says it, and that makes it true. When Mary amiably persists, Tremlett asks what Mary expects to gain by following her own ideas instead of Tremlett's, which Tremlett holds because they are the common view.

Mrs. Tremlett's loyalty to conventionality shows that attitudes are harder to change than clothing is. She insists everyone can tell factory hands as far as they can see them. Nevertheless, she is amiable to the workers Mary confronts her with, and so she becomes a test case of a second sort. Not only does she show that individuals can rise in social status by looking a different part, she also demonstrates that prejudice based on convention does not necessarily lead to the abusive behavior it intends to justify.

While Mary is intrigued at transforming Mrs. Tremlett into a gentlewoman, she insists she is not one herself. When even Mr. Bell lapses into conventional attitudes on the subject of young ladies, in contrast to his liberal views about factory hands, Mary is quick to set him straight. She warns him not to explain to her the "etiquettes" which govern "other young ladies" since she has nothing in common with them and so finds their rules "very heavy harness."

The protest marks her departure from the standards of the conventional world, although her first step shocks even herself. When she begins wondering if she could turn one factory hand into a man of learning and convert another into a woman of fortune, it is too "strange" a scheme, even for Mary. On the other hand, she cannot help recoiling from the "millocrats" she is expected to take as her peers. And Mrs. Tremlett's doggedly conventional attitudes keep her from becoming more than a chaperone. If Mary is to avoid utter loneliness, she will have to act on her beliefs.

Companionship for Mary is not a simple matter of patronizing factory hands. Her disappointment with the Drake family shows that there must be likeness in character to build on before even generosity will gain friends for her. It is not until she surrounds herself with Michael's associations that she finds companions whose personalities make them socially congenial.

Michael's brother, Edward, and his friend, Fanny, are as unconventional as Mary is. They have been able to maintain their integrity in spite of factory pasts which keep them barely human in conventional terms. Mary suspects that cotton fluff in the hair is not a permanent characteristic, since she has already seen what social training can accomplish with even so unpromising a candidate for change as Mrs. Tremlett was. Since Edward and Fanny are far more likely candidates, Mary's experiment is entirely successful in their case. Like Tremlett and the Drake sisters, they begin as dependents. But unlike Mary's earlier candidates, who have been only partially responsive, Fanny and Edward flourish. Cultivation builds upon their real strengths in a way which turns them into genuine friends.

Michael's escape from the underside of the normal

world follows a parallel track. On first appearance, he is altogether a factory hand. Concealed by cotton fluff and rags, his individuality does not appear until he is dressed in decent clothing, for the satiric amusement of guests at Dowling Lodge.

Michael is sensitive, as well as attractive, though neither trait is much called for on the factory floor. Dressed in the outgrown clothes of one of the Dowling children, Michael is required to take part in a family play by reciting verses which say he is grateful for the change. He cannot keep from having his clothes replaced, but he does refuse to be told what his thoughts and feelings are. He breaks down in the midst of the false recitation and begs to be sent back to the factory as a less distressing way to live. When he is allowed to visit the factory, he begs to put his rags back on. He is afraid Edward will not believe they are still brothers if he appears in his elegant Dowling clothes.

This kind of tenderheartedness saves Michael from being overwhelmed by his surroundings, just as Mary's satiric gift separates her from the normal world. Torn from his family while still a child and abandoned in the notorious Deep Valley Mill, Michael might easily yield to bitterness. He is saved by the fact that both despair and revenge are outside his emotional range.

In Michael's case, refusal to resist is not passivity. He endures his situation for years, finally losing his temper because of protective feelings, rather than in self-defense. Roused to a murderous rage when the child at the loom next to his is beaten, Michael becomes afraid that he may eventually act on this dangerous emotion. He maintains his self-control by withdrawing from the rest of the workers inside his mind, and when this no longer protects him from the seething rage he feels in behalf of others, he escapes from the Mill.

The nature of this turning point shows that Michael was willing to accept himself as a victim of widespread crime committed by factory owners, but he will not consent to become a criminal like them. To Michael, impulses which would make him no better than factory owners debase him far below the level of the factory hands.

Since Michael's next stage is as a shepherd, his experience offers an illustration of Mary Brotherton's "education" in the social results of different kinds of work. When

Alternative Groups / 31

Mary first began to investigate the factories, she bothered everyone who would listen by being astounded that rural poor are respected while factory poor are not. Trollope makes Mary's point vivid by sending Michael off with his flock. When Michael's factory rags are replaced with shepherd's clothing, and his health improves from outdoor exercise and better food, he seems a different person, to the outside world.

Trollope has already shown that a change of clothes has no impact on character, and so Michael remains the same inside, just as Mrs. Tremlett did. As his confidence returns, he seeks out Martha Dowling to thank her for being kind to him when he was a child. He knows she talked his mother into signing the papers which condemned him to Deep Valley Mill, but he also knows she was her father's dupe and does not condemn her innocent berayal of him. She gives him all the cash she has on hand, and since it is conscience money, he keeps it for her sake. However, she turns to him for help when her bankrupt father is dying, and Michael gladly uses her money to pay her father's immediate debts so the man who has tormented him can die without police guards in the room.

Michael's generous reaction emphasizes his lack of interest in revenge. Unlike Martha, who was herself betrayed, her father is inexcusable in every way. Michael's feelings are influenced by Dowling's character, but the contempt and outrage he feels do not undermine Michael's loyalty to his own code. Refusing to use Martha's money to save the father she loves would seem like giving in to the values of Dowling Lodge and Deep Valley Mill. At Dowling Lodge, Michael refuses to act as if money is more important than decency, just as he fled from Deep Valley Mill rather than risk becoming a murderer by defending other victims.

Michael's experience at Dowling Lodge completes his separation from society by showing how totally his values are at odds with the standards of the mill world. Like Mary Brotherton, he is uneasy about the result of his difference from other people. But, also like Mary, he is determined not to compromise his beliefs, even if total isolation is the result.

The feelings which separate Michael from the factory world also make it hard for him to think of joining Mary's group, even when he sees that doing so could relieve him of his unwanted loneliness. In a reversal of his anxiety about his brother's pride when they were children, he now objects to displaying himself before his "well-taught" brother in the guise of a shepherd boy. Martha wants him to escort her to Germany where she will visit Mary while he is reunited with Edward, but Michael is offended at the suggestion that he pretend an equality he does not feel.

As usual, Trollope uses a change of clothes to symbolize a change of role. Michael insists upon dressing as a respectable-looking manservant in order to accompany Martha into Edward's presence without giving himself away. His distrust of the situation he is entering into is no more than reasonable, in view of the almost universal rejection he has been subjected to in the past. And he has no way of knowing that Mary Brotherton has assembled her "family" in order to replace a society whose values affront her on the same basis which alienates him.

The unquestioning and unreserved welcome Michael receives makes it impossible for him to doubt the feelings of the group, but his own problems are too complex to be resolved so simply. His sensitive spirit has been permanently marked by the dependency he suffered at Dowling Lodge, and he is too proud and wary to place himself in a similar relation to Mary Brotherton. As Michael and Mary negotiate this difficulty, it becomes apparent that it is Michael's sense of himself as a shepherd who used to be a factory boy which makes him feel he cannot join the group.

Nonfinancial differences between individuals are a social problem which Mary has learned to understand. Heartily agreeing that the members of the group must be equals in order for them to live the life they all prefer, she asks Michael to go to the same university which cultivated Edward's mind and confidence. A couple of years of study, accompanied by training in social skills, will put Michael on an equal footing with the rest of them.

This resolution is the final step in Michael's education. He had hoped Mary might set him up in a small business so he could use financial independence as a basis on which to feel less inferior to his educated brother. But Mary knows money has never been a question between the brothers, and so there is no reason why it should become one now that they are adults. In fact, they are already equals financially, since Edward has no more money than Michael has.

Michael's hope that his earnings might balance his

Alternative Groups / 33

brother's learning shows how hard it is for him to realize he has found a social group where gold is not the basis on which personality is judged. When Mary substitutes education as a way of determining equality, Michael accepts the offer immediately, both as a route to self-improvement and as a symbol of his independent preference for the value system which is the basis of the group.

As is routinely the case with novels of this type, Trollope's group does not cut itself off entirely from the rest of the world, even when it is complete. Martha Dowling spends some time with them, and she is happier with Mary's group than she is at home in England. Nevertheless, she has spent her life being mistaken about the value of everything and everyone around her, and she is no more ready to make a clear response to this small society of friends than she was to cut through her ambivalence toward her father and his world. Her father's death releases her from his direct domination, but it does not change her nature. Too passive to separate herself from Dowling standards even when she finally sees them for what they were, she remains tied to the conventions of her past and cannot commit herself to the definite act which would be required if she joined her friends officially.

Trollope uses Martha's role as an occasional visitor to help define the group. The values held in common are active enough to make passive people fall away. But commitment is not required of casual short term residents, and so Martha is welcomed, as she is, whenever she presents herself. Her acceptance as a permanent outsider shows how carefully the group provides for the individuality of the people involved. They have gathered on the basis of birth, friendship, adoption and finally marriage, but these apparently conventional relationships have no impact on the actual link which ties them to each other.

Trollope uses Mary's experiment to demonstrate that education and social training are enough to erase the surface discrepancies of wealth and rank with which Michael Armstrong began. It is a presentation which transfers the basis of social division away from any comfortable assumption that social destiny is governed by birth. Peers must find each other by watching for shared value systems. Many people will accept a world which splits uneasily between millocrats and factory hands, since they are willing to accept habit as truth and look on change as too much trouble. But it is equally true that independent personalities on both sides of the social chasm place greater importance on individual qualities than on the simplicity of norms. Such unusual people will persist, even when so "strange" a way of judging forces their separation from the world.

Elizabeth Gaskell's interest in an alternative society took a different form from earlier retreats from the world. The population in her Cranford is a neighborhood rather than a consciously selected group of friends. It already exists as a contrast to London and Drumble when the novel begins, and additions arrive as neighbors rather than as self-aware recruits.

The most obvious result of these differences is the lack of defensiveness which Cranford enjoys. People living there have not had to pass inspection, as David Simple's friends do. They are not in danger of arrest or social reprimand, as Michael Armstrong and Mary Brotherton are.

Such a lack of pressure lets them take themselves and Cranford for granted. Some of them have always lived there, as Miss Matty has, and so they never feel the need to figure out what living there means. Others have always "vibrated" between Cranford and Drumble, as Mary Smith does, and so lifetime habit explains their presence. Still others are brought to Cranford by changes which have little to do with society, as in the case of Captain Brown, who gets a job on the railroad and expects to live near his work.

Such a community might at first seem too casual to serve as an alternative social group, yet Gaskell's description of life in Cranford makes its utopian basis clear. Members of the community live up to definite standards, though the pattern is far from coherent as they explain their individual views. Everyone in Cranford has a strongly developed individuality which would make all of them vulnerable if they went in for "verbal retaliation." They protect each other from this unfortunate exposure by being "exceedingly indifferent" to opinions, never trying to persuade anyone or even gain a consensus on conflicting ideas. When discussion is called for, they meet in a formal gathering, but each lady talks about whatever subject interests her at the moment, and they are "contented" to have all talked at once on their separate topics. The procedure works perfectly well, since, when they do listen, the only result is that they endure each other's ideas as patiently as they put up with other kinds of "eccentricity." In other words, Cranford uses considerate and forebearing behavior as a substitute for the ideological basis which underlies conventional utopias.

Some residents realize how eccentric Cranford is. Mary Smith, for example, points out that her friends in "the world" identify personal characteristics as "bugbear faults" and make use of them to "cut and come again," attacking weak spots under the guise of helping people improve. The neighboring town, Drumble, takes such assaults for granted, but Mary knows there are other ways to live, since she spends as much time as she can in Cranford. The contrast makes her feel "banished" when her father's claims keep her in the world.

Other residents assume that Cranford attitudes are universal, and when the world does occasionally intrude, behavior normal to life in Drumble seems like personal eccentricity to them. Miss Matty's reaction to the bank failure which makes a pauper of her is typical. As a stockholder in the bank, Miss Matty feels responsible to the people whose notes are now worthless. This makes her grieve for the bank officers who caused the failure, since she assumes they must be feeling even more sadly and helplessly responsible than she does. Mary lives in Drumble as well as Cranford, and so she knows self-interest among the managers provoked the disaster, but such a possibility never crosses Miss Matty's mind. She takes Cranford values so totally for granted that she automatically expands them into the rest of the world.

By allowing Cranford to be as unconscious of itself as Miss Matty is, Gaskell frees herself from the justifications which take up so large a part of the earlier novels of this type. Instead of arguing the need for a social option, Gaskell casually assumes Cranford's existence. Her concern is with the practical and commonsense methods which are effective at securing unpretentious peace and satisfaction, day by day.

One test of any utopia is its method of keeping its membership inside the limits of the rules. Cranford's method is remarkable. When someone behaves "badly," the Cranford ladies find a way to forgive the offense. The "reason" for any lapse is irrelevant, in Cranford. The ladies forgive what they cannot approve of because it is their own nature to do so, not because conventional views of justice say they should. For example, Miss Jessie is forgiven for singing out of tune and for dressing like a little girl because she cheerfully bears the nervous irritability of her dying sister. Miss Barker is excused for dressing better than the other ladies since she is only wearing out the stock left over when her family business closed. Mr. Hoggins is forgiven his coarse name since changing it to Piggins would be very little help.

Citizens of Cranford bear each other's good behavior as cheerfully as they endure all other inconveniences. For example, Miss Jessie bravely faces sympathy and friendship when her father dies. She knows her longing to be alone with her grief is less important since it is a purely personal need.

Gossip is transformed into a Cranford function, as well. All the Cranford ladies know every detail of each other's lives, and yet this exposure does not produce the usual bad results. Instead, knowing everything helps them protect each other, since they can take advantage of their grasp of details to describe each other's characteristics in the most favorable possible way. Miss Jenkyns sometimes does not spell exactly in the "modern fashion," for example. And stage fright turns Miss Matty "enigmatic" when she writes to someone who intimidates her.

Making allowances for the individuality of others is not simply a habit of language. Some kinds of eccentricity are not even mentioned, though they may place a considerable strain on the behavior of everyone else. For example, when Mrs. Jamieson falls asleep at a party, the rest of the group is severely taxed. Talking in a loud voice is inconsiderate since it might wake her, but a soft voice is an equal offense since it would exclude Mrs. Forrester, who is too deaf to hear anything less than a shout.

In a community which deals with sleepiness and deafness as equal eccentricities, it is not surprising that the manliness of men is accepted as an eccentricity, as well. The Cranford ladies are uncharacteristically in agreement on the subject of men. To be a man is to be "vulgar" and inconvenient. Men have to be "attended to." Conversation has to be "found" for them. They speak too loudly and violate the "snugness" of parties.

The basis of this judgment is impressively scientific-- Miss Pole points out that her father was a man and so she knows the sex "pretty well." Miss Matty is able to agree that men are troublesome, since she realizes her own experience has been exceptional. Her father was "neatness itself" and wiped his shoes before coming into the house "as care-

Alternative Groups / 37

fully as any woman," but these details describe only her father and have nothing to do with "men."

This accommodation is a kind of summary of Cranford's ability to make needed adjustments which will bring belief and experience into line. What men "are" is an opinion. Opinions are ignored. When a particular man behaves well, he is of course accepted just as if he were a woman. Once he is a member of the group, his gender is forgiven along with all his other eccentricities. Gaskell uses this pattern throughout the novel to show how Cranford deals with its own members, as well as with the world.

In the opening sequence of the novel, the Cranford ladies define themselves by acculturating Captain Brown. Predictably, they dread his arrival, since he is known to be a man. They feel his being so entitles them to resist him with "small slights" and "sarcastic compliments." At first he seems to justify such treatment since he coarsely "alleges" poverty as his reason for not renting the house everyone assumes he ought to choose. In Cranford, no one mentions being poor, and so the ladies hope to drive him out of the community for such a breach of tact.

He makes other significant mistakes, as well. For example, he sees a fragile woman having trouble carrying her groceries home on an icy day and carries them for her. The ladies expect him to pay a round of visits the next morning and apologize for behavior which shows he has noticed that the woman is too poor to hire a servant to carry her packages. But Captain Brown breaks the rule of apology, as well, as he innocently persists in behavior he considers appropriate.

His doing so turns out to be reasonable, even in Cranford, since the Cranford ladies condemn behavior on bases which are just as irrelevant as those they use in order to forgive. Captain Brown's actual offense is that he is a man, not that he is helpful, or that he is frank about being poor. Gaskell establishes the point clearly by showing how the ladies normally deal with awkward truthfulness. When Miss Jessie Brown admits to a shopkeeping uncle, Miss Jenkyns tries to "drown" this "confession" under a "terrible cough." Her father could expect the same treatment if he had not added the mistake in gender on top of his other faults.

When his sex is used as an excuse to set aside the usual code, Captain Brown proves himself an ideal recruit for the community by behaving more like a Cranford lady than the ladies do. He answers sarcasm in good faith. When Miss Jenkyns lectures him on Dr. Johnson and warns him not to read Dickens, he "screws his lips up" and drums on the table, but he does not answer back. And he feels guilty enough for even his silent thoughts that he stands beside Miss Jenkyns' chair and tries to smooth over the chasm in taste between Johnson and Dickens. It is Miss Jenkyns who fails to rise above opinions and continues to sulk.

His crucial defect is solved when Captain Brown finds his role at tea parties. He "waits on empty cups" and carries food around so automatically it is clear that he thinks the strong should help the weak. Such behavior makes him a "true man," in Mary's partly worldly eyes. It also shows that he has managed to fit in as one of the Cranford ladies. Just returned from Drumble, Mary notices that no one in Cranford any longer fears that this particular man will interrupt the snugness of the group.

Captain Brown's acceptance is a flattering compliment since gender is not always forgiven or set aside. Miss Jenkyns, for example, chooses to wear a cravat and a bonnet like a jockycap so that her dress will reveal her as a "strong minded woman." She certainly does not intend to dress like a man, since she "knows" women are superior.

The gender question is often an element in the conflicts which surround arrivals and departures from the community. For example, when Miss Matty's brother, Peter, leaves Cranford, he is a fallen woman as well as a lively young man. Gaskell uses this unconventional episode from Peter's boyhood to show how Cranford deals with behavior which violates its code.

Peter does belong in Cranford, on the basis of his character. His only prize at school is for being the "best good fellow that ever was." He is "too easy" with his friends, and so they get him into "scrapes." His unfailing sweetness irritates his more rigid sister, who punishes him by thinking him "ungenteel" and by refusing to laugh at his jokes.

The un-Cranford-like judgmental aspect of Miss Jenkyns' attitude bothers Peter, since he is a gentlemanly boy. He is always helpful to old people and children, but he loves practical jokes and uses the gender question to tease anyone who resists his playfulness.

Establishing a background for Peter's most serious breach of Cranford's code, Gaskell gives a preliminary example of Peter's method. He insists "the ladies" will believe anything, but he illustrates his point by playing a joke on his father. Peter dresses up like a lady passing through town in order to call on the author of a published sermon. His easily duped father is extremely proud of his sole publication and readily falls for the trick. He even goes to the extreme of offering to send a copy of his sermon to the supposedly admiring lady, who is really Peter in disguise. Since Peter is required to make the copy, he is "punished" in a properly Cranford way--he does suffer for his mischief, but not because retaliation is artificially applied.

As Miss Matty tells this story, she has trouble deciding whether to call Peter "him" or "her," but finally she settles on "her" since "Peter was a lady then." It is a confusion which is the basis of Peter's final boyish escapade. When everyone is out of the house he dresses up in his sister's clothes, swaddles a pillow in infant clothing, and goes strolling in the garden, cooing and talking to the pillow in his arms. Coming home, his father sees a large crowd of townspeople peeking through the railings in front of his house. He naturally assumes they are admiring a rhododendron he is excessively proud of and decides to invite them into the garden to inspect the "vegetable production" he imagines they are awed by. When he gets close enough to realize the "production" is not "vegetable," he makes them watch while he bursts into the garden and strips Peter of his clothing--"bonnet, shawl, gown and all." He throws the pillow-baby at them and then flogs Peter while they watch.

The reactions of Peter and his family show how Cranford works. Peter stands unflinching for his punishment, and when his father pauses to catch his breath, he simply asks if he has "done enough." Peter then bows to the audience, like a gentleman, goes into the house to say "god bless you forever," to his mother, and leaves Cranford without either explanation or complaint. What started as a joke turns out to violate Cranford standards so basically that self-banishment is the only possible response, for the person who has broken the rules.

"Sorrow" is what other members of the community feel. Peter's father must laboriously learn the standards which come spontaneously to Peter. He feels justified, at the moment of the flogging, but he quickly realizes what he has done and admits he did not think "all this" would happen as a result. After the immediate sadness fades, he sometimes starts to "lay down the law" in "the old way." But then he remembers and puts a hand on the shoulder of the family member he has been dominating and asks in "a low voice" if he has hurt them. He becomes so humble and gentle--so Cranford-like--the rest of the family cannot bear it. Peter's mother tries to reassure her husband by talking constantly about the wonderful future which will result from Peter's new career in the navy. She acts as if she were quite glad of "that unlucky morning's work" which sends her into a last decline and ends in her dying without ever seeing her only son again.

This painful episode shows that Cranford values can be acquired. Peter's father is too vain and too quick-tempered to be spontaneously suitable for membership in the community. But such deficiencies do not isolate him since small vanities are as widespread in Cranford as in the rest of the world, and irritability sometimes erupts into "peppery words." In fact, his eagerness to adopt more Cranford-like behavior turns out to be more of a burden to his remaining family than consistent lapses would be.

Cranford's willingness to make allowances for even severely provoking behavior is symbolized by the community acceptance of Miss Jenkyns, who never yields any opinion, even in the face of death and grief. For example, she interprets Captain Brown's death as an affirmation of her own integrity, and no one contradicts her. In fact, Captain Brown's death has nothing to do with her. He jumps in front of a train in order to throw a wandering child to safety. But what Miss Jenkyns notices is that he was walking down the street reading <u>Pickwick</u>, just before his heroic death. This detail makes her realize that Captain Brown has been "killed for reading" defective literature. Satisfied at having finally overpowered him on the subject of Dr. Johnson, she is able to relent sufficiently to describe him as a "poor, infatuated man," though even death does not soften the more crucial literary judgment.

Except in the individuals who test these qualities, patience and forebearance are such dominant attitudes in Cranford that the community might at first seem ready to put up with almost anything. It is true that the ladies are generally meek and "undecided to a fault." Nevertheless, they are capable of their own kind of heroic action when it is needed.

Gaskell uses the bank failure which ruins Miss Matty to show Cranford in a coping mode. The ladies work together effectively, regardless of their inability to speak in the form of a conventional debate. Miss Pole calls a meeting so that everyone can pledge something toward Miss Matty's support. The idea is heartily embraced, in principle, but contributions have to be by secret ballot, for the sake of both the poor and the better off. Mrs. Forrester is ashamed to give so little, though she pledges a noticeable percentage of her own barely subsistence income. Mrs. Fitzadam is equally embarrassed to admit how much she is able to give, since doing so might imply a glorying in more ample funds.

Individuals make separate plans, as well, since no one assumes a gesture of sympathy is the only act required. When Miss Matty tells Martha, her servant, that she can no longer pay her wages, Martha insists on marrying at once in order to take Miss Matty in as a boarder, provided Miss Matty can bring herself to have a man around the house.

Mary's plans are equally careful of Miss Matty's personal tastes. She suggests that Miss Matty sell tea, which is neither "sticky" nor "greasy." Miss Matty cannot be expected to endure stickiness or greasiness, even if she can overcome her doubts about becoming a shopkeeper.

The other problems surrounding this enterprise are solved in a similar way. Everyone's gentility is shocked at the thought of Miss Matty descending to buying and selling, but the loss of status is minimized when her shop sign is displayed where it cannot possibly be seen. Miss Matty solves a different kind of integrity issue by asking the manager of the general store what teas she might offer in order not to compete with his stock. And this established shopkeeper proves himself to be a true resident of Cranford by sending customers to Miss Matty in a steady stream. Miss Matty relieves her conscience over accepting money from the public by giving long weight to everyone. Cranford retaliates by bringing gifts in exchange--cream cheeses, newly laid eggs, fruit and flowers.

This form of rescue contrasts significantly with the way bank failure is handled in Drumble. Since the bank failed in the world, and since Mary's father lives in the world and deals with money routinely there, Mr. Smith is sent for in the hope of getting experienced advice. But when he arrives, Mr. Smith brings the attitudes of Drumble with him, and they prove to be as ineffective in Cranford as they would be in the world. He goes over Miss Matty's papers and explains them in a way which makes no sense to Miss Matty, though she has understood the implications of her situation perfectly clearly on her own. His contribution ends with his description since he has nothing to suggest beyond the fact that she is ruined. He ends up endorsing the plans Cranford has devised, though he objects to the idea of consulting competing stores and extravagantly overestimates Miss Matty's income from tea by assuming she will think of profit margins rather than of how much candy she can give away without making children sick.

The fact that Mr. Smith has nothing to offer is not the important point, to Cranford. He is a busy man who has interrupted his own life in order to go over the situation with Miss Matty, and this is the detail which Cranford notices. His own affairs are in an "anxious state," which might cause people in Drumble to wonder whether he manages himself well enough to claim to give advice to others. But in Cranford, his predicament only means that his taking trouble is all the more generous, because it is so inconvenient. In the end, all parties hold steadfastly to their own point of view. Mr. Smith offers Cranford nothing except his pity and disbelief, and Cranford presents its usual generous sympathy in return.

Gaskell bases <u>Cranford</u>'s structure on this unconventional type of cause and effect. She builds her plot around the premise that events do have results, though acts are unlikely to be causes in the usual sense. True citizens of Cranford make choices according to their feelings. Opinions do not count. Since they never even consider attempting to live rationally, outcomes are automatically disconnected in their minds.

Part of the novel's remarkable humor comes from the way the Cranford ladies think. They do not consider the future when they make a choice, and this lack of prediction leaves them free to explain every kind of event according to their heart's desire. As a result, the aftermath of a choice is seen in terms of the truth of its feeling, rather than its rational inevitability, since that is the method the Cranford ladies use.

Miss Matty's love affair shows that even tragedy can be transformed, if logic is set aside. When they were young, Miss Matty and Thomas Holbrook loved each other and would have married except that Miss Jenkyns was offended by a man who farmed his own land instead of having a manager do the work. When the lovers meet thirty years later, the encounter renews Miss Matty's wound, as her behavior shows when Mr. Holbrook dies soon afterwards. The day she hears that Mr. Holbrook is dead, Miss Matty tells her servant, Martha, that she may entertain one young man, though he is not to be a "follower." Miss Jenkyns never allowed the servants to have followers, and Miss Matty will not defy her sister, even though she is now dead. On the other hand, Miss Matty has learned from her own love affair's sad ending, and so she will not allow rules which she has suffered from to repeat their cruelty in other lives. She is eventually rewarded for this generous response since her permission means that Martha's Jem has made himself available for the marriage which makes it possible for Miss Matty to continue to live in her own house as her former maid's boarder. But this kind of justice is irrelevant, since the only result Miss Matty had in mind was that Martha's happiness should be greater than her own.

These outcomes are not rational, but they are appropriate, if examined carefully. Miss Jenkyns has restricted the happiness of others, and so it is fair for her rules to be set aside. In contrast, Miss Matty is unfailingly considerate of the feelings of others. Since even grief turns her behavior toward greater generosity, she deserves solicitude in return.

The structure of Peter's adventures also confirms the Cranford process. As a boy, only his skill in the art of practical joking kept him from being an ideal candidate for Cranford. When he has to leave, his generous nature and sweetness of temper produce a kind of little Cranford in India where he settles down to spend his life. One of the people he helps on the other side of the world happens to describe him with effusive gratitude, during a temporary stay in Cranford. The half worshipful story convinces Mary Smith that she may have discovered Miss Matty's long lost brother. Tactfully silent about her hopes, she sends a letter explaining Miss Matty's predicament, and so Peter's thoughtless goodness finally leads to his being told that not all his family is dead. No feature of this outcome would be considered rational, by the standards of the world, but no result could be more reasonable, where feelings are concerned.

Time has had no impact on Peter's character, though his judgment has improved. When he returns to Cranford,

he no longer dresses up in clothing borrowed from either
sex, but the tendency to joke remains. His stories about
life in India are such tall tales they seem to come from the
Arabian Nights rather than from reality. Most of the Cranford ladies conclude that he has become "very Oriental" and
are satisfied. However, Mary notices that he does not
launch into his most spectacular accounts when his sister is
within hearing, and he spares the rector, as well. Mary
does not analyze it in a rational way, but her observation
eventually reveals a pattern. Peter did not at first expose
Mary to his wilder imaginings, since she spends time in the
world as well as in Cranford. But when she asks what seem
to him to be gullible questions, he stops protecting her from
his yarns. As he explains himself, it becomes clear that he
still thinks some people in Cranford are "fair game." The
difference is that now he confines his jokes to people who
seem to want them. If Mary asks to be taken in, he will
oblige. And Mrs. Jamieson provokes his most spectacular
performances because he believes she needs the "strong
stimulants" which his absurdities provide.

  This last sequence is in keeping with the novel's
structure since it brings the plot to a conclusion without
depending on conventional logic for the purpose. Peter
tells Mrs. Jamieson the mountains in India are so high
that he once mistakenly shot a flying creature which turned
out to be a cherubim. As a result, she forgives Lady Glenmire for marrying a man who enjoys bread and cheese for
supper. Because Peter has ended this long-standing feud,
Mary says that everyone is "better" when Miss Matty is near.

  If the world's standards are used to analyze such a
flow of logic, there seem to be no cause-and-effect connections between any of the events. It is not reasonable that a
totally unrelated story which is both impossible and blasphemous should cause a snob to set aside her "delicacy" and in
the process add credit to the saintliness of someone else who
is not involved in any way.

  But causality in Cranford depends upon entirely different patterns. If Mrs. Jamieson enjoys herself, regardless of the reason, she will forget that Mrs. Hoggins used
to be a lady, and their interrupted friendship will resume.
No matter why the feud is ended, Miss Matty will be relieved to have hard feelings set aside. And since Peter
wants his sister not to be "harassed," her personality does
trigger the sequence which brings peace.

Gaskell adds small echoes from the world in order to make clear how Cranford judges. Peter brings enough of the outside with him to be interested in predicting results, even though the connections he works with are pure Cranford. He willingly jeopardizes his soul, in Mrs. Jamieson's opinion, in order to enter the assembly room with one of the feuding ladies on each of his arms. And he warns Mary of his intentions, since she brings enough of Drumble with her to analyze events, even though she uses Cranford standards in the process.

When the last episode is looked at in terms of the emotional connections Cranford judges by, the flow of events is clear as well as satisfying. Mrs. Jamieson is roused from her apathy, Mrs. Hoggins is restored to respect, Peter goes on enjoying his jokes, and Miss Matty's love of "kindliness" is served because "friendly sociability" resumes. Peter's success at predicting nonrational results shows that, in their way, Cranford values are as reliable as logic is in the world.

Miss Matty, with her "soft" dignity, is an appropriate symbolic center for such a community. She thinks her "best work" is to "do odd jobs quietly," but the rest of the group knows that what she actually does is teach the sweetness of temper she shares with her brother. It is a lesson which must be demonstrated rather than explained. And this characteristic helps prove how right such a symbol is for Cranford. Discussion would remove it into the realm of an opinion, and opinions are ignored.

In keeping with twentieth-century habits of mind, the group at the center of Judith Rossner's Any Minute I Can Split is a commune, rather than a set of friends, and it thinks of itself as an "intentional community" rather than a neighborhood. This arrangement sounds altruistic and intellectual when its newest member describes it to outsiders. Properly utopian, Roger talks as if every baser urge and impulsive gesture has been refined away by idealists who are using themselves as experimental lives for the benefit of the rest of the world. He insists cities have failed as a way of helping people live together in groups, and his privileged urban listeners agree that even Philadelphia is becoming disorderly. He goes into detail about "the farm" as a pilot program for the future. Its experience will show how much land is needed for survival farming when the cities break up.

The commune will establish the best size for population units and will explore living arrangements and social organizations to find out what works better than urban housing and city government.

Roger is not the only resident who makes the farm sound regimented through submission to an abstract goal. Another recent member, Hannah, is perfectly willing to lead tours of the farm and answer questions about communal living. As she talks, the people staying there sound like a tightly organized unit dedicated to self-regulation. In her vision, individuals control their own destiny by creating their own environment. She presents this idea as true for the commune, but it is even more true for her, personally, since everything she owns, including her children, is kept in a trailer which is always ready to pull out at a moment's notice.

Both these explanations are so theoretical they give the impression of a community of philosophers huddled in long, intense discussion of abstract goals adjusted to the greater good. It is true that most of the residents eventually try to define the farm. For Margaret, it is a refuge from marriage. Dolores sees it as a way of living with her ex-husband in a condition of respect and affection rather than the tolerance and irritation which marriage brings. It provides Mira with a "slum" as background for the great lady role she affects. David has never figured out how to become attached to people in the world outside, but his emotions are aroused on the farm. De Witt wants to be needed so he will have a chance to be "nice" to people in a variety of ways. The "younger group" is searching for anarchy. Depending on who does the describing, the farm sounds like a place to be vegetarian without inconvenience, to raise organic beef, to live with a married lover, to escape "cultural bags," to be an earth mother, to find ego support, to be a celibate wife, to see how it feels to drop out of the FBI.

Such a morass of views suggests what would happen if the residents tried to establish a common ideology or an official, strong leader in the way that is expected of communes. Those of the residents who do think in terms of group values make claims which are as individual as the opinions of the more self-absorbed members, and so the result is approximately the same. Opinions are not completely ignored on the farm, as they are in Cranford, but beliefs are not what the residents share, and so the inten-

Alternative Groups / 47

tion of this intentional community is important primarily in conversations with outsiders and newcomers.

Long-term residents deal with calls for abstract views in the same way they deal with any other disruption. When outsiders tour the farm school, for example, most of the residents decide individually that anything they say might turn out to be irrelevant. Therefore, each refuses to answer questions. Only the newer members, like Roger and Hannah, misunderstand the group completely enough to feel comfortable giving clear explanations. What they say is strictly their own opinion, but they fail to notice the discrepancy, at least at first, since no one contradicts them directly. As in Cranford, beliefs of all sorts are routinely left intact, unless residents happen to feel irritable about something irrelevant. Both Roger and Hannah are able to see themselves as unofficial mouthpieces because they have such aggressive personalities that they mistake tolerance for passivity and patience for approval.

The actual basis for the group is demonstrated by the event which provokes a formal meeting. When the farm's absent owner decides to sell the property, the commune reacts in its usual way--individuals talk informally about their anxieties. It is not until Roger decides to rescue them by buying the farm that they feel pressured into making an official response.

At first it seems perverse that they feel more threatened by salvation than by loss. But buying and selling property is an outsider's view of what is going on. De Witt has something entirely different in mind when he mildly repeats his opinion that Roger's offer to buy the farm ought to be talked about by the whole group. De Witt refuses to say what disturbs him since he will not lay "something heavy" on the transaction if no one else is worried. However, De Witt is "in charge," insofar as anyone is, and so the carefulness with which he avoids taking over the group's mind is even more important than the problem he foresees.

The meeting sounds like any other conversation on the farm. Some of the residents are willful and self-absorbed as they harangue about their usual hobby horses. Others reassure and pacify, as always. But this time, exploring personal reactions is official, and the effort brings into the open a problem which would not have emerged from more idle quarrelsomeness. From an outsider's point of view, it ought to be ideal for someone on the farm to own the property. But the group's view is more alarmed. If Roger buys the land, he will no longer be a resident. He will become a landlord.

"How one has to be" when "indebted" has been a problem for the group. They have been extremely disturbed by Mitchell, the man who now owns the land they live on. When Mitchell sends word that he is coming down for the weekend, everyone's routine changes. One of the women launches a frantic cleaning campaign, another refuses to do even her normal, minimal tasks, two of the men walk away for the weekend, one of the women withdraws into her bedroom, and De Witt amuses himself at the chaos.

In person, Mitchell does nothing to justify such an upheaval. He has not asked for rent, so the farm is free to ignore profits and have mere self-sufficiency as a goal. He does not try to take over, because his interest in communal living is an outsider's curiosity--he does not have the kind of personality needed to succeed as a full-time resident.

Since Mitchell does not personally deserve the hostility he provokes, his treatment shows that trouble comes from the landlord role, which is a concept from the world outside. Mitchell has not tried to insist upon the rules of the rest of society, but he cannot help bringing the world with him when he visits. His sports car makes the farm look shabby instead of comfortable. He talks of taxes, which the commune never thinks about. His wife speaks to him in a way he accepts as sympathetic, but she seems aggressive to people on the farm.

If even a man like Mitchell is alarming in the role of landlord, Roger would clearly be disastrous. Roger's personality is "visibly difficult." While no more than an equal resident, he has already created tension by believing his willfulness, energy and money entitle him to an oversized voice in the community. As landlord, he would be convinced his dominance is proved, according to the standards of the world outside.

Since Rossner puts off this crisis until after the group has had a chance to work on Roger's attitudes, the episode focuses on acculturation rather than on the destructiveness of strong-arm tactics in themselves. As he walks in the door, Roger's first remark is an insult and a cliché. Residents automatically respond to the attitude rather than the remark, and his training begins. He is under continuous pressure to set aside the "cultural bags" of wealth and power and sexual domination. Since he enjoys the extended-family benefits offered by communal living, his behavior does respond, even though he continues to be vicious in relationships where he feels safe and to jeer at the idea of being kind for the sake of other people's needs.

The stresses created by Roger's domineering ego are further modified by the fact that the commune has already weathered a power struggle. Hannah, also, takes disruptively strong stands, from the moment she arrives. Her conversations are a problem because she preaches against drugs, for example, and proclaims that mothers who want to work should drown their children first. Members of the commune who use drugs and who do not enjoy unremitting contact with their children worry about her attacks, but they dodge around her opinions rather than confront her. They believe she smothers her children and occasionally say so to each other, but they do not expect their judgments to matter.

Like Roger, Hannah does not limit her disruptiveness to rudeness and complaint. She insists on using the community as a captive labor pool in support of a school she organizes to protect her children from truancy charges. Most of the residents obligingly agree to teach whatever they know, though individuals who never offer work of other kinds also refuse to volunteer for the new scheme, and no one objects.

The appearance of cooperation is deceptive. Hannah fails to notice that everyone responds merely as an individual--anyone who cooperates does so because the new activity seems interesting, not because Hannah's high-handed descriptions persuade individuals to submerge themselves in a "relevant" community project. Hannah's beliefs about the project would not cause tensions automatically, since no one on the farm minds what codes other people find to live by. But Hannah expects all the classrooms to function like clones of her, whereas the volunteers think of their own classrooms as their own.

This discrepancy turns into an authority crisis for Hannah, and she begins withdrawing her children from class after class. Because the commune always considers relationships to be private and individual, the other teachers take each episode with Hannah's children as a personal matter and think about it in emotional rather than educational terms. But Hannah's behavior is ideological. She believes she is protecting her kids from other people's ineffective teaching and from other people's badly behaved children.

A more sharply focused power struggle develops between Hannah and De Witt. As unofficial center of the group, De Witt usually makes himself extremely approachable to new residents. Yet he is immediately wary of Hannah, sensing her drive to convert the farm into a conventional, strong-leader structure in order to establish herself as its head.

This personal conflict helps define the values and strengths of the farm. Hannah insists she hates sex--she hates "the way it feels"--and yet it turns out she "can be had" by De Witt. At first it seems his universal ability to charm has involved her in spite of her ideological stand on the topic. But she maintains a symbol of separateness by parking her trailer in such a way that she can "split" at a moment's notice. And since she spends most of her time in the trailer rather than in the house where the rest of the residents live, the trailer gradually becomes a refuge from the farm in the same way that the farm is a refuge from the world outside.

As soon as Hannah feels secure about her importance to the group by misunderstanding their cooperativeness regarding the school, she quarrels with De Witt. The sequence makes it clear that sex was political, for her, rather than tender, as it is for De Witt. And since she cannot gain power with it, in this community, she has "been had."

De Witt eventually "wins" because he sees any struggle as personal rather than symbolic. He has no reason to feel treated since his importance to the commune does not rest on authority and so it cannot be challenged directly. He is as vulnerable as any other man in his sexuality, but that is a private problem which he solves by the practical method of stopping his visits to Hannah's trailer and by charming more interested women.

With nothing to fight against, Hannah defeats herself. Strong ideas, stated violently, are no more effective as routes to power than work and sex turn out to be. She is not the only vegetarian or health nut in the group. She makes a quarreling point out of rejecting the past, but everyone on the farm tends to be silent on that subject, so her conflict about it dwindles into repetitions of quarrels she had with a husband she left in the world outside.

Hannah's struggles show how she basically misunderstands the commune. She was invited to move there by one of the long-term residents who admired her without making clear exactly what it was about her that appealed. The group makes her very welcome because she is charming and her children are delightfully resourceful. When her appeal wears thin as her arrogance becomes obvious, everyone is patient with the change in the same way they tolerate anyone else's depressions and outbursts. But tolerance is not enough for Hannah, and when her children are expected to behave as individuals like all the rest, she feels her central image of authority has been challenged. The uproar among the children is only ridiculous, to other residents, but Hannah sees it as a final denial of her claim to power. She will not participate in a group on an equal basis, and so she "splits."

Hannah's flight helps establish limits to what the farm will tolerate. Bids for authority are accepted, just as any other self-image is, so long as other residents are not pushed into roles they do not choose. But Hannah insists on controlling other people's lives, beginning with her children and extending to the people who teach them and the children who play with them. It is her refusal to negotiate which expels her from the group.

In contrast, Roger may succeed as a resident since he is flexible about details, even though he is more agressive than Hannah in the way he talks. When he understands that the idea of a landlord is awkward for the commune, he thinks of alternatives. He offers to buy the house separately from the rest of the farm and assign the subsistence area in undivided shares to residents who will then feel they have an equal voice in living arrangements. He even manages to be a good sport about speculation that shares might be sold to support trips to California, though he plans legal ways for blocking that kind of individual treatment of symbolic participation in ownership.

This willingness to negotiate is the quality which turns out to be absolutely required for success as a resident, as David's experience shows. David has "cleared out" his own head with "acid," and so strength of will is not one of his possibilities. He develops an almost marsupial attachment to Margaret while she is enormously pregnant, and his dependency continues into an earth mother-as-sex goddess phase after her twins are born. Margaret accepts this relationship since nobody else minds. But David feels betrayed when she is equally passive toward Roger's claims as husband and father. At first, David tries to make his dependence into a sufficient claim. When that does not force Margaret back into her Jocasta-like role, he sulks and hides. When she fails to respond to his aggressive moodiness, he tries arguing. But life on the commune has begun to influence Margaret's passivity, and so, for the first time, she answers back. David is so outraged that he beats her up and "splits." De Witt underlines the point by explaining that David was not jealous of Margaret's husband so much as he was envious of her ability to change.

Margaret's development on the farm is important to the novel since it allows Rossner to distinguish adaptiveness from passivity. Margaret's original lack of direction causes as many problems as aggressiveness in new arrivals does. She has related to her husband primarily "as victim," and so when she leaves him, she runs away rather than separate from him. She comes to the farm simply because David knows it exists. When the birth of her twins attaches her to the group, she limits her worries to being afraid that she may not know what she is supposed to do or might fail to notice when she has done something wrong. Attracted to De Witt, she has such an inadequate self-concept that she cannot enjoy an affair for fear she is nothing more than an "obligation" to him.

Being treated like everyone else is as much a surprise to her as it is to Hannah, though the reasons behind her reaction are quite different. Hannah is offended at seeming no more important than anyone else, but Margaret is astonished to find herself no less important than anyone else. De Witt reinforces the message by helping Margaret find affirmative ways to talk about herself. As a result, she gets out of the habit of worrying about how she is "supposed" to be and begins thinking only about questions she considers real, such as being a good mother and doing her share of the farm work.

By the time Roger comes looking for her, she discovers that dreading him is a bad habit she does not need to resume. When she first arrived at the farm, her dependency showed up in dreams of Roger falling in love with the twins in a way that would spill over onto her as a kind of secondary child. But by the time Roger actually does fall in love with his daughters, her dreams have moved on to a more

Alternative Groups / 53

active vision of herself running down a beach beside a "grown-up type" like De Witt.

When Margaret decides she wants to identify what it is that makes her different from the thousands of other women, she has achieved the transition from passivity to individuality. Roger's arrival is a setback since she has old habits to overcome, but De Witt reminds her in front of Roger not to get on the defensive and suggests what she can say to identify herself when Roger is insulting. With her new "serenity," she sees that Roger's rages and storms have nothing to do with her as a person, and so she is no longer bothered by them.

The last stage in her adjustment to the commune is triggered by Roger's willingness to adapt to the group on his own basis. Margaret is as bothered by his ability to shift his position as David was by her ability to "grow." It hurts her feelings for De Witt to become friends with Roger, because she thinks of them as alternatives. If they find common ground, it will erase some of the differences she sees between them. It will also contradict her belief that they are connected with each other only through their relationship with her. When De Witt seems willing to become Roger's partner in a commercial organic beef operation, she is terrified that Roger's influence may turn De Witt into a remote, self-important, woman-neglecting cowboy, even though she knows De Witt's goal always is the escape from boredom offered by anything that does not last too long.

As usual, in books of this type, contrasts with the rest of the world help to establish the nature of the community. Rossner brings her novel to a close by sending Roger and Margaret on a formal trip into conventional society. They visit both their parents to show off the twins, as would be expected in the outside world. But their reactions reflect the fact that life on the farm has given them the confidence which comes from knowing there are other ways to live.

Contrasts are persistent and vivid. Margaret smells her mother-in-law, freshly scented and bathed, and tries unsuccessfully to recall her last shower, now that the farm has freed her of the "lopsided notion of femininity" which used to govern her life. The twins are everyone's pleasure and no one's burden on the farm, but they become disasters in the elegant apartment where Roger's parents live. It turns out that one person cannot control two crawling babies, though this fact does not emerge on the farm, where babies are not considered one person's solitary problem. The babies only seem different in the new environment, but Roger really does behave differently, as he joyously returns to his old relationship with his mother by turning loud and abusive and demanding money.

Roger's passive and accepting parents might seem to invite the treatment they receive if it were not for a parallel trip to Margaret's widowed father. Not only has her father failed to keep in touch with Margaret, he has taken the further step of marrying again and rejecting the marriage which produced Margaret because that marriage did not take place in the church.

Since the parents, as individuals, are so different, Rossner's point becomes clear. It is the role rather than the person which governs behavior in the world outside the farm. Neither Margaret nor Roger fits the expected pattern very well, but this does not keep the parents from performing their part of a role which they accept as relevant. When Roger and Margaret appear, making the claims of children, their presence in their role is endured. But this reaction from both sets of parents does not result either in the tolerance of the farm or the love dictated by the idealized concept Margaret gives up so reluctantly.

Emphasizing the impact of conventional roles, Rossner explores an extended family operating on the basis of blood relationship. At the summer beach house shared by several generations of Margaret's family, Roger and Margaret are again free to take a walk together since other people will look after the twins. As on the farm, there are drifting groups of drug-fogged vegetarians. But at the beach house, the young are categorized as nieces and nephews rather than as identifiable individuals. Enjoying the water, Roger and Margaret consider buying a beach house instead of the farm. But Margaret knows that such a project would use the world's model of an extended family rather than the pattern she has come to value on the commune. At the beach, she would be stuck doing all the work, as is conventional for mother figures in the world. Consciously rejecting this "lopsided" role, she finally understands clearly what it is the farm has offered her.

On the farm, normal roles seem like "crazy ideas" which have been "invented." They do not apply unless they are "acquiesced in." De Witt's function as emotional center of the commune is to bring any role into the open so it will not apply out of thoughtless habit or lack of energy to resist.

Because he functions as a facilitator rather than a leader, De Witt's personality is important to an understanding of the commune. Significantly, the residents describe him in as many different ways as they describe the farm. He is a "spooky do-gooder," a substitute father, a genuine adult, a brother, a plural husband, a business partner, a man who "forces" lovers to "need" him.

Contradictions are left unadjusted since the labels reflect the personalities of the people who offer them rather than describing De Witt himself. His own summary is that he believes in himself. The importance of this value is established as he helps newcomers find a way to believe in themselves, too. When Roger arrives in search of his traditional victim, Margaret, De Witt helps him take over his own life without having to rely on the support of an abusive relationship. When Margaret arrives, feeling gross and disfigured, he helps her find a value for herself which does not depend on sexuality.

De Witt's need for variety also is symbolic of the farm. In the world, he has functioned as a psychiatrist, a chiropractor, an accountant, a lawyer and a real estate broker, although he has not been licensed in any of these roles because of his distaste for specialization. All these possibilities are professions, however, while the farm extends variety into life outside the nine-to-five experience typical in the world. He has always wanted to deliver a baby, and Margaret offers him the opportunity to deliver two. Hannah creates the opportunity for him to get involved in a school. Roger makes beef ranching possible. None of these experiences is important in itself, but all of them interest De Witt, since he is "suited for anything" that does not last "too long."

The world's attitude toward variety and change is very different from De Witt's. During the trip back into their pasts, Margaret and Roger both discover that they are locked into roles which restrict their growth. With their parents, they act like permanently sullen kids. Alone together away from the commune, they become angry, feel trapped, and begin to blame each other.

By contrast, the farm makes it possible for them to get along even with each other because it offers them variety.

The lack of accepted roles means that every relationship must be negotiated on the basis of the individuals involved. Since their trip convinces them they cannot accomplish this kind of relationship on their own, each willingly chooses to return to the farm, where De Witt is the psychic center.

Despite its twentieth-century surface which features sullenness, disorder, violence and hate, Rossner's novel turns out to include elements of all the earlier utopian types. Like the group in David Simple, this commune is consciously designed. Like Michael Armstrong, Any Minute I Can Split suggests that the world might be better off if social reeducation could take place on a massive scale. And like Cranford, Rossner's novel guarantees freedom and variety by showing that individuality flourishes most successfully in a network of unique and voluntary relationships which set roles aside.

This type of achievable utopia which is not doomed to fail has proved to be continuously intriguing to novelists. The works they produce are extremely different from each other in tone, but they have in common the dream of a voluntary association of individuals who allow for the uniqueness of others as carefully as they defend their own. They also include a realistic understanding of the way the conventional world responds to behavior of this kind.

Such novels often gather like-minded people around a symbolic central figure who feels strongly enough to take the first step. Geraldine Jewsbury's Constance Herbert, for example, accomplishes its happy ending by surrounding the heroine with a supportive group. Constance has insanity in her genetic background and so cannot marry or have children as a way of accumulating companionship and love. A small coterie of friends and relatives supply this lack. Constance buys a country house where the group live together in happy unconventionality. They maintain enough contact with the outside world for marriageable members to find mates. But this turns out to be an arrangement of Amazons, since the function of outside males is the biological one of supplying children, so that withdrawing from the world does not accidentally narrow their lives by depriving them of relationships friendship alone cannot supply.

In Felix Holt, George Eliot is ideological in a somewhat different way. She uses differences in social class values to shake the heroine's conviction about the inevitable

Alternative Groups / 57

rightness of the values with which she has grown up. A broader vision finally makes it possible for the heroine to reject both money and social status as ways of judging. In order to replace the world she cannot admire, she relies upon the company of an equally alienated hero whose philosophical practicality has offended his mother and jeopardized his life in the conventional world of politics and profit.

This kind of utopian group which develops and emphasizes individuality occurs as a secondary pattern in some twentieth-century novels which are interesting in other ways as well. Dorothy L. Sayers, for example, uses an academic setting to cast aside the usual hierarchies of class, rank and parentage. In Gaudy Night, academic women discover the equality and individuality available to people of any background who devote themselves to the life of the mind in a social context where only talent counts. And though Jane Rule's The Young in One Another's Arms is most intriguing as a representation of Canadian-American border politics, it also includes a kind of accidental boarding house which maintains itself as a voluntary group by setting up a subsistence business. The activity in common does not invade individuality since no one is committed to anything and every participant remains entirely free to come and go.

The pictures of the world withdrawn from in these novels are as varied as differences in place and time and author's attitude can make them. And this variety outside helps establish some consistent patterns in the utopian groups described. All these groups accept temporary visitors as amiably as they greet new active members. Both members and visitors are always free to come and go. No one is forced to leave, even when they break the rules in basic ways. Such decisions involve only the person making the choice because the basis of judgment is so intensely personal-- satisfaction in varied individuality is the reason to join, and a preference for conventions and roles is the reason to leave. Ideologies which sound more structured are entirely personal statements, which anyone is free to make, and everyone is welcome to ignore. Once unique individuals find such a group to enrich their lives, they think everywhere else is exile.

Notes

1   Malcolm Kelsall, "Introduction," The Adventures of David

Simple (London: Oxford University Press, 1969), p. xii.

2 Kelsall, p. xiv.

3 Kelsall, p. xxvii.

4 "Preface," The Life and Adventures of Michael Armstrong, The Factory Boy (1840; rpt. London: Frank Cass, 1968), p. iii.

5 Michael Armstrong, p. 186.

6 "Preface," Michael Armstrong, p. iv.

3. INTERNATIONAL OPTIONS

Maria Edgeworth, Castle Rackrent
Geraldine Jewsbury, Zoe
Edith Wharton, Age of Innocence

others:
Frances H. Burnett, A Fair Barbarian
Jane Rule, The Young in One Another's Arms
Maria Edgeworth, The Absentee

    When Frances Trollope sent her group of factory young people to Germany in order to free them from their pasts, she implied that it is better to be separated from surrounding society than to be in constant contact with a culture which misunderstands or disapproves. But permanent isolation is not always the goal of writers who take an international approach to social alternatives. Rather than being cut off from foreigners, travellers can learn new languages, change their wardrobes, keep current on different topics for casual conversation, and even adapt to another church when doing so will free them from the drawbacks of an exile's role.

    Writers who see national borders in cultural terms are likely to bring outsiders into close and constant contact with strange communities, using their surprise and their adjustment to show how important private habits are to personality. In this type of fiction, characters may tackle a new community in the aftermath of a demoralized retreat from the culture where they were born. Exiles may find a society which suits them almost by accident, without dreaming they could belong anywhere. Or they may have set out deliberately toward a network of assumptions and tolerances which they believe will allow them room to breathe. Whatever their reasons for getting involved with a new country, they function as case studies in how travel can provide a smorgasbord of cultures.

Novels making use of this principle sometimes provoke critical responses which demonstrate rather than analyze the remarkableness of the approach to national stereotypes. Outright blame, or neglect, is bad enough, but praise for the wrong thing can be even more disconcerting, as Maria Edgeworth's Castle Rackrent shows. Edgeworth is given credit for the innovation of staging her drama in the muddleheaded mind of a "simple" narrator.[1] Such praise helps rescue Edgeworth from neglect and silence, but it also tends to conceal her actual accomplishment. Castle Rackrent's narrator, Thady, is many things during the book--"honest," "poor," and "faithful"--but he is not "simple." Rather, he is Irish. He maintains his cultural identity in the face of persistent pressure from English norms, and his ability to do so proves he is the opposite of simple, in both meanings of the word.

Castle Rackrent's "Preface" defines the function of the story's narrator by insisting that it takes unselfconscious domestic behavior to reveal "real" character. Private happiness and personal grief constitute the "real rewards" and the "real punishments" which make definitions of virtue and vice convincing, since nothing beyond the external social role emerges from a study of public appearance and action. For this reason, a gossiping tale in the idiom of the locality is more accurate and more informative than any official survey. Since Thady has lived in the family for "two hundred years, me and mine," he is the ideal voice for the Irish view.

Castle Rackrent is unusual, even among novels of this type, since it examines the possibility that nations, as well as individuals, may change the value system in which they began. At the time the novel was written, Ireland's union with Great Britain was being debated in primarily political terms. But Edgeworth was interested in the emotional meaning of the proposed change. As the oldest daughter of the Edgeworths of Edgeworthstown, she had reason to know that the most crucial question, for Irish lives, was not political at all. The real question was cultural. Would Ireland lose its identity upon union with Great Britain? If it did, what would the loss mean?

Before Edgeworth could speculate about cultural change, she needed to define the traditional values which govern Irish views. She used the Rackrent family for this purpose, following it through four generations, from establishment by Act of Parliament to downfall through apoplexy and gambling. As the story unfolds, the plot moves forward on the basis of a generally English standard regarding causes and effects. But Thady includes a running commentary on the story he tells. Since both his method and his analysis are Irish, he does not contradict conventional attitudes. Instead, he substitutes an internally consistent and philosophically stimulating interpretation governed by attitudes so different that doubts are raised about every event and detail, even down to the meaning of individual English words.

Edgeworth's method is to use each Rackrent as an embodiment of some major element of the anti-Irish stereotype conventional at the time. Thady then explains how the Irish interpret behavior which seems so easy for outsiders to condemn. Sir Patrick, for example, is an infamous drunk. His drinking has the conventional result, in terms of the plot. By the time he dies of the shakes and apoplexy, he is so deeply in debt that his corpse is arrested on its way to its grave.

If it were true that everyone lives by an identical value system, details such as these would not need to be interpreted. But what events mean in any work of literature is a second question which is separate from what happens in the plot. And unless the values of both writer and reader are utterly conventional, the implications of experience depend upon the standards embodied in the individual work, as Edgeworth shows.

Drinking, for example, is not a symbol which stands for the same thing in every mind. Thady is proud of Sir Patrick's ability to sit out the best man in Ireland. When his hands shake so much he can barely raise his glass, Sir Patrick's only reaction is affectionate regret over how his father would feel at the sight, since he used to praise Sir Patrick for being so steady handed when he first taught him to drink as a small boy.

Bankruptcy also turns out to be subject to interpretation. Thady explains that Sir Patrick is the finest host in Ireland and gives clear evidence to support the claim. For example, Sir Patrick has the chicken house refitted as a hostel to accommodate friends and the "public in general" who "honor" him with their company quite "unexpectedly" but so continuously that the castle cannot hold them all. Even his final fit does not interrupt his hospitality, since his guests "sit it out" and do not endanger their enjoyment by sending for word of his health until morning.

It is the emotional results of this hospitality which interest Thady. He explains that the whole country range with the praises of this gentleman who lived and died beloved by rich and poor. Since Sir Patrick is such a general hero, interrupting his funeral procession in order to seize his body for debt is the work of "villains." Their claim of acting on behalf of creditors is merely the "disguise" of the law, which brings down the wrath of the "mob." It also justifies the heir's refusal to accept Sir Patrick's outstanding bills as debts of honor, since involving the law means "an end of honor to be sure."

In terms of conventional stereotypes, the heir, Sir Murtagh, is a quarrelsome man, too involved with the law to notice or care that his wife is a rack-renter. But for this generation, too, Thady understands personality traits differently. He repeats like a refrain the information that Sir Murtagh was "a very learned man in the law." The advantage of this is that he knows he can confiscate trespassing cattle, and so he does not like for Thady to talk about the possibility of mending the fences which would keep his tenants' animals where they belong.

Sir Murtagh also enjoys "having the character" of legal learning, though it leaves him "too incredulous" about other belief systems. For example, he "thinks nothing of the Banshee" which has been heard beneath his window. He also ignores a serious cough. The death which results from this "incredulous" behavior is entirely appropriate--Sir Murtagh breaks a blood vessel in the passion of his "last speech." The fact that he was yelling at his wife rather than a judge does not deny him his audience--the kitchen "was out on the stairs," and so he was heard more attentively than he would have been at the courts.

In eulogizing Sir Murtagh, Thady describes him as "the best of husbands" and then explains this means he looked into his affairs and made money for his family. Evidence in support of such a summation is the fact that his widow was left to enjoy a "fine jointure." The money came from her own efforts, since Sir Murtagh's lawsuits used up so much more than his income that he was driven to sell off part of the estate to meet his costs. Financial details such as these are crucial in the usual view, but to Thady, the fact of the situation is the fine jointure. His concern is not a conventional pity for the new widow. What he cares about is that the jointure makes it possible for her to leave "to the great joy of the tenantry."

Thady points out that he never said anything "one way or the other" while "my lady" was part of the family. To a non-Irish mind, the statement is false in both implication and fact. The form of the statement seems to promise an attack, now that the widow is no longer "the family," but all Thady does is get up to see her "safe out of sight" at three o'clock in the morning. On the other hand, during the time he claimed to have been silent, what he really was doing was describing her habits in great detail. His descriptions are phrased sympathetically, however, and that is the point, to Thady, since to "say something" is to criticize.

Thady's method of talking about "my lady" without "saying" anything shows how his monologue manages to include both English and Irish information. He does not say she starved her servants. He says she was a "strict observer, for self and servants" of fast days, but not holidays. She was "very charitable." This means she set up a charity school where children on the estate learned to read and write for nothing. He then adds that they paid for their learning by spinning for my lady. The yarn they worked with was "duty" yarn, which their parents had donated. They wove it for my lady without wages since the looms were a gift from the Linen Board to the people on the estate, and my lady arranged for the gift. Thady explains that she was a "good wife," since she provided luxurious dinners for her husband out of the "duty" fowls, "duty" turkeys and "duty" geese which she "racked" from the estate. She was such a "great economist" that she would accept even money, "if offered properly."

In other words, the widow Rackrent lived up to her name, even though it was hers only by marriage to a man whose father had been born an O'Shaughlin. Thady notices the details of rack-renting, and he speculates about possible explanations. He suspects my lady might have Scotch blood, for example. And his search for a national stereotype to cover the situation in a way he can accept extends to Sir Murtagh. The costs of the law keep Sir Murtagh so perpetually eager for money that he "makes English tenants" of everyone on his estate. These external value systems—"Scotch" and "English"—can be brought to Ireland, and the Irish will be helpless to resist them, but they will only be endured and not adopted.

Sir Murtagh's younger brother, Sir Kit, is more "like the family" since he values a guinea "as little as any man." But when he leaves the estate in the hands of an agent and lives at Bath as an absentee, the result to the estate is almost as disastrous as rack-renting. As usual, Thady does not discuss absenteeism directly. Instead, he notices a "family likeness" between the brothers which contradicts the contrast between their personalities and characters.

Representing both an English and an Irish point of view, Castle Rackrent's plot includes the worst aspects of absenteeism, even though Thady consistently explains events from the point of view of "the family." When Sir Kit moves to Bath, for example, he is living "to the honor of his country abroad." When gambling debts force him to send constantly for more money, Thady blames the agent since Sir Kit could not possibly need "so much money, and he a single man."

Sir Kit finally marries in order to rescue the estate, just as his older brother did. Again, the sacrifice turns out badly. Sir Murtagh's wife--a Skinflint before marriage--outlives him, though Thady excuses him for such a poor choice on the grounds that Sir Murtagh could not have known she would do so. Sir Kit's situation seems better since his wife has her property with her in the form of a diamond cross. However, she refuses to give up her diamonds. Sir Kit locks her into her room and says she will have to stay there until she cooperates. She stands her ground, and so Sir Kit begins making himself agreeable to unmarried women in the neighborhood.

Sir Kit's reaction might seem extreme to unsympathetic eyes, but in fact he is perfectly justified, on several grounds, as Thady explains. If Sir Kit does not have access to his wife's funds, for example, it cannot be true that he is married, in any meaningful way. This is a relief to Thady, since it frees him from thinking of the woman as part of "the family" and so he can "say something" about her. He points out that she should have "shown more duty" since Sir Kit "condescended to ask so often" for the diamonds which would rescue the estate at least temporarily. Her "duty" in this matter is even more clear because Sir Kit never made any secret of the fact that he married her for her money.

Thady is careful to show that Sir Kit's irritation was not unprovoked. Imprisonment comes only as the last event in a long series of blunders on her part. Sir Kit forgives her for complaining about the smell of whisky punch. He also forgives her for "heresy." She is "a Jewish" and gives orders that pork is not to be served. Sir Kit forgives the mistake, though of course he overrules her so that ham and sausage remain the center of their diet, as is traditional at the Castle.

Mistaken reactions to Ireland are a serious matter. Thady points out that Sir Kit's wife "laid the corner-stone" of all her "misfortunes" by laughing at the name of the bog of Allyballycarricko'shaughlin. After all, even Thady does not know "how many hundred years" the same "bit of bog" has been in the family. Since she has just been added to "the family," she is not entitled to an opinion about an association of such antiquity.

As the last Rackrent, Sir Condy is even more like "the family" than Sir Kit was, in terms of money. As a kind of warning of what is to come, Thady points out that Sir Condy was "very little altered for the worse" by what he saw of the "great world" before inheriting. Sir Kit had the excuse of gambling to account for his costs, but Sir Condy simply exhausts the estate, for no consistent reason. One of his major expenses is an election which he wins by seeing that there is "not a soul sober" except "just when polling." However, this is less of a drain on the estate than would otherwise be the case, since the costs of the campaign come after he is already "ruined."

Like every other condition in Ireland, being "ruined" is subject to interpretation. For two years, it has been no more than a "great report," since the sheriffs during those years were particular friends and the sub-sheriffs were "gentlemen."

In this case as well as in all the others, however, the conventional interpretation is not the one which actually applies. Safety from the "vultures of the law" does not guarantee the survival of the estate. Thady's son, Jason, buys up all the outstanding debts and presents a single total to Sir Condy which has so many "noughts" that he is "dazzled" and signs over the entire estate.

Thady's attitude toward this transaction grows out of Edgeworth's concern with the possibility of change in national identity. While the Rackrent family goes through four generations without deviating from traditional behavior and values, the Quirk family needs only one generation to accomplish a total reversal in ways of judging. Thady persistently explains his point of view in terms of "the family," by which he means the Rackrents. Jason is his son, but that relationship does not make Jason Thady's "family," to start with, and Jason does not become "the family," even after he takes over Castle Rackrent.

Through her explication of the Irish sense of what "the family" is, Edgeworth illustrates the nonpolitical, emotional aftermath which inevitably would follow upon a loss of national identity for Ireland. "Honest Thady" "washes his hands" of Attorney Quirk. He insists to his turncoat son that the "lawful owner" must not be "turned out of the seat of his ancestors." The people on the estate prove Thady's point by rioting in front of the Castle as a way of rejecting Jason's claim to becoming their landlord.

Jason might defend himself by pointing out that he has been on the estate for one generation longer even than Thady has, whereas the O'Shaughlins were transplanted onto it only four generations ago. But Jason cannot prove his claim in terms of Irish logic since he has adopted a different set of rules. His doing so demonstrates what happens when fully structured value systems conflict directly. Jason and Sir Condy were schoolboys together, and yet only Sir Condy has maintained the genuinely Irish outlook. The two men document Jason's loss of Irishness in their reactions to every issue. Jason is terrified of the crowd mobbing the castle, but Sir Condy cheerfully steps out onto the balcony where his people can see him link his arm with his usurper. Jason is self-righteous over the huge stack of outstanding bills and debts with which he confronts Sir Condy, but Sir Condy turns aside and calls for whisky punch.

When Jason says to Sir Condy that they both will behave "like gentlemen," he points to one of the clearest contrasts between traditional Irish values and the outside values which come in conflict with them. Both men do behave like gentlemen, given their own standards in the matter. Jason wants to free the estate he has secured at so much cost and trouble, and so he offers to buy up the jointure Sir Condy has attached to it in favor of his wife in the event that she becomes his widow. To make his offer vivid, Jason brings golden guineas, which is the conventional English method of persuading the Irish.

The jointure is as significantly Irish as Jason's offer is English. Sir Condy signed the papers granting it when his wife announced that she was leaving him. Doing so was no more than "justice to himself" since it would keep her friends from saying he had married for money rather than for love. In true Irish fashion, of course, he married for neither. He flipped a coin to see whether he should marry Belle for her estate or Judy for her beauty, but neither Belle's money nor Judy's beauty lasts long enough to matter either to the estate or to Sir Condy.

The result of cultural change in Castle Rackrent is embodied in this final negotiation between the two value systems. Sir Condy accepts the guineas so that Jason will leave him in peace, and Jason hurries away in clear technical possession of an estate which he will never own, according to the standards of the people who have lived on the estate for "two hundred years and upwards." Thady's story ends with the "catastrophe." Continuing would mean transferring his attention to his son, and Thady is "not very well able" to tell about anyone so irrelevant to "the family."

By using Thady as her narrator, Edgeworth demonstrates a value system which probably could not be made convincing through direct exposition. Thady's method is to observe behavior in a perfectly frank way and to recognize what he is seeing. In speaking, he is equally honest, since, as he says, there is no reason to lie about happenings which everybody knows as well as he does. The structure of his ideas, also, is entirely reasonable. That is, he states judgments and organizes evidence in support of them. The connection between concept and detail is not conventional, but it is consistent, and it is based on Thady's values.

The result of this procedure is to demonstrate Edgeworth's conviction that two cultures may coexist without the dominant culture ever knowing what is going on. Half-suppressed reactions of a subjugated nation may follow a logic so "unknown" as to be unrecognized outside the population which has been overrun. In such a case, neither education nor tradition necessarily governs a person's culture by birth. Instead, individuals are left free to identify with the national profile which most comfortably assumes the values which make sense to them.

Like Maria Edgeworth, Geraldine Jewsbury treats

national identity more as a state of mind than as a political reality. Her characters sometimes are active travellers, but international comment in the narrative is not tied to their itinerary. Instead, Jewsbury uses constant reference to national types as a kind of shorthand to help in describing and analyzing characters. In Zoe, for example, a man may be "insipid" in the way of English husbands. A woman may analyze her own feelings while they are passing, like a French woman. Religious feeling may be as fanatical as it is in Italians.

Descriptions of this type sometimes contradict the facts of the individual's nationality by birth since Jewsbury applies the concepts to personality without regard to geography and politics. In her use, national stereotypes simply show patterns of belief about human nature. So relaxed a tone makes choice easy and trauma-free. When individuals do not like the customs of the country where they were born, they feel perfectly entitled to look elsewhere for a more congenial set of rules.

Alternatives may be found through travel, or they may be discovered in the company of unusual visitors. Both these methods serve the needs of Jewsbury's title character. Zoe makes choices among local opinions as she travels. And after she settles in England, she maintains only minimum contact with the standard local society, preferring to surround herself with a selection of friends who tolerate and understand her.

As Jewsbury represents it, choosing "customs" is an entirely pragmatic matter. Even before she is old enough to think about questions of behavior, Jewsbury's heroine becomes a problem to people who assume that culture is dictated by birth. Zoe is a terrible shock to the very English aunt who is to raise her after her mother dies. Mrs. Martha heartily agrees with most of the people in the community in seeing anything non-English as "outlandish." When Zoe arrives from Europe as a toddler, she speaks only French and has dark Mediterranean eyes. Mrs. Martha tries not to look at these appallingly foreign-colored eyes. But it is even harder to avoid noticing Zoe's tendency to "romp like a ploughboy." The child does love reading, but even in this area, she breaks the rules. She is so avid that her typically English cousin warns her she will become an "idiot" from pouring over books. And she refuses to admire "Goody Two Shoes," the one book it would be appropriate for her to find fascinating.

Life as an English girl suits Zoe in some ways, despite such problems. Her exotic looks and manners attract as many people as they repel, so she is not isolated or ignored. She does not need to fascinate everyone since she "despises" the people around her enough to make general popularity meaningless as a goal. Independent from the beginning, she is strengthened by situations which would be devastating to less spirited girls. For example, her cousin tries to undercut her pride by telling her that she is illegitimate because her parents were not married until after she was born. The attack does not serve its purpose since Zoe's reaction is "not like other people." Instead, the information causes her to feel more interest in her mother. It also serves as a warning that she will need to depend upon herself.

Jewsbury establishes this behavior as adaptive, rather than passive, by setting limits to the forebearance required of Zoe's independent spirit. Zoe accepts her cousin's taunts, but she cannot submit to the pitying, self-sacrificing protectiveness of the neighborhood boy whose typical English gallantry moves him to offer to marry her in defiance of her delapidated moral state. She convinces herself that nothing could be more unbearable than English squeamishness about anyone who does not fit perfectly into English forms. Now that she is old enough to be marriageable, she faces unremitting pity and contempt, in England. Therefore, she insists on going to her father in Paris.

The move succeeds in its most basic function, since it marks the beginning of Zoe's insistence on finding the social context which best serves her need for self-respect and freedom. Still, it is disastrous in its details. Zoe has still to learn that rejecting one offensive social group does not guarantee the automatic discovery of a more congenial alternative. Looking back she sees that English girls are allowed considerable freedom, so long as "love, marriage and handsome men" do not fill their minds. By contrast, French girls are prisoners until they marry. While she lived with her English aunt and uncle, Zoe was allowed unlimited outdoor exercise. But her father's life abroad has made him a Parisian in his attitude toward daughters. As a result, he does not permit Zoe even to go for a drive, except when he is occasionally willing to accompany her. In England, Zoe was surrounded in the usual way by young people of both sexes. But the equivalent rules in Paris limit her social contacts to her father and the card-playing cronies who call on him.

Even at this young age, Zoe is pragmatic about the result of her actions. Exploring her imprisonment, she discovers that marriage is the only "honorable emancipation" for women in Paris. Resourceful and independent, she begins to estimate the husband-like traits of each of her father's friends. None of the cardplayers is acceptable on even the minimum basis of transforming her into an "independent married woman." But one of her father's more presentable former friends turns up unexpectedly, and Zoe seizes her opportunity like a "school-girl" looking forward to her "holidays."

The importance of freedom to Zoe can be evaluated in terms of the objections to marriage which must be set aside. Gifford is her father's age. It is not Zoe herself who dazzles him, since what attracts his attention is her physical resemblance to her long-dead mother, whom he admired. In addition, Gifford meant to enter a monastery rather than marry. He wavers from this long-standing dedication only because travel has isolated him from the support of his usual society and the ideas which normally surrounded him.

Zoe dismisses all these problems. Her concern is that Gifford knows the story of her birth and adored her mother anyway. Her only other interest in the transaction is the fact that marriage to anyone will bring her the "rights and privileges" which France accords to adult women but not to girls.

Fortunately for Zoe, rules about marriage turn out to be portable. Gifford is English by birth, and marrying reminds him of the fact. His repatriation could turn into a serious problem for them both, since "English" wives are supposed to "employ" themselves "rationally" by doing needlework, whereas Zoe thinks her value lies in something more than sewing with colored silks. She is in fact English, since both her father and her husband carry an English passport. But a woman like Zoe can never be mistaken for an "English wife," no matter what the details of her biography might imply.

Regardless of his return to English views, Gifford is in no condition to be intolerant of Zoe's difference. His own state is a contradiction, in England, though it came to him by birth. He is a Catholic. This fact modifies his identity, since Catholics suffer under a kind of "theoretical hatred" in England, even when they seem "English" in other ways--by being "good-humored," for example, or by having a "mania" for "being sincere."

The contradiction helps both Gifford and Zoe when they move to his estate in the English countryside. Their conventional neighbors do not accept a blending of English and Catholicism. And though the community generally maintains an indulgent silence, the pressure of even unstated opinion keeps Gifford from achieving the complacency of a "regular English husband." When left undisturbed, he thinks of both his identities as inevitable. But his non-Catholic neighbors have the same basis for their hostile views. Since their opinions are as passionately held as his own, he is forced to accept the possibility that both religion and culture might be considered options rather than inevitabilities. Zoe in particular is likely to have such a reaction, he believes. She reads a "vast deal" more than a woman should and thinks about what she reads so dangerously that he concludes it is a "thousand pities" his wife is "not a man."

Gifford's reaction shows that Zoe's sense of herself as a wife of the French type is no more inconvenient than is her status as a "free thinker." Gifford objects to both. Nevertheless, their marriage has a European tone which he cannot change, and so he limits his reaction to occasional statements about unorthodoxy. His closest approach to attempting a conventional husbandly control comes in the religious area since he worries more about Zoe's soul than about her social irregularities. He asks the local priest to discuss ethics with Zoe. Unfortunately for Gifford's plans, the priest is impressed by Zoe's highly rational freethinking mind and overwhelmed by her warmth and beauty. Never having had to guard himself against women, the priest is converted before he realizes his danger. He finally leaves the Catholic church instead of pulling Zoe into his faith. Gifford regrets that Zoe has "undermined" the priest, but he is too resigned to her nature to hold her strength against her.

Zoe's social unorthodoxy gives most trouble in terms of her influence on Gifford's daughter by an earlier marriage. As an absorbedly devout Catholic, Clotilde is persistently un-English in attitude and behavior. Gifford's firmly conventional niece insists that Clotilde's failure to behave like a modest English girl comes from the influence of the "flashy foreigner" Gifford has afflicted her with in the shape of a stepmother. Gifford ignores the accusation since he feels his daughter should not be judged by conventional notions. It is only when

Zoe agrees with him that he reconsiders his tolerance. Zoe insists that "conventional go-carts" are good only for helpless people and certainly do not apply to Clotilde. Hearing his own idea transformed into such scornful and wholesale contempt, Gifford recoils from arguing special cases. He insists there is "a value and beauty" in "grateful allegiance to conventionalities" which Zoe fails to understand. And he further defines the limits of his mental independence when he paraphrases his niece's opinion and warns Zoe that he will not tolerate her influencing Clotilde toward her own indifference.

Occasional conflicts such as these do not mar the marriage, partly because Gifford's behavior in general is remarkable. Jewsbury emphasizes his tolerance by offering a contrasting glimpse of the life Zoe would have faced if she had married the young neighbor who self-immolatingly offered to rescue her. It is her conventional cousin who flourishes as the squire's wife, producing children and supervising the household and never looking beyond her "own domestic circle."

Zoe's idea of doing her duty by her husband leads her in a completely different direction. An obliging hostess to younger members of Gifford's family, she helps them find a niche for themselves in society while not interfering with their personal views. Socially charming, she is dazzling and besought in London, even though she feels a prison sentence would be easier to bear. Convinced that religion is nothing more than "cobwebs to catch flies," she nevertheless decorates the chapel, attends prize day at the Catholic College Gifford establishes, and entertains Gifford's Catholic friends without any awkwardness. A devoted mother, she produces two fine sons and supervises them so sympathetically that Gifford feels free to write a will which leaves them in her sole charge. Dedicated to domestic peace, she is gracious with Gifford's lapses. When he says she would not understand a legal case he is involved with, she does not remind him of her superior intelligence. Instead, she quietly pursues her own plans. When he is offended by one of her books and burns it, she does not refer to her rights. She simply buys another copy and keeps it tactfully out of sight.

Gifford is an ideal husband for a woman like Zoe. As a Catholic, he cannot accept English customs wholeheartedly, and his life abroad also has tended to loosen the hold of English customs on his way of judging. These ambiguities in his own situation make him more tolerant than a "normal" husband could hope to be. He is intelligent enough to recognize

Zoe's "genius," and he is sophisticated enough to admit that her mental superiority will automatically interfere with any efforts she might make at behaving conventionally. Since Gifford recognizes that Zoe is living up to her idea of her duty in her own way, their marriage flourishes by accommodating attitudes which would destroy a more thoroughly "English" household.

Zoe's reaction is less surprising than Gifford's since she always adjusts her expectations to her reality. After she has had a chance to compare her marriage to the English standard, she recognizes her good fortune. Gifford is dull, and sometimes his social and religious faiths are limiting. Still, he accepts her nature, once he knows it. And this is so remarkable a generosity that Zoe develops a sincere liking for him which is not love but is far warmer than her initial almost impersonal gratitude to the man who made it possible for her to escape into the social freedom of a French marriage.

In Zoe, there are national styles in lovers as well as in marriages. Gifford's niece is "too thoroughly English" to think she can care for anyone except her husband, but Zoe is not limited by such ideas. She falls in love with Father Everhard, the priest who was supposed to save her soul for her husband. Her being free to do so is "French," and so it does not seem to her to violate her marriage.

On the other hand, Everhard Burrows in love is "English" to the core. He is from a very old family whose English Renaissance roots integrate his religion into the rest of his personality in a way which is not available to Gifford. The people who live near the Burrows' Manor House are anti-Catholic, as modern English are supposed to be, but they know that everyone used to be Catholic. They talk themselves into patience by recognizing that the Burrows family remained good Catholics, as well as good people, when Catholicism was suppressed in England. Looked at this way, the religious question is English in its essence. Its role in history is echoed in Everhard's personal experience when he discovers that he would have made an ideal Jesuit, if that order had not been suppressed.

Identifying himself with the suppressed minority of an oppressed minority, Everhard clearly faces problems with his social role. Unused to women, he is more at ease with Zoe's saintly stepdaughter than with Zoe. But Zoe needs the companionship of a mind as good as her own, and her sophistication enables her to make him fall in love without realizing what is happening to him. Unsuspicious until the very end, he translates his emotional upheaval into a spiritual form, accepting Zoe's voice as the "voice of his soul."

The identification is unexpected, in some ways. The first time Everhard heard of Zoe, she was described as Gifford's "heretic wife." The label is accurate enough, as far as it goes. But the role it implies is entirely false, as Everhard quickly discovers. Zoe insists that anyone who really does believe should be left in peace. She saves her intolerance for use against people who pretend to a belief they do not hold. It is hypocrisy, rather than faith, which offends her.

Since Zoe's doctrine is as attractive as her person is, her influence helps Everhard set his life in order. His childhood wish to serve the church came from his affection for the kindly old priest who raised him. This simple vocation is undermined as his intelligence matures. Studying for Holy Orders turns out to be disillusioning since he becomes convinced that the church is not the only "form" which "Truth" takes. This discovery does not provoke a turning point, however, since he lacks the emotional independence and the energy to launch an entirely different life. He has an offer to go into trade in London, but he is too English to accept such work. His obliging aunt is ready to arrange a brilliant European marriage for him, since he is welcomed in Parisian society as un jeune homme charmant. But his tastes are against this alternative, as well, since it is the "voluptuousness" of celibacy which really attracts him. Since nothing else is offered, he submits himself to Holy Orders without faith, as the least afflicting alternative.

Everhard's responses amplify Jewsbury's international theme since he searches for the truth of his own nature by reacting against nation after nation. The Italian Catholicism in which he has been trained is too fanatical to interest him, and yet it cuts him off from anyone else. His total isolation turns Zoe into a godsend. She accepts belief without herself believing in a way which proves to Everhard that tolerance can form the center of a healthy personality.

Under Zoe's subtly flirtatious attention, Everhard's mind and personality blossom. He imagines he is attracted to a life which does not involve "yokes" and fails to understand why he gravitates to Zoe in a way which forms new social and mental habits. Zoe does not wish to awaken him to his unconscious love since she is a "coquette in grain," and so their attachment deepens peacefully until an accident warns Everhard of his danger. A fire leaves Zoe fainting in Everhard's arms, and the conflagration is repeated as a "fire" in Everhard's veins. He is astounded at his passionate response to Zoe's defenselessness, and Zoe apologizes for "letting" him "betray" himself since it was the "last thing" he wanted to do.

Helped by Zoe's tact, Everhard loses only his naivete without being deprived of his innocence. He leaves the area in order to avoid a repetition of inappropriate passion, but he does not reject his genuine feeling for Zoe. Recollected at a safe distance, she remains a source of "gladness" which is so central to his being he never thinks to wonder if she is "constant."

In contrast to this "cold and remote" faith, Zoe's French-style lover assaults her feelings like a tropical storm. Mirabeau loves her "like hatred," and she is so confused to find herself in love with two men at once that she considers writing to Everhard and pleading with him to protect her from her passionate response to the man who has taken his place in her life. She has no husband to defend her from herself, since she is now a widow. Still, she finally decides not to appeal to Everhard for fear she might be taken at her word and required to give up Mirabeau.

Her feeling for Mirabeau is as intense and demoralizing as her love for Everhard was calming. Everhard's Jesuitical reserve and yearning attachment to "metaphysical philosophy" lose their appeal under the assault of Mirabeau's "radiant" intelligence. His eyes gleam like lightning, his voice is deep and mellow, and his shaggy black hair is "not confined." "More than mortal," he seems to have come from another planet. His "genius mastered hers" and the result is a delightfully tormenting turmoil.

Everhard's intricate conversations are not at all Mirabeau's style. He courts in silence, spending hours in a physical closeness interrupted only rarely by brief phrases of passionate tenderness and references to eternity. Zoe is so moved by his procedures that she admits her happiness in his presence is intense enough to feel like pain. When she decides to exert her own dignity in self defense, Mirabeau disappears without an explanation. He returns without comment only after she is humbled by anxiety and neglect.

Zoe has always been approached in the most perfect deference, and she is stunned by Mirabeau's invasive insistence on both his defects and his power. He describes himself as "scarred and thunder-riven," an "outcast" who is "soiled and defaced." Nevertheless, he insists he loves her more than she can love herself and this makes him her "master." He is no "credit" to her, but she is "swallowed up" in him and should stop her "childish pretense" of independence.

Both Zoe's lovers believe they have a mental affinity with her, but even in this point, they are so different they scarcely seem to fill the same role. Mirabeau tells Zoe women suffer only the hell of consequences, whereas "noble-minded men" dread the hell of remorse. When Zoe gently answers that "some women" regret wrong action in itself without regard for blame from others, Mirabeau recognizes a "point of sympathy" between them.

The one thing these men genuinely do share is a misunderstanding of the essentially social function of a lover in Zoe's mind. It is a mistake which allows them to read false meanings of their own into her actions. Mirabeau's demands are no more justified than Everhard's trust was. Mirabeau believes Zoe is "strong and wise" and will give herself "freely" out of an eagerness for her "whole being" to be "molten into" his. While she sedately plans on their being "friends all our lives," Mirabeau is offering the "whole force" of his soul. He assumes they will rise above society, but Zoe sees a social context for even metaphoric intensity such as Mirabeau's. And when a sympathizing friend finally reminds her of her reputation, Zoe mentions marriage. As a divorced Catholic, Mirabeau cannot marry. He is as maddened by the admission that he is subject to rules outside himself as he is by the discovery that Zoe has been "cold-blooded" and "calculating" while he has been in love.

Their final conflict is the opposite of Zoe's resolution with Everhard. Mirabeau insists she accompany him to France, where his career is newly launched. While he is busy "conquering" and "ruling," she will be his "support" his "angel," his "counsellor." Zoe sees a different picture. Mirabeau has already "loved and abandoned" a hundred women, and she angrily refuses to love him as a "weak woman" who is willing to throw away her sons and social position solely in order to follow her man.

The refusal to disappear into Mirabeau's "destiny" is hard for Zoe, but she is rewarded for maintaining her own values. Peacefulness returns to her after Mirabeau storms back to France. Once outside the range of his overwhelming personality, she is able to see that he intended only to engulf her rather than to "modify" her character. The difference means that his influence does not linger after his dominating physical presence ends.

Slowly recovering her former balance, Zoe remembers how Everhard associated himself with her interests and occupations rather than loving "himself in disguise." Working out the contrast in detail, she admits that Mirabeau saw her sons as his rivals, and they return the favor, remarking that he likes to make people do what "they don't want." By contrast, Everhard's spirit is constantly present as she works with her sons' education. Since she considers motherhood to be her most important role, Everhard's identification with it allows his memory to return unscathed by Mirabeau.

Further proof that she chose correctly comes as her later life replaces everything Mirabeau offered--except passion. Her older son becomes a Member of Parliament before he marries, and Zoe serves as his hostess. It is a more stately and more honorable version of the tasks she would have performed as Mirabeau's adjunct. In addition, she has the comfort of a lifelong friendship with Clara, who would have been lost to her, along with her sons, had she given Mirabeau her "whole being," as he demanded.

Jewsbury presents friendship as a need separate from love for any individual who is outside the normal code. Like Zoe, Everhard must have a "confidante," though he is too much a "Jesuit" for any woman to fill this need. Paralleling the emotional response which drove him away from Zoe's part of England, his intellectual involvement with her extraordinary mind encourages him to leave the church which has never served his needs. Still unsure of his own nature, he tries to become a kind of secular Jesuit by immersing himself in the daily life of an utterly unenlightened village in Wales. He is not suited to a totally friendless life, however, and so he is relieved when ranting missionaries run him out of town as a way of polarizing the emotions of the ignorant villagers whom Everhard is too sophisticated to reach.

Recoiling from the primitive life, he seeks a different

audience by writing a book which explains the ideas he has developed under Zoe's influence. He has spent so long with these thoughts as his only companionship that they seem self-evident truths, to Everhard. But they are so far outside the limits of normal opinion that his book is greeted with "one simultaneous yell of horror" from educated English readers.

As usual in this novel, geography helps him define his social needs. He feels he must leave England, since its population seems to him to have "gone mad." He already knows France is too fashionable and Italy too decadent for his tastes. Choosing among the European countries which have not yet disqualified themselves in his opinion, Everhard wanders to Germany, as Frances Trollope's refugees do. And in Germany, he finally finds a congenial group who take his views as a matter of course. These slightly idiosyncratic thinkers "seek after good" while "mutually tolerating" each other. In such a social context, Everhard is finally freed from his "false position." He is able to spend the rest of his life in happiness and peace among minds as good as his own.

What England finally offers to the widowed Zoe, and Germany provides for the defrocked Everhard, Clotilde finds in Italy. In the eyes of her "respectable English" cousin, Clotilde is immodest to the point of depravity because she falls in love with a man who has not offered himself to her. But Clotilde is more devastated by the sensation of passionate love than she is by the disappointment when her half-acknowledged lover deserts her. She has always been devout to a fault, and only in Italy can she find a convent sufficiently absorbed in God to serve as a congenial context for her needs. The appropriateness of her choice is shown in her inward peace and confidence and in her remarkably rapid rise to become Mother Superior over the nuns who trained her.

Since Jewsbury shows that both Zoe and Clotilde find a place for themselves in a country which has proved galling for someone else among their social contacts, Zoe does not contrast national types in order to make absolute choices among them. Instead, Jewsbury makes the opposite point. The existence of extremely different national "customs" makes personal freedom and comfort possible by maintaining a range of options which individuals of integrity can choose among if they find themselves ill-suited to their place of birth.

Without this European variety, unique individuals would be in trouble, as most of the characters are until they find their place. The problem is that society "shows no mercy" to individuals who are "different from other people." "Singularity" is always in "bad taste," since the one thing everyone everywhere agrees upon is that "mutual toleration" is not a possibility. For this reason, anyone who feels out of step with a particular society is not entitled to settle for being either defensive or odd. Instead, everyone must look for the social context where they will seem normal enough to be interesting, rather than drifting like some pathetically lost "link between two species."

Fortunately, the different nations of Europe differ from each other on everything from the function of women to the meaning of amiability and the proper length for hair. With so much variety to choose from, no one needs to be misunderstood, trampled, or alone.

Americans who cannot fit into the roles offered by their society face a more elaborate problem. Less exposed to other nations, and conscious of a history which is still too brief to show how time routinely changes customs, Americans tend to grow up not even grudgingly aware that social systems can differ in basic ways and still be valid for the people who accept them. One result is that social enforcement becomes easier for those who are well suited to conventional American standards. On the other hand, an apparently unchallenged belief in uniformity makes acculturation far more destructive for individuals whose instincts and responses take them outside the norms.

Traditional critical response to Edith Wharton's The Age of Innocence is a demonstration of how this works. This international novel is usually discussed as a kind nostalgic, poetic, historical regionalism which celebrates and traps in amber one city, one time, and one social class. [2] In fact, the novel Wharton wrote is a study of three extremely different personalities who use geography and cultural relativity as tools for self-discovery.

In The Age of Innocence, Wharton uses "Old New York" to show how American social networks deal with members of the group. She depicts New York society as strikingly uniform in its treatment of individuals. Everyone is expected to behave as people "always" have. However, the results depend upon the personality of the individual being socialized. A person who fits the New York pattern may be in a "rut" of tribal habit. Individuals who are partially aware that they do not quite fit in may think of New York uniformity as a "prison." But New York natives who are helplessly different will be brushed aside as "foreign" when New York discovers how boringly simple its culture seems to them.

Wharton embodies the "straight up and down" patterns of New York in the character and behavior of May Welland, who "always" says and does the "right thing." May is "straightforward," her composure is routinely "boyish," and even on her wedding journey, she maintains her "boyish smile." Her "too-clear" eyes are shadowed only by her hat brim, since experience "drops away from her" without leaving a trace. She is so impervious to influence of any kind that her circulation seems to involve "preserving fluid" rather than the "ravaging element" of blood.

Since May is perfect in the role of a "Civic Virtue," her husband finally stops trying to see a difference between her "real" self and the tradition and training behind her. He is chilled by the "niceness" which makes her beauty "ineffectual," but he also realizes that May will be protected, even without the ability or wish to charm, since New York automatically "rallies around" anyone who so perfectly embodies the standards of the social group. The reaction is merely a reflex, since New York is a place of "habits" rather than "opinions." Inclusive, but not profound, its behavior seems like that of a "deaf-and-dumb asylum" to individuals who know there are alternatives. Its hold on its residents is a "narcotic" rather than an ethical standard which can be argued, adjusted and understood.

This silence is a necessity rather than an oversight. The "crystalline" atmosphere May embodies can be maintained in its absolute form only so long as it is not discussed. If society were to allow itself to begin talking about ideal behavior, cracks in the pattern would be discovered almost at once. For example, one of New York's two "great fundamental" clans is more worldly than the other. Their difference produces an undercurrent of tension in the very center of the group. So long as no one mentions what unruliness implies, individual lapses are manageable as temporary bad manners, to be corrected, or irritating habits, to be admitted silently and endured. For example, Professor Emerson Sillerton is like New York in being "set in his ways," but he is a thorn in society's side since he is "different from other people" without even realizing it. "Catherine the Great" is even more of an embarrassment since the "twinkle" in her eyes suggests she knows perfectly well that she is being willfully "peculiar" by building her house away from the homes of the rest of the clan, using the wrong color of stone and installing French windows.

People like these are tolerated in a shocked way since they are constantly present as part of the tribe. But some family members wander in addition to deviating, and in such cases New York is relieved to let their "foreignness" deny their identity by birth. "Poor" Medora Manson, for example, habitually returns to New York between marriages. Her marriages take place in a foreign rite, however, which leaves her family free to think of her as "the Marchioness." So un-American a title lets them feel justified in closing their feelings against her.

This reaction is not individual so much as it is New York's automatic assumption that women give up their claims by birth when they marry and acquire a foreign title. Priding herself on the bluntness which is her form of New York "honesty," Catherine Mingott points out that "the Countess Olenska" would be a "silly goose" to try to turn herself back into "Ellen Mingott." She has the "luck" to be a "married woman and a Countess," and New York will not allow her to pass herself off as an "old maid." The absoluteness of these categories is a reminder that there is only one respectable way to be unmarried in New York, and since experience does not "fall away" from Ellen, she cannot exist there under her birth name.

Wharton's New York is able to enforce this narrow view because isolation is a value as well as a geographical fact. When New Yorkers travel, they respond to the foreignness of other countries by becoming "more uncompromisingly local" and by falling tactfully silent in the presence of foreign intellectuals whose neglect of everything but their minds leaves them seeming "common," in New York eyes.

This habitual lack of transaction between New York and everywhere else is protective for people like May, whom it suits. But Newland Archer sometimes vaguely suspects that other nations may be made up of alternatives rather than of defects. Unlike May, who is "terrifyingly" in tune with New York in both instincts and training, Newland occasionally sees "his" New York through an "inverted telescope." He is even momentarily relieved by the sense of "other lives" and "other cities" and another world "beyond his world," although this expanded point of view finally reinforces his isolation rather than offering him an escape. When most repelled by "his" New York, he sees it from the "wrong end" of a telescope which converts him into a "dwindling" figure and his fiancée into a "faint" figure. Unfortunately this kind of vision offers him nothing beyond minimizing and depersonalizing them both. His ability to sense that other worlds exist does not set him free.

Wharton uses Newland Archer's ambivalence to show how social norms maintain themselves. In the beginning, Newland "holds his views" without feeling they need to be "examined" since they are identical to the responses of all the men he thinks of as "his kind." He considers himself superior to the other "specimens," but he "instinctively" accepts the general doctrine anyway, because striking out on his own would be both troublesome and "bad form." This complacent acceptance seems to be entirely satisfactory as long as it is not compared to any other way of life. But Newland's whole world is shaken when he encounters a new kind of creature who is completely outside his previous experience--a "nice" woman who "looks at life differently."

Ellen Olenska's impact on Newland is the "curious" one of "reversing his values." Where he has taken as a matter of course his "masculine pride" in the "proprietorship" of a fiancée of "abysmal purity," he suddenly finds himself saying that women should be "as free as we are." The purity he is "supposed" to want begins to seem "factitious" to him, and he shudderingly realizes that the blindfold which protects young ladies from the world's grime may actually be a "bandage" protecting eyes which are blind because evolution has stopped developing a sense of sight which is never used. However, he is no better satisfied with the opposite extreme. Ellen's eyes are simultaneously "meditative" and "kind," and Newland feels "frightened" by the knowledge their complexity implies.

This habit of recoiling from both options rather than making a choice is the aspect of his character which keeps Newland in New York. As long as betrothal visits are considered "usual" by everyone, he accepts them unthinkingly. But after he begins to sense what Ellen sees, such rituals become a kind of circus parade in which he is "shown off" like a "wild animal cunningly trapped." He used to think the customs of "his little tribe" had "world-wide significance," but Ellen's watchful presence causes him to develop a horror of "sameness." He begins to suspect that New Yorkers are mere "patterns stencilled on a wall." New York's formerly innocent gaiety is shockingly transformed into "children playing in a graveyard."

Once he begins to examine the ideas he has "inherited," Newland is surprised to find life can go on in the old way. He has glimpsed a "real life" filled with "real people" who live where "real things" happen to them, and the discovery turns his old life into a "sham," a ritual of "trifles," a performance.

Coming to believe that traditional life is "beyond enduring" is not the same as figuring out how to make his own mind less "empty and echoing." He can easily, if somewhat painfully, admit that his old life involved merely habit. But if he begins refusing to do what has always been done, he involves himself in making constant, deliberate choices. Doing so is a violation of his nature, since his personal reactions tend toward ambivalence rather than willing commitment.

Left to himself, Newland would recoil from every definite stand and thereby achieve a kind of balance by default. Such a personality can be coerced into normality against its preferences by persistent pressure from an encompassing social group. And this is the mechanism by which Newland is "trapped" into the early marriage he asks for so half-heartedly and conventionally. Forced into a definite action, he laughs hysterically rather than trying to negotiate for his freedom. "Imprisoned" in the marriage he longs to escape, he fascinates himself with the "strident laughter" of "inner devils" rather than rehearsing ways to escape from his "friendly" captors.

In this context it becomes clear that Newland's relationship with Ellen involves considerably more than her foreignness. Marriage to May embroils him in commitment, very much against his will. By contrast, adoring Ellen is infinitely satisfactory since it commits him to nothing at all. His feeling for her is "closer than his bones," and yet he does not even cross the room to stand beside her. For Newland, yielding to passion means dreaming of a "kind of sanctuary" where a visionary Ellen is "throned" among his secret thoughts and longings. Feeling trapped by May, he wants to go somewhere he and Ellen can escape "categories."

The real structure of this yearning is made clear by

Newland's refusal to take even the first step away from categories by leaving New York. He meets his needs by mentioning New York's worldy opposites in a barely controlled voice--Japan, Samarkand, India, or simply "travel." Going to an actual Ellen would lead to different daily details from those which follow upon his submission to May, but it would be equally destroying in the largest sense because it would require commitment from him. And that is what his whole nature wishes to avoid. For Newland, "real" life takes place inside the imaginary chapel in his mind. Ellen's undemanding presence there constitutes a rescue from an "actual" life which becomes more and more "insufficient." Satisfied by the remoteness which an image instead of a woman can supply, Newland finds himself "blundering" against traditional views like an "absent-minded man" tripping over his own furniture.

Going numbly through the social forms, Newland listens to his friends laugh and watches them talk while he, himself, floats somewhere between the chandelier and the ceiling--he has an out-of-body experience rather than leaving the room. Walking through the wedding ceremony, he detaches himself from both personal and social commitment by believing he has his eyes shut, and by allowing his spirit to drift into some far off "unknown." Appropriate to Newland's sense of what is happening to him in the publicity of Grace Church, Wharton puts into the minister's mouth the first words of the Burial Service rather than the opening passages of the Marriage Service.[3] After a few months of marriage, Newland tells May he is dead, that he has been dead for "months and months," but the confession ends with the bitterness and does not lead him on into a useable protest.

A man who sees death and dreams as the only practical method of changing his life is not likely to escape from the "dangerous sweetness of security," even when he realizes that "resignation" is one of its "principal constituents." His journalist friend, Wimsett, urges him to get down into the "muck" or else to emigrate, but Newland smiles "condescendingly," not bothering even to explain that a gentleman must "abstain" from such outrageous responses.

"Abstention" is the key to Newland's personality, and it is because she makes it possible for him to explore this quality more fully that Ellen proves to be so disruptive to his life. He has already tested the world of "Europeanized" Americans" and discovered them to be as "unreal as a carnival."

He thinks of the experience as the "greatest fun in the world," but only when the adventure is brief. The people who live such a life permanently turn into "malodorous hot-house exotics." The "complicated love affairs" of such "cosmopolitan women" are intensely distasteful to him, and it is in this context that he first examines Ellen's situation with the double vision of a family member and a legal adviser.

Like the rest of "his kind," Newland persistently sees Ellen as either a wife or a mistress. He accuses the family of trying to make her become Beaufort's mistress. He accuses Ellen of planning to "replace" him with Beaufort. And when Ellen grievingly confesses she loves Newland, he contemptuously fits her in the "familiar role" of married mistress.

It is Ellen's patience in refusing such assigned roles which is her real attractiveness to him. He is "tranquillized" by her ability to maintain a "perfect balance" between loyalty and honesty. He can trust it to be not an "artful" balance, since her explanation of her unprecedented attitude is interrupted by tears and "falterings." Ellen's "naturalness" is convincing, since "no one cries" in New York. Ellen's delicate refusal to fit either of the roles New York demands of women forces Newland to recognize a world of cruelty and hypocrisy and "elaborate dissimulation" behind the ruthless "solidarity" of a family opinion which will always sacrifice any individual for the well-being of the group.

Ellen looks at things "as they are," in contrast to New York's unflagging blindness. When she finally understands Newland, as well as New York, she recognizes that her ability to maintain a delicate balance is a more positive form of the ambivalence which leaves him helpless. Grimly realistic, she acts on the implications of Newland's feeling for her, when she understands it. She insists that they must be apart in order to be "near each other." The problem is that Newland forces her into a role, whenever she is physically present, just as the rest of "his" New York does. Unfortunately, the only role available is that of assignations, which is "detestable" to both of them. They can love each other only when physical separation leaves them free of the New York categories which mutilate Newland's perception of them both.

Newland is very glad to be told that they must separate, since it is a proposal which offers him exactly the life of detachment, of meditation rather than conversation, which he craves so helplessly. Life in May's environment seems like the grave to him as soon as he realizes it is not the only way a decent man can live. But life in Ellen's world would be vividly worse for him, because he "chokes and splutters" in her "stimulating" atmosphere.

It is apparently the sulphur in Ellen's air which gags Newland, since he speaks of Hell, rather than Europe, as her former address. He refers to the "contortions of the damned" and insists he would "rather see her dead" than back in "that hell." When Ellen's aunt acts as a go-between for Ellen's estranged husband, Newland thinks of her as a "messenger from Satan" who has come straight from Ellen's "hell."

As an individual who cannot help being different, Ellen takes a less "simple" view. She readily admits the "abominations" of her past life, but she is equally quick to recognize the splendors and attractions of the world, which "tugs" at her with "all its golden hands." She pleads with Newland to "hold out"--not to be like "all the others." She insists that she will no longer feel lonely and afraid, if they can succeed at loving each other. It is a resolution made possible because she defines loneliness as living with people who "ask one to pretend."

New York does ask Ellen to pretend. When she wants her "freedom," she is told she cannot divorce. She is warned not to live in a respectable but "eccentric" street, even though it is her only access to social variety and economy. She must not attend musical evenings since the "best" people do not host them. She cannot speak affectionately to her maid, since doing so is "foreign."

This difference in vision is too basic to be solved. When Ellen's European husband offers to take her back, New York assumes he has been overwhelmed by a "longing for domestic life," but the situation is not so "simple," in European minds. Ellen's complex awareness makes even older New Yorkers seem "immature" by contrast. Catherine understands her, but the rest of the family seem to think she does not speak their language. Newland sometimes even translates her phrases into French in order to grasp their overtones. And foreign phrases intrude into his own conversation when he is thinking of her.

Still, for Newland to snap at May in Latin is not the same as for him to understand Ellen. The man who "speaks her language fluently" is Beaufort. Beaufort has the "habit" of "two continents" and "two societies." In addition, his world is enlarged by his easy association with artists and writers. These more sophisticated circumstances mean that Ellen is at ease in Beaufort's company, even though his "careless contempt" for "local prejudices" diminishes him in Ellen's eyes. Since Beaufort participates in New York hypocrisy and Newland shares its fussiness, Ellen is left to "find her own level" outside New York. She needs "good conversation" in a setting of "immemorial manners." Neither New York nor the men who live there can offer her that. She is like "no other," but there is room for her in Paris, a city so complex that she will not "hunger mentally," or be "enslaved," or be deprived of "moral freedom."

Wharton emphasizes the geographical limits of New York by sending Ellen to Paris with an establishment of her own. Her family wanted to force her to return to her husband, but New York cannot control her in Europe, as it manages to do in America. The entire "tribe" persists in its conviction that she must be a mistress if she separates from her husband. When she refuses to cooperate, they transform her anyway. Even May accepts it as true that Ellen is Newland's mistress. In fact, Ellen and Newland have avoided becoming lovers at a considerable sacrifice of their happiness in favor of May's. This irony helps define the New York mentality as perversely simplistic rather than as "innocent."

As the "tutelary divinity" of her tribe, May is "victorious," in New York. Ellen's foreignness is an excuse to "eliminate" her from the tribe. And Newland settles down to being a "brick" in a "well-built wall," after he is deprived of contact with the "pleasureable excitement" of Ellen's energetic life. But losing touch with a world where action follows swiftly after emotion means that Newland is cast adrift rather than rescued. Losing the focus of his ambivalence, he becomes so "absent" that he is occasionally startled to find other people imagine he is living among them.

The permanent discrepancy between Newland's inner and outer life shows how self-deluding May and her family are in assuming it is their action which separates what they think of as the guilty pair. It is only when Newland acts freely that the real basis of their situation is revealed. Old Catherine serves as a catalyst by appealing to Newland for help in fighting the family in Ellen's defense. She points out that Ellen is a brave woman and adds that she has always admired courage "above everything." Old Catherine is right in thinking Newland loves Ellen, but she is wrong in supposing that action follows emotion in his instincts. He can kiss Old Catherine's hand in gratitude for the value she places on Ellen without feeling any urge to answer her or to break away from the rest of the family. He justifies his inaction by thinking that "he and his people" have always placed "decency" above courage, and "breeding" above feeling. But what is even more central is the fact that he, himself, has always recoiled from commitment to anything. Since Old Catherine is only an individual, and nothing less than the tribe can trap him, and since Ellen refuses to entice him, Newland's shadowy form appropriately stays in New York where his ambivalence is undisturbed and his emptiest instincts are enough to get him through the day.

Wharton underlines her point by following the career of another member of the tribe who is driven out for making mistakes which are too basic to be ignored. To New York, Beaufort's bankruptcy is a man's equivalent of the degradation Ellen is supposed to have achieved. Like Ellen, Beaufort is doubly disgraced since he refuses to be crushed by the disaster. He spends some time searching for a congenial environment and finally settles in Buenos Aires, where he is able to resume an interesting social life. His properly despondent New York wife finally dies, leaving him free to marry his faithful mistress and dote on the daughter she has already presented him with. Far from being punished for this eventual happiness, Beaufort is vindicated at second hand when his "bastard" appears triumphantly in New York and even dares to marry the oldest son of that preeminently "good citizen," Newland Archer.

Ellen's escape is also vindicated by events. Newland imagines that Ellen lives in quietness and obscurity, in the aftermath of their brief love. But years later he sees that she actually lives in a "modern building" in a quarter of Paris which is "pervaded" by a "golden light." It is a shock to realize that, if she thinks of him at all, her memory can be no more than a "relic" in a "dim chapel" which she must be too busy to visit every day.

Finding that Paris is a true home for Ellen leaves Newland with his appropriate geography. Always wishing to

avoid choosing either New York or "Japan," he can now admit
that thinking of Ellen is "more real" than seeing her. He
sends his aggressive and delightful son to call on her, knowing she will understand why he does not come, himself. He
enjoys thinking about visiting Ellen because it makes his
heart beat "wildly," but he feels that very private sensation
is sufficient. For him, it never has suggested action to follow. Since he trusts Ellen to understand his attenuation in a
way he could not trust May, he can let her know of his silent
reverie and then leave without seeing her in exactly the way
he used to send her flowers with the sender's card removed
from the envelope.

Newland does not belong in Paris, though he is free
enough to know what Paris is. Habit allows him to stay in
New York, though he is tranquilly absent when he seems to
be there. His detachment from both worlds and from the
people who live vitally within them helps Wharton establish
the freedom with which her characters choose the environment
which suits them. May is triumphant in New York. Ellen
enjoys "tangible companionship" in the "incessant stir of
ideas" in Paris. But for Newland, "thinking over" a pleasure
is more satisfying than "realizing" it. It is involvement and
commitment, rather than New York or Paris, which make him
feel trapped. His "real" life takes place in dreams, and so
it makes very little difference which address and which woman
he detaches himself from at any given moment. His choice
to live in dreams makes more clear the nature of the social
and emotional freedom Ellen demands and the courage she
shows in finding it.

A much more lighthearted presentation of the way
Americans differ from Europeans occurs in Frances Hodgson
Burnett's A Fair Barbarian. Burnett shows the impact of
American frankness and energy on an English village which rules
itself through behind-the-scenes manipulation and through automatic disapproval of the young. The young American woman
who comes to pay a visit to her English aunt shocks all of
Slowbridge society, but she charms most of them, as well.
The young men are bewitched by attention which is carefree
rather than flirtatious. The repressed young English woman
who befriends the American heroine ends by adopting her values to the extent of deciding to choose her own husband and
sweetly telling her grandmother that she would have been
"more frank" if she had received kinder treatment as a child.

At the opposite extreme from the freedom and liberation Americans represent in Burnett's novel, Jane Rule depicts the United States as a police state. The Young in One Another's Arms describes the experiences of young men who cross the Canadian border to avoid the draft. Though Canadians are tolerant and humane, even the sanctuary of an informal group home does not protect these refugees from the constantly hovering shadow of the United States police. If they had only fugitive warrants to dread, they might find peace. But crossing an international border does nothing to redeem a state of mind, as Americans show by turning each other in or lapsing into old ideals. In order to benefit from the change of country, refugees must wish to set their aggressive past aside. Because of a Canadian commitment to patience and tolerance, individuals who genuinely want to align themselves with a noncoercive society are able to live at peace with themselves even under the shadow of police helicopters and raids from the south.

The English/Irish border also supplies a choice between natural and urban life and between personal and social codes. In The Absentee, Maria Edgeworth examines the emotional result of being educated abroad. The young Irish lord who is an "absentee" in this novel enjoys the cultivation of an English university education, but he is disgusted by the way English women snub his mother and tradespeople cheat his family and friends. Returning to Ireland to investigate the estate which supports him, he is able to find ways of avoiding the dishonesty and the social cruelty which are unfortunately widespread. But learning to do without the intellectual life he enjoyed in England is more difficult to manage. Still, on balance, there can be no question of where his real identity lies. He solves his problem by selecting from both national ways of life. He moves to Ireland where he can "do good." And he relieves the intellectual isolation his choice might bring by setting up as a host for international visitors.

In each of these novels, individuals who choose to set aside their birth environment need a great deal of energy and a clear sense of their own standards. Not only must they resist the mindless pressure of a society which assumes it is universal, they must also be prepared to maintain themselves as somewhat apart from the country they adopt. If foreigners are accepted at all, they usually are allowed some relaxation of the rules, which makes being different somewhat easier than it might be for people who stayed where they were born. Any social separation is a struggle. But individuals in search of a more suitable environment may find that the struggle itself is a help since it calls attention to their situation and therefore attracts other people whose values turn them into peers.

Notes

1 Ernest A. Baker, History of the English Novel (New York: Barnes & Noble, 1929), vol. VI, p. 32.

2 R. W. B. Lewis, Edith Wharton (New York: Harper & Row, 1975), pp. 429-33.

3 Lewis, p. 430.

4. ETHNIC ALTERNATIVES

Aphra Behn, Oroonoko
Nina Bawden, Under the Skin
Nella Larsen, Quicksand
Margaret Walker, Jubilee

others:
Rosa Guy, Edith Jackson
Nella Larsen, Passing

The way people interpret and adjust to cultures which try to overrun them has fascinated novelists from the beginning. What happens when marauders appear? Will military power enforce a change of social courtesies? When a planted king speaks a different language and prefers a different kind of food, will the nation change its diet? If new gods turn new wrath against old habits, will the people accept the change in fears, or retreat into their own more comfortable taboos, or weave a second punishment schedule onto their familiar rules?

The problem is acute enough when the populations look very much the same, as in Edgeworth's Castle Rackrent. But when skins differ as well, difficulties multiply since individuals are automatically assigned to groups according to their color, without a qualifying glance at how they act and feel. In such a situation, people whose values are unusual rather than conventional have even less than the average chance of maintaining their independent individuality.

English novels dealing with this area normally show cultures coming into conflict directly, often through political activity. In a modified form of the struggle Castle Rackrent depicts, nonwhite cultures may be confronted with alternative beliefs. Fiction which accepts the idea of cultural variety will show how individuals on both sides of the division tend to reexamine their instincts when they find out there are other ways to live. Final responses will be governed by personalities--some people become more tolerant when they see options, while others become rigid in defense of the values they have learned from birth. It is when individuals might wish to retreat from their inherited society and try out new values that the ethnic question makes a basic difference. A sense of new peers is complicated by the color of the skin.

American novels take a different approach, because American ethnics are normally included in the general population rather than being thought of as a distant and exotic race. Lacking the support of obvious georgraphical divisions, ethnic Americans often are not overtly recognized as having a special kind of problem since they are not supposed to have a genuinely separate culture. Nonwhite individuals who do not accept their conventional role as ethnics are often greeted with a special kind of disbelief, as if their isolation from the conventional center of American society should not be admitted as anything more than the typical outcast role assigned to any American holding unusual views.

Writers of any color may explore this topic in English fiction since national boundaries are usually featured along with race. But conventional American fiction routinely does not depict distinct and valid value systems for nonwhites living among the pale majority. Therefore, American examples in this field usually have ethnic authors.

The difference produces a greater than normal separation in the two English language traditions. American novels deal in psychological and ethical distinctions, whereas British novels are more direct about the basic question in itself, since they treat it as if it were primarily political.

This distinction has been important from the very beginning of the novel in English. When Aphra Behn wrote Oroonoko, she included many of the same elements Daniel Defoe used thirty years later. Behn's novel was enormously popular among her contemporaries, but her assumptions about her material were extraordinary, and so Defoe's less startling Robinson Crusoe is routinely preferred by literary historians as the "first" novel.[1]

A crucial difference between the two novels is Defoe's treatment of Crusoe and Friday. Both men assume that a master/servant relationship between white and nonwhite will be resumed, even in total isolation, since it is "natural." His novel therefore takes both domination and submission as inevitably linked, in the same way he depicts eye color and speech habits as attributes associated with the skin.

Aphra Behn's less self-congratulating view was that people think in terms of their own culture. Not only do societies place different values at the center of their system, but individual members behave differently when isolated from the group which trained them. Some people live up to their culture's highest ideals, regardless of where they are, while others may degrade themselves according to the methods they bring from home. But whatever they decide distance and separation mean to cultural assumptions, their reaction will come from their personal integrity rather than from the color of their skin.

In order to make her point, Behn depicts three cultures, each having a different skin color. She gives fair warning of her cultural neutrality by beginning her description with the population native to Surinam and showing that these people are innocent not because they are childlike, in the way savages conventionally are described, but because they are good. They are "modest," though almost naked, and since they seem to have no "wishes," they are like "our first parents" before anyone had learned "how to sin." Their purity shows what a good teacher "Nature" is, especially when compared to "religion," which absorbs itself in "offenses" unknown to such "tranquil," non-Christian innocents.

These people are the color of a "new brick," and they respect each other's beauty with a "decency" of act and glance which is destroyed only by white men who teach them "vice." If left without civilized advantages, they enjoy a sense of justice which is not tarnished by a knowledge of either "fraud" or "cunning."

Since these natives overwhelmingly outnumber the whites, they cannot be enslaved despite their vulnerability to deceit. But political independence for both groups does not do away with the need to share ideas between two cultures which come into constant contact. For example, colonial survival requires that the natives must teach the whites where to go for game and how to identify other kinds of local foods. The helpful natives are repaid when the colonials give their own special knowledge in exchange--the whites demonstrate the art and function of lying.

Behn is careful to show that this kind of interaction is
not merely the automatic and partly unintentional impact of a
complex society on a simpler world. She follows up her description of the beliefs of the Surinam natives with an analysis
of another nonwhite culture which suffers in a similar way.
In the second case, the social rules are so complicated that
life at this black court would be a satisfactory challenge for
the most decadent of European courtiers. Coramantien natives
have a value system which is elaborate enough to contradict
itself and therefore leave room for self-deluding interpretation,
manipulation, deceit, self-righteous betrayal, casuistry and
fraud.

Unlike the natives of Surinam, imported Coramantiens
do hold some values in common with colonial whites. They
take slaves and sell them, for example. They value glory
above domestic virtues. And they see relations between the
sexes primarily in terms of power.

Agreeing on some topics turns out to be a mixed blessing for individuals in both groups. Since both Coramantiens
and whites accept slavery as a concept, they fail to notice how
crucially different their ideas about that situation are. Coramantiens become slaves only when they cannot be ransomed
after a defeat in war. Therefore, in realms where their own
definitions apply, high ranking Coramantiens are not slaves
unless they have lost their family and friends, as well as
losing a war.

But in the minds of the whites, Coramantiens are
black, and Blacks are slaves. This view means that Coramantiens who are transported to Surinam will normally be
treated all alike, without regard to original rank or personal
merit or reasons for imprisonment. Symbolic of this complete depersonalization is the fact that they are bought by
blind lot. Slavers guarantee nothing individual about the lots,
which may vary in the number of slaves, in the percentage of
children, in the ages and health of the workers, as well as
in the kind of work they may be fit to do.

Slave owners who accept such a group transaction obviously have no reason to think of their slaves as cherishing
rules of their own which they expect to live by. And this in-
sensitivity is encouraged by one aspect of Coramantien culture. When they become slaves for reasons their home culture respects, Coramantiens resign themselves to their new
life. Their owners are quick to conclude that graceful submission

in itself is a characteristic of all Coramantiens. They do not realize that the surrender to slavery is only a second stage of a more important surrender on battlefields at home.

As long as all Coramantien slaves arrive in Surinam as a result of war, their definition of slavery has little practical impact on daily relations between the races. But when Coramantiens are betrayed into slavery rather than being defeated in war, the difference in values becomes a central issue. Not having surrendered, Coramantiens expect to be dealt with in terms of their rank and personal qualities. Unfortunately, slave-owning whites who notice personal excellence usually interpret it solely in economic terms. A beautiful, resourceful or intelligent individual is obviously more valuable as property. If an independent spirit is detected, it is likely to be taken as nothing more than trouble among a usually peaceful subject population. This contradiction in what the two groups think their behavior means leaves the white colonials unprepared for any display of integrity among the Blacks they claim to own.

Misunderstandings about integrity are a central issue in Oroonoko. Part of the problem is that honor is not a very common topic among the whites. Oroonoko is casually betrayed into slavery by an "English gentleman" who invites him aboard his ship as if returning his host's hospitality. As soon as the young prince and his companions are drunk, they are trapped and chained and transported as slaves. When Oroonoko vows to starve himself rather than be sold, this white gentleman's conscience is untroubled as he lyingly promises Oroonoko his freedom at first landfall.

Oroonoko has difficulty understanding what has happened. He knows Europen codes regarding hospitality define the relationship between a host and his guests in a way which is similar enough to his own culture's view. When host and guest are citizens of different nations, the only difference should be that the relationship is even more generous and flattering than usual.

Oroonoko is right about these similarities. What he does not know is the additional European rule which excludes Blacks from ceremonial categories. To the English captain, Blacks are slaves. Therefore, the Englishman thinks Oroonoko is neither a prince nor a host, regardless of his parentage and grace.

Emphasizing that this gentlemanly sea captain is not merely an unfortunate example of white integrity, Behn repeats the pattern in Surinam. After he is sold, Oroonoko is again promised his freedom, though he is not given it. He is promised that his wife will be freed, also, but she is not released. He is promised that his child will not be born into slavery, but both parents are kept in bondage as the birth approaches. When Oroonoko finally loses his faith in white integrity and organizes a revolt among the slaves, he is promised freedom if he will surrender. When he yields to the pleas of a white man he respects, he is whipped instead.

Part of the reason Oroonoko has so much trouble learning to distrust the promises of whites is that he is uncertain exactly where blame lies, and he is too generous to hold others responsible for what is not their fault. For example, he notices that whites routinely say they respect their god, and this seems like a contradiction to Oroonoko. He explains that he is sorry to hear the English sea captain pretending to any worship, since irreligion would be better than adoring a god who "taught him no better principles." Much later, as he resists the betrayal which leads to his whipping, Oroonoko has refined his views somewhat. He insists the gods of white men should be despised for teaching "principles so false" that an "honest man" must never "eat and drink with Christians" unless he has his "weapon of defense in his hand."

This willingness to blame their god instead of the whites themselves increases Oroonoko's difficulty in grasping white morality. When Christian views of death and judgment are explained to him, Oroonoko responds by doubting the integrity of a god who allows sinning worshipers to pay their debts in secret, much later, in a different life.

Inconsistency among the whites also makes difficulties for Oroonoko. If slavers and slaveowners routinely promised the opposite of what they actually intended to do, he could adapt by planning around such a system. But he notices that some whites actually do seem to live according to the standards all whites claim to hold. Such a contradiction convinces Oroonoko that there is no relationship between professed belief and action, among whites, and he is left with no way to evaluate them as a group in terms of their own standards. Instead, he must judge each of them according to his own ethics until he has known them long enough as individuals to detect their personal patterns of behavior.

Oroonoko's problems of interpretation have a double source. He is perfectly prepared to accept the idea that the rules which apply between equals are different from those which govern slaves. For example, when Trefry, his owner, explains that he and his slaves all are "undone" in love for the same slave woman, Oroonoko says he understands why she might be allowed to refuse her fellow slaves, but he does not see why Trefry hesitates to "oblige" her to "yield" herself to him, since he is her owner.

Oroonoko's attitude changes instantly when he discovers it is Imoinda, his own wife, who is resisting Trefry. Like Oroonoko, Imoinda was betrayed into captivity. Neither of them deserves enslavement according to their own rules, and so they both hold themselves apart from their countrymen whose bondage is justified in everyone's mind. The difference is so obvious to Oroonoko and Imoinda that they assume it is clear to their would-be owner, as well.

Oroonoko demands special treatment for himself and Imoinda because they have no reason to think of themselves as slaves. Trefry does grant them immunity from all but the name of slave. However, his motives are not the ones Oroonoko assumes, and so his actions contribute to the mistakes in judgment which the two men make about each other, regardless of their genuinely affectionate goodwill.

Trefry has courted Imoinda rather than raping her, partly because he does not approve of using "strength and force," and also because she manages to appeal to his better nature. He delights in love and prefers to place "decency" above "passion." Most of his official peers laugh at this response, since sensitivity is ridiculously inappropriate to their ideas of slavery. But Oroonoko sincerely applauds Trefry's hesitation, even without knowing who the woman is, since her persuasiveness may show that she is noble.

This conversation shows a genuine affinity between the two men. Imoinda's ability to persuade Trefry against his appetites shows that she could rightly be included, if the three of them combined in friendship to set themselves apart from conventional standards in order to live by a value system based on their personal views.

Such an outcome would benefit Trefry at least as much as it would benefit the two slaves. He is a gentleman of wit and learning, a skilled mathematician and linguist. Because of his cultivation, Trefry has trouble finding intellectual and moral peers among the besotted white colonials who surround him. He is understandably charmed by the companionship of a man who is more than his equal in every way. As a prince and heir to his grandfather's throne, Oroonoko has been carefully educated. He speaks a variety of European languages and knows the national histories which go with them. His judgment and wit are as well trained as his mind, and his conversational ability has been polished by an intricate court life and by a high-minded love. Even while he is in chains, his personal qualities are so obvious that Trefry treats him like a brother instead of like a slave.

Trefry's affection and respect encourage Oroonoko to assume that his injustice has been recognized and responded to. He lives graciously in the governor's mansion while he waits for his official freedom. When the colonials flock around to look at him, he receives his guests like the host he has always been. Since he does not drink, he has little in common with the debauched white men Trefry also deplores, and so he spends most of his time with the women, for whom he performs in his usual role of escort and protector.

This life is lullingly pleasant, for a while, since Oroonoko has always enjoyed the companionship of Europeans who visited his grandfather's court. Eventually, however, the idleness of white society begins to irritate him. He is accustomed to measuring himself in terms of glory on the battlefield. And he is used to an elaborate court protocol, where dancing and music stimulate peacetime appetites as charming interludes to war.

By contrast, only recreation is available to him in Surinam, and that is simply not enough for his "large soul." He quickly tires of games, since other men are no real competition for a man of his abilities. He turns to hunting "monstrous" tigers and "wonderful snakes," but most animals are not dangerous enough to stir his pulses. To be sure, he is knocked out by the "numb-eel," but that is simply embarrassing to him since it happens in a moment and is not a competition.

Oroonoko cannot try to solve his boredom by returning home, since his grandfather's betrayal of Imoinda makes exiles of them both. His only recourse is to look for New World opportunities to exercise his skills. Longing for ways to win glory in battle, he offers to kill a creature feared as the Devil, though it takes on the appearance of a tiger. He sees it as a worthy challenge since English hunters have tried everything from poisoned arrows to guns against it and have been routed. In his usual charming way, he asks the ladies what "trophies and garlands" they will make him if he succeeds where their own hunters have failed. Covered with their promises, he goes off to bring back the tiger which has seven bullets healed into its heart.

This half-flirtatious confidence in his manly appeal shows how completely Oroonoko misunderstands his role among the whites. His owner does not treat him as a slave, and he knows he does not deserve to be one, and it never occurs to him that society in general might disagree. He fails to notice that other slave owners have begun to be afraid of him, since there seems to be no limit either to his courage or his skill. When bitter conflicts make the white women afraid to visit Indian villages, as they used to do for recreation, Oroonoko offers to escort them in safety. His cultural understanding and tolerance emerge when he expresses "esteem" for the Indian war captains even though their code of self-mutilation is "too brutal" a form of "courage" to please him. And his excellence as a diplomat lets him bring about so good an understanding between whites and Indians that a secure peace is established as a result of his visit.

Well-rounded superiority of the sort Oroonoko enjoys is likely to provoke jealousy and backbiting, under any circumstances. For this reason, Oroonoko would be in trouble even if he were not a slave and were not Black. For example, he and an English gentleman are out walking with a group of white ladies when a tiger approaches. The ladies run away. Oroonoko is normally unarmed, but he borrows the gentleman's sword and advises him to follow the ladies. The man obeys, but Oroonoko's solitary courage endears him only to the ladies and not to the gentleman he also protects.

Oroonoko's presumption on the rank he used to hold produces similar results. When he first arrived in Surinam, many of his fellow Blacks recognize him as the invincible warrior whose skill and courage sent them into slavery. According to the culture in which they were all trained, they fall on their faces before the prince who conquered them. When eventually Oroonoko exhorts them to cast off their servitude to the degenerate race which has left its own country in search of freedom to be more completely depraved, they declare themselves ready to follow him. However, they reveal themselves as genuinely enslaved when they desert him at the first appearance of pursuing whites. And when they are issued whips, they willingly line up and join in degrading him.

Such experiences enable Oroonoko to discover what has been an unstated basis for all his past relationships. His beauty and charm make his grandfather envy him, his courage causes his followers to desert him, and his color allows Europeans to torture him.

If everyone were color-blind, Oroonoko's isolation could be relieved by Imoinda, who adores him and shares his values, and by Trefry, who values his companionship above that of any other person. Under other circumstances, these three people could withdraw from both Black and white society and form a friendship group similar to that found by David Simple or by Michael Armstrong.

But Oroonoko suggests that the ethnic question finally cannot be set aside. Trefry's personal honor makes him as gullible as Oroonoko is. He mistakenly believes, as Oroonoko does, that the deputy governor's promise of freedom for Oroonoko is sincere. Since the mistake is the same, it ought to produce similar results. Instead, the concept of justice which Trefry and Oroonoko apply is irrelevant to the standard English view. Both these friends believe that Oroonoko has been imprisoned by mistake, which means the only possible response should be to set him free. But the English community in general describes a different justice, just as they describe a different hospitality, when differences in color enter in. Any personal friendship between the two men is simply set aside by the community in order to deal with Oroonoko's pride. The result is that Trefry must live with the horror of having accidentally betrayed a man he deeply admires. And Oroonoko must face death by torture at the hands of a community which has never seen him as anything but Black.

Behn has already established the crucial difference Oroonoko's color makes in the way English justice is defined. She lists Oroonoko's French tutor among the prisoners the Egnlish sea captain traps. The captain promises they will all be set free on Surinam. And when they arrive, he does release the Frenchman, since he is not Black.

In contradiction of this absolute way of judging, a slight blurring of the color barrier brings the novel to an embittered close. In order to kill Oroonoko thoroughly enough, white colonials borrow a ritual of mutilation from the natives of Surinam. It is an ironical cultural exchange of sorts, but for people to meet only in terms of violence implies no hope for future tolerance, even among races who come into direct enough contact to learn each other's patterns.

Instead, it suggests what has become a standard attitude in fiction of this type. Cross-cultural understanding is difficult to accomplish, even under ideal circumstances. The problem is increased when ethical, political, social, aesthetic, moral, spiritual, economic and domestic values all can be reduced to an irrelevant reference to the color of the skin. Therefore, where international borders are marked by a difference in color, individuals will not be allowed to ignore the dividing line in order to identify their peers on the basis of like-mindedness. Anyone who persists in such a way of judging will be punished as well as isolated and misunderstood.

When Nina Bawden took up this question nearly three hundred years later, she saw many of the same problems. In Under the Skin, English intending to be friendly without regard to color are still hesitant and often ineffective. Africans who offer trust in response to courtesy are still betrayed. And class distinctions are still an added burden for targets of prejudice.

The major difference brought by the passage of time is that the concept of a hero has disappeared from all races equally. Oroonoko was spectacular in every way, and was recognized as being so in every culture where he lived, but Bawden's central character in Under the Skin is simply a "pleasant youngster" who is "delightfully handsome" as well as being bright. Oroonoko lived at the center of government, both at home and while technically a slave. However, Jay Nbola's white contacts in Africa are colonials who, even to their countrymen, "aren't much" as men and are sometimes more a "set of reactions" than they are an "intelligence." In England, Jay's association expands upward far enough in social class to include a typical "John Bull." The difference in social class is important among the English, but it proves to be irrelevant in regard to Jay, whose color supersedes all other considerations.

The twentieth-century loss of the heroic mode means that a tragic outcome is not required, and so, at the end of his novel, Jay is only beaten up, instead of being killed, as Oroonoko is. But Oroonoko's greater physical suffering does not stand for a more tortured journey toward sophistication since the cross-cultural shocks which educate the two men are much the same. Betrayal and mutual misunderstanding are the central fact of relations between races in both novels, and so their characters share the emotions which disillusionment brings. That Jay is left alive when he recoils from white society means only that "guilt" has been added to English attitudes. It does not imply that any of the negatives have been removed.

In order to define her topic, Bawden places "the color bar" into a broad spectrum of prejudice. Jamaicans run into the same kind of trouble Blacks face in London, but Welsh are targets, as well, even though they suffer from no color question and their separate national identity can be ignored when English find it convenient to set the political division aside.

On the other hand, being altogether English is not necessarily a protection. People are slow to admit the humanity of the deformed. And though midgets technically are not deformed, there is a prejudice against anyone who is not "full size." At the other extreme, being oversize through fat is just as categorically despised.

Not all prejudice is visual. Bawden is careful to include targets who do not deviate from the norm in any visible, current way. Tom Grant, the central English character, is of modest background, but even after years of marriage and of professional success, his wife's higher family status is not forgotten. Tom's mother is attractive and healthy and graciously alive, but none of this protects her, even in her own home, since she is old enough to have become "mad." And when every other category would support equality, there is still the "feminist" question--no one can be expected to understand a woman's mind. Even women have trouble with this prejudice, blindly judging a total difference between a wife and a "bit," a mother and a "frigid," childless woman.

In such a welter of discrimination, it might seem that particular prejudices should become less important. And individual cases do sometimes work out this way. For example,

Julia spends years of prurience despising her estranged husband's live-in mistress. When the two women finally meet, in late middle age, Julia is shocked to find that Georgiana is harmless and almost dowdy. Ashamed of her wasted anger, she wishes she could make amends.

Tom's "mad" mother provokes a similar response. Tom defends her right to stay in her own home, with the help of a nurse, but her doing so causes trouble since everyone is sure "mad" people ought to live in hospitals. Tom's in-laws even offer to "upgrade her in class" in order to have her treated like an "unwanted relic" of the professional classes. When the nurse dies suddenly while Tom is unconscious with pneumonia and concussion, Tom's wife and her family are finally able to place his mother in a hospital and feel justified. Tom admits that she is being cared for, not just attentively, but "affectionately." Nevertheless, the admission does not free him from an anxious sense of generalized guilt.

The problem comes from the fact that Tom's mother is not helpless. She recognizes people from her youth instead of current family members, but this limitation does not interfere with her ability to get through the day. She looks younger and more alive than some of the people who are trying to have her confined because of her age, and in one sense she really is younger, because she lives among her memories of being young. Not seeing herself as pathetic, decayed and helpless, she refuses society's attempts to make her manageable by assigning her to that role. As long as Tom protects her rights as a separate individual with preferences and strengths which are not cancelled by her "madness," she is a source of worry, embarrassment, and confusion. But when she is at last put into the niche society assigns old women, then she can be showered with support, affection and respect.

This sequence forms a kind of précis of the problem faced by Blacks. As long as they confine themselves to the expected role, they are politely treated. But when they show a willingness and an ability to judge and analyze, they run into trouble immediately.

To furnish a background for Jay's attitudes, Bawden opens her novel with an African sequence in which roles are somewhat different. In Africa, Jay is part of the majority, though the dominant force is the English colonial government. In Jay's country, Tom is a minority's minority since he is sent there on a short term research assignment outside either structure.

In this context, Tom is considered "white," though he has little in common with the attitudes, interests and abilities of the white colonials who are his official hosts. The local administrator explains with satisfaction that he builds a new courthouse in the shape of a squash court wherever he is posted. Tom manages to respond politely that it is an "individual" contribution to colonial rule. But his private thoughts are that the English leave "curious legacies"--squash courts instead of a concept of justice and "the accent of Eton and Harrow" instead of education.

Tom feels no more affinity for the one white person who cultivates friendships among the Blacks, since Chirk is the kind of man who cannot make friends in any context. He is so patronizing a host for Black government workers that Tom is ashamed, although the regular guests seem less concerned. For example, Milly has considerable self-confidence, which comes from being a schoolteacher and from being beautiful. She makes Chirk's patronizing behavior unimportant by ignoring it while she leafs through his record collection looking for dance records so she can teach Tom the new dances which he is too out of date to know.

Among all the people he encounters in Africa, Tom feels most affinity for Jay. Meeting him at Chirk's, Tom cannot read Jay's thoughts in his face, but he does not assume his problem comes from racial differences since Milly is no better at reading Jay's feelings. The problem turns out to come from Jay's politeness--he has been puzzled by the fact that Chirk has no English friends, and he is guarded in a situation he does not understand. Chirk does not serve alcohol when entertaining "decent young Christians," but Jay is delighted by Tom's invitation to go for a beer together.

As soon as they are isolated from both African and English social contexts, the two men have no trouble understanding each other and quickly discover how similar their basic attitudes are. Each is distressed at being linked with a population which does not share his views. Both believe in the "principle of Self-Help." Neither judges all members of any group as being automatically alike in character and feeling.

Both Africans and English reject the idea of their

like-mindedness, however. For example, Tom warns an African fishmonger that selling small fish will deplete the future supply of food. The merchant laughs graciously before he answers each of Tom's complaints, in order to soften his resistance to disapproval coming from a white. But when Jay joins in the discussion on Tom's side, the merchant looks sullen and switches into Swahili. Assuming Tom will not understand, he separates his two critics in order to express his contempt for Jay and his opinion.

Tom has a similar experience when he asks to bring Jay to the club as his guest in order to see a slide show. Officially, Tom is within his rights, but permission has to be granted by the board, anyway. He asks "boyishly," hoping a nonconfrontational approach will help them live up to their own rules. Jay is "awfully keen on England," which means he would be more likely than anyone else to enjoy the show. Nevertheless, Tom is forbidden to bring him because the pictures might include a white wife in a bathing suit. Tom's retort that Jay probably "wouldn't mind" makes clear whose attitudes he shares, but that in itself causes additional trouble since it turns Tom into a problem to other whites without changing Jay's situation in any way.

Tom knows that he and Jay are not identical. When he is around Jay, he longs to be more "eager" and "warmhearted." Jay "speaks from his heart," which makes Tom envious since he has "forgotten how." In contrast, he feels "cluttered up" with the effects of "centuries of other people's opinions." Jay's friendship becomes intensely important to Tom since it might be a route to the emotional sincerity which Tom longs for. In his warmhearted way, Jay believes they are friends, and Tom is sure it is only the "opinions of others" which keep the two men from taking up a friendship which would be automatic if race did not divide them in other people's eyes.

Bawden uses the friendship between Jay and Tom as a way of measuring the way social pressure is compounded by differences in culture as well as race. Tom knows that Europeans are "grossly inhospitable" by African standards, and so he invites Jay to be his guest during the year he is to spend at a London University. The gesture is merely normal, by Jay's standards. But for Tom's family, it is extremely awkward since long-term residents in London are either paying guests or family members.

The half-conscious decision to deal with Jay as if he

were a family member causes shock for everyone. When Jay catches cold, Tom's wife, Louise, bullies Jay as if he were a "favorite younger brother." Unfortunately, this means she forces him to drink milk, which he hates, and so being waited on and pampered is not a clear gain.

Louise's teenage niece, Veronica, falls in love with Jay, partly through conventionally idealistic white guilt and partly through a response to Jay's personal charm. Veronica has been in love with her uncle Tom for years, without distressing anyone. However, when she expands her crush to include Jay, the family feels justified in abusiveness of every kind.

A major source of difficulty is that Jay has standards of his own. When Louise begins to scold Tom for cynicism, Jay says that African women do not shout at men. Louise is astonished by even so mild a remark because she has been thinking of their relationship as one in which she will do all the judging. It is a shock to find that Jay makes judgments of his own. It is even more bewildering to discover that he judges on the basis of a different set of rules.

Louise adjusts to this novelty by delighting in everything about Jay which emphasizes his difference. She is intrigued by his view that it is immodest for a married son to stay in his mother's house, where he will be "naked in bed with a stranger." And she is amazed by the extent of Jay's admiration for England, partly because he outdoes her in patriotism, and partly because England is not wonderful at all, for Blacks.

The rest of Louise's family is less adaptive. Jay is appalled to find that Louise's brother, Reggie, has a medical degree but does not practice since he can make more money in other ways. When he meets Reggie at a family party, Jay sympathetically laments England's neglect, which forces doctors to give up their professional dedication in order to make a survival wage. Both Reggie and his daughter assume Jay is sneering. Reggie is furious, and Veronica is delighted to see her father being successfully teased. And Jay is too sincerely outraged on Reggie's behalf to notice the disturbance he has caused.

An ice skating party at the country estate of Louise's father produces a similar disaster. Jay comes limping back to the house between Veronica and Louise, explaining that one of "these savage women" has wounded him accidentally. He is bleeding from a cut on his leg, and they make amends by fussing over him as they wash and bandage the wound.

The scene goes beyond the conventional when Jay's responses get him into trouble both when he is individual and when he is universal. Being a good sport about the accident, Jay says he "feels like a pasha" since he is "being waited on by two charming ladies." His use of a non-English image is a reminder that he is as "exotically out of place as a peacock." And since Veronica enjoys waiting on a "pasha," she suddenly decides she would like to become a nurse. Louise deflates Veronica's enthusiasm by saying she would "never stick it." Jay is a father, and so he is experienced in responding to the hurt feelings of children. He automatically soothes Veronica in the tenderly reassuring tone of any kindly adult to any disappointed child. The episode is really no more than courteous, but Veronica's grandfather is appalled by Jay's independence of judgment and his assumption of the right to comfort Veronica.

The grandfather's abusive reaction brings into the open the conflicting opinions which a polite silence has masked. Half jealous of her niece's erotic immaturity, Louise quarrels with Jay while explaining that the men in her family assume he is taking advantage of Veronica. Jay is horrified at the assumption that he cannot be trusted to behave in a "decent and civilized manner." He begins packing immediately, apologizing for causing trouble between Tom and his brother. Tom is offended to hear Reggie referred to as his brother, since he despises fat, and Reggie has a face which might as well be "painted on an eiderdown." Using his own standards, as always, Jay is shocked when Tom denies family feeling for his wife's brother.

The complexity of the situation emerges in the conflict between Tom's view and that of everyone else involved. Tom insists that Reggie has been "abominably rude" to his guest, but Tom is probably the only person who really thinks of Jay as a guest. Reggie's mother tries to restore peace by saying that Reggie has been a "naughty, tactless boy," as if she were hushing up a schoolboy squabble. It is a reminder that Reggie has been "abominably rude" to several members of his family. He rationalizes Tom's attitude toward Jay by deciding he is a homosexual. He has no trouble persuading himself that his sister is promiscuous and his daughter is depraved. In such a context, his remarks about Jay become almost mild.

Jay finally consents to this family role, even while realizing it is not what he and Tom had wanted. He writes a wayward-son type of letter after he moves out, offering "comfort" since they will have been worrying. And when Tom warns him not to go home after he has been beaten up, he goes to Tom's mother as the most obvious safe place.

Bawden suggests the real function of this treatment by contrasting it to Jay's situation once he is living his own life. In the neighborhood he chooses for himself, he is able to enjoy the "ritual" of being Tom's host. And he defends residents who are victims of other prejudices with a "belligerent flourish," since he turns out not to be the lowest on a neighborhood pecking order which includes Welsh and career criminals as well as Blacks and midgets.

Inevitably, Jay misunderstands this situation. He assumes his right to judge is recognized since he is neither a guest nor a relative and is paying his way like anyone else. But the rest of the community admits only that he is not quite the lowest on the social ladder. Not realizing there are several categories above him and only one below, Jay scolds and frightens a pair of street boys for writing anti-midget graffiti. The boys' Welsh father attacks him publicly enough to land both of them in court for brawling.

Bawden uses the court sequence to reveal the discrepancy between public and private forms of British justice. Tom testifies to Jay's character. His case is also helped by the fact that his attacker has an extensive police record. The judge summarizes these points and lets Jay off with costs and a warning, but he requires the boys' father to pay a large fine.

This reassuring outcome has immediately distressing results. Jay's African friend, Thomas, decides to thank the judge for upholding justice without regard to color. His fulsome harangue offends the judge. Tom recognizes Thomas as "only tedious," which is a problem without regard to color. But to the judge, Thomas' praise implies an assumption that justice might not have been done. He is furious to find that he has been judged as well as judging.

A second result is a scene which recalls the structure of the fishmonger episode early in the novel. Tom and Jay are both beaten up as a warning to leave the neighborhood where official justice has disturbed the informal and more widely accepted hierarchy. As in Africa, the stronger feeling is expressed against a member of the same race. In this case, Tom is beaten badly enough to land in the hospital, unconscious for days, whereas Jay is hurt only enough to be a terrifying sight when Tom's mother's old nurse opens the door to him.

Jay's beating would not in itself drive him back to Africa, if it had not taken place as one in a series of eye-opening conflicts. Reluctantly losing his illusions, Jay tells Tom that England is full of people who "behave like friends" but who finally think the most important thing is his "dirty black skin." Giving up his original joy at being in Tom's country, Jay insists it is better to have enemies than to "make friends of such people." He is touched by Tom's appearing in court for him, but the otherwise universal misunderstanding makes it impossible for the two men to act on their like-mindedness in any social setting, and Jay accepts the situation.

One of Jay's charms is his ability to strike "just the right note" toward people who have been helpful in the past but who are now "outgrown." It is this skill which keeps his departure from being a rout. Like a good son in trouble, he allows Louise's father to pay his plane fare back to Africa. When he is back home, he names his new daughter for Louise. Since family circumstances can be pleaded quite honestly, he receives a promotion in his African job, even though he did not complete his full year of studies. In addition, his grant will be renewable if he should ever decide to give England a second chance.

All of these arrangements are a sop to England rather than to Jay. For example, Louise tries to get Tom to agree that it all worked out "rather well." Tom uses his injuries as an excuse to rave bitterly against such a self-satisfied attitude. Nevertheless, he recognizes that concepts of brotherhood must include Cain and Abel, that anyone who loves his neighbor as himself is neurotic, that hate is so seductively simple an emotion that racial hatred is a nearly universal "infection."

In Under the Skin, only "oddities" like Louise's stepmother, Georgiana, escape this infection. Georgiana is "always grateful." She asks only that she be allowed to be nice to everyone. Tom thinks the world would be happier if more people were like Georgiana, but there is no chance for this to happen since no one would ever think of "modeling themselves" on so humble and considerate a creature.

Instead, most people relate to others in terms of insecurity. Feeling unvalued, they try to find ways to cut other people down. Tom insists, for example, that Reggie "ought to be" insecure, whether he is or not. And Julia launches a new attack against her estranged husband even while she thaws toward his mistress, suddenly telling Tom that sex could not be the basis of the relationship since her marital experience was like "posting a marshmallow in a letter-box."

Given this social pattern, personal merit turns into a handicap rather than an aid. The more attractive, intelligent, decent and charming Jay is, the less manageable he becomes, as an individual. Since his quality causes him to stand out above other people, the only way he can be related to in a framework of insecurity is to grant him nothing but the color of his skin. Jay, himself, finally realizes that, in England, he is no more than "an exhibit," a "sort of freak."

That such a response is a reflex rather than a conscious choice is implied when Louise explains a girlhood experience to Tom. She remembers reading the story of a Chinese bandit who fell in love with a white woman. It gave Louise a "terrific thrill" to think of "condescending to someone who is stronger." In order to show that the idea is not merely a teen-age vagary, Bawden extends the reverie into adult critical speculation, allowing Louise to decide that Lady Chatterley enjoys the "idea of being raped by an inferior."

Since Louise is far more conscientious and liberal than most English people, the expression of this feeling from her suggests a hopeless future for friendships such as Tom and Jay imagine. However, Bawden offers a small countercurrent at the novel's end, as a counterbalance to the suspicion that Tom and Jay are unique and therefore likely to be defeated in any social context. Jay's young son, Philip, also comes to England to go to school. Unlike his father, Philip fits in easily, immediately acquiring the "clear, high, carrying tone" which will identify him for life as a prep school boy. Reggie thinks he is a "poor little beggar" who "won't know where he belongs." But Tom insists Philip will be "one of the New Men" who will "belong everywhere."

Bawden does not shift hope to the next generation

altogether, however. When Tom receives a posting to Africa, everyone can rejoice sincerely. Louise is delighted since she believes it will compensate him for the loss of Jay's companionship in England. Jay is happy because he knows Tom will enjoy the move. And Tom's reserved superior likes the idea since fieldwork offers a "moral simplicity" which Tom cannot find in his work as a teacher in England.

Fieldwork's "moral simplicity" involves the belief that prejudice is not wicked or evil but is merely the behavior to be expected from "stupid and unattractive" individuals. Since a full ethical range exists among the English who live in London, consistently unattractive behavior there comes as a shock. But white colonials are frankly recognized as "not much." Their stupidity about race is in keeping with their quality, and so its offensiveness is kept within bounds.

Building on this very muted hopefulness, <u>Under the Skin</u> ends with Jay's coming to meet the plane when Tom and Louise arrive in Africa. While they are still out of earshot, Jay turns to say something to his wife. Louise wonders what Jay said, but Tom knows that Jay's thoughts are exactly like his own. The novel began with Tom thinking, "He does look black." It ends with Jay saying, "They do look white."

The equality implied in this exact reversal suggests that friendship may have a better chance in Africa. It is a place where Tom can be relaxed and happy. When he laughs after telling Louise what Jay is thinking, it is a reminder that Jay laughs not at people or at jokes but from happiness. It is encouraging for the novel to end with Tom laughing for Jay's reasons. The combination suggests that friendship may be able to survive in spite of universal pressure, as long as the friends themselves remain determined that it will.

In contrast to the highly social representations typical of English fiction, American novels frequently use the tradition of a search-for-self in order to explore ethnic identity problems. Since Black Americans can be dealt with as simply Americans who must struggle with more or less the universal identity conflicts of growing up, the additional problems facing them emerge slowly, as a second level of crisis, after the usual intellectual, social and biological quandaries have at least partly fallen into place.

Americans who struggle with the social result of belonging to a minority group are not helped toward self-definition

Ethnic Alternatives / 113

by the kind of clear cultural divisions which international borders reinforce. Instead, the assumption which surrounds them is that everyone's basic values are the same. In such a situation, a difference in skin color is assumed to have no impact on value distinctions which are universally held. Nonwhites may be expected to feel that a culture which favors whites is narrowing for everyone else, but such a reaction is not believed to justify an attempt to redefine normalcy. As a result, nonwhite Americans must discover the idea that variety is abstractly possible before they can begin to wonder if they may be unconventional in more than skin color.

Their situation is made harder by the fact that society assigns them to an ethnic group in a completely simplistic way, even though dark-skinned individuals may be very much aware of the mixed ancestry which is so widespread a fact of American life. Some people accept this convention as easily as they adjust to other social norms. But it is a situation which allows American fiction to explore the dilemma of individuals who are not entirely "white," not entirely "Black," and not at all conventional.

In Quicksand, Nella Larsen makes use of ambivalence as well as travel to depict the dilemma of an individual whose multiracial parentage sets her apart and keeps her aware of options. Helga Crane is the "biscuit" brown child of a "white immigrant" who was deserted by the gambler who fathered Helga. Since the mother's second marriage was not racially mixed, Helga becomes the only nonwhite in an extended family of aunts, uncles and cousins, as well as half sisters and brothers. "Mutual antagonism" over the difference in color segregates Helga from these white relatives. At the same time, living in a white family keeps her from meeting any of the Black social groups to which she is automatically assigned. Larsen uses the resulting double isolation to define the identity and value conflicts facing individuals who have clear connections with both groups.

Helga has only one American relative who can think of her "calmly," and even he is convinced that her "Negro blood" will keep her from "amounting to anything." Nevertheless, he is a personally kindly man, and so he rescues Helga from the hostility of her white childhood by sending her to a Negro boarding school. Accustomed to thinking of herself as an "obscene sore" on the lives of her family, the fifteen-year-old Helga is overjoyed to discover that there are groups of people who think being dark is not the same as being "loathsome." It is her first experience of being treated like a valuable individual whose skills are needed by society. Helga responds by flinging herself into school and into self-cultivation and recoiling gladly from her "white" past.

Helga's story is in many ways a typical American quest for personal identity. She becomes a schoolteacher because she dreams of "doing good" for her "fellow man." When classroom realities disillusion her, she rejects such dreams as "immature" without being able to rid herself of a typical professional snobbishness about any frankly materialistic occupation.

This double distaste is present in her attitude toward pay as well as work. Helga admits that money is "necessary" and even "desirable," but she "dismisses" its importance. Provided for by rich Black friends in New York and by rich white relatives in Copenhagen, she cherishes the artistic indulgence their way of life supplies while deploring the materialism which makes it possible.

Such careful distinctions isolate Helga in every social context. She feels lonely when she is unemployed among people who work, when she is sophisticated among idealists, and when she is cynical among enthusiasts. As usual in such cases, she withdraws in order to be in touch with herself instead of her role. But in Helga's case, being alone does not bring relief because the most important contradiction is inside her. She is searching for something beyond the "bareness" of her "own small life" at the same time that she yearns for the "blessed sense" of belonging to herself rather than to a race. As she investigates the identities made available by her appearance, intelligence and family history, she gradually concludes that such a combination must be a dream, rather than a goal.

In the beginning, her difference seems personal. At Naxos, a showcase boarding school for Black children, she faces what might be routine adjustment pressures by identifying herself so clearly as to become engaged to another new teacher who is experiencing the same transition. However, James Vayle quickly becomes "naturalized," whereas Helga remains "a little different." She becomes convinced the school intends to destroy the individualism of both faculty and students by "cutting" them to "the white man's pattern." She is upset that one of her friends straightens her hair, for example, and she rebels against the school's insistence on somber clothing since dark skins need vivid color to bring out their natural beauty. Talking herself into resigning as a way of rejecting the white man's pattern for Black lives, she decides someone should write "<u>A Plea for Color.</u>" Significantly, she does not consider writing such a work herself. Instead, she is satisfied with visualizing a document which would serve the double purpose of urging Blacks to wear bright colors at the same time that it celebrated the vividness of more colorful skins.

Harlem offers the kind of glorying in color which Helga called for as she left Naxos. When she first arrives, she has the "magic sense" that she has come "home." To be sure, the "prominent 'race' woman" who helps her locate a job and a friend to live with warns her not to mention that her "people are white," but the suggestion does not seem a trouble spot since Helga never refers to her background easily, under any circumstances. She is bewitched to find herself among people whose tastes and ideas she shares. She delights in Harlem's conversation, its parties, its vividness, its variety. Satisfied and "unenvious," she gladly turns away from the "sober mad rush" which makes "white New York" seem like a "monster," in comparison.

Her first happiness cannot last, however, since white New York is always there. Harlem dwellers use its shops, galleries, restaurants and theaters without seeming to notice that they absorb white standards of living and ape white tastes in entertainment. As she becomes more familiar with Harlem life, Helga begins to notice her friends' obsession with "race." Their "deep and burning hatred" of white people confuses and wounds Helga, since half of her heritage and all of her childhood experience are a part of the "despised" white race.

Her reawakened ambivalence comes to a crisis as she watches Audrey Denney, a beautiful black woman who associates with whites and Blacks equally and gives parties for them together. Helga admires the "assurance" and "courage" of the "beautiful, calm, cool" young woman who ignores race and pays attention only to individual people. But other Harlem dwellers insist it is "disgusting" and "obscene" for Audrey to include white people in society, since the "most wretched Negro prostitute" is better than any president of the United States.

Helga is unable either to answer or to forget such remarks since she is not a "rebel." She struggles with her "envious admiration" of Audrey in uneasy silence, trying to meet Harlem's demands by convincing herself she wants to ignore and be ignored by the "pale and powerful" segment of the world. She has enjoyed Harlem as a "mosaic" which ranges from "sooty black" to "pastry white." But the price of membership for her is to lie about her white mother. When she realizes that the self-deceiving politics of her friends have forced her to deny half of herself, she recoils from the Harlem to which she cannot "belong."

Copenhagen confronts Helga with a different set of problems. On the basis of childhood memories of her mother's wealthy sister, she feels "appreciated" and "understood." Her aunt and uncle encourage her to wear bright colors, to emphasize the air of remoteness which causes trouble for her in America, to think of herself as "unique" rather than as a misfit, to enjoy luxury and admiration.

But being the only member of her race turns out to be as distressing as it was to be "boxed up" with "hundreds" of people she has not chosen. Eventually she begins to feel like a "curiosity," a "stunt," a "decoration," a "curio," a "peacock," a "savage," a "new and strange species of pet dog." She assumes she is a work of art to the famous artist who does her portrait, but the painting turns out to be some "disgusting sensual creature" who looks "wicked." The artist makes an indecent suggestion just before the last brush stroke, and when Helga ignores it, he later offers marriage. The second offer serves only to put Helga in touch with her hatred for her situation. The artist justifies himself by insisting that she has the "warm, impulsive nature" of an African woman and the "soul of a prostitute." The explanation shows that his painting really does reveal his view of her, and it is an image she will not tolerate. Her aunt and uncle urge her to accept the marriage, which is advantageous in every conventional way. Yet, Helga cannot excuse the lack of respect which warns that being considered unique is not the same as being treated like an individual person. The distinction forces her to realize she is homesick for Negroes and the sense of a nonmaterial world which their society provides.

The spiritual world of the Reverend Mr. Pleasant Green constitutes Helga's last hope for self-acceptance within a group. She wanders into a Harlem mission house to escape a storm and discovers a part of life she has not seen before. She is repelled by the women who "crawled over the floor like reptiles," but she is fascinated by the congregation's "Bacchic vehemence." Such "primitive violence" seems to return her to the "mysterious grandeur" of "simpler centuries. " The religious fervor which at first seems "foul, " "vile, " and "weird" finally hints at "some One" who would be interested in her in a stable way. Overwhelmed by the isolate's feeling that what she does matters to no one, she gives in to the smothering ritual which leaves her unsure whether she has been "lost" or "saved. "

In the "miraculous calm" which follows, she lures the Reverend Mr. Pleasant Green into a marriage which will end her ambivalence by committing her to a clearly defined way of life. She is compelled by his sense of security, which comes from thinking only of the soul, and she hopes that a life of dedication to the minister will release her from the absorption in money and things which has troubled her in all her former efforts to find her appropriate social niche.

She is slow to admit that a life which ignores the body in order to concentrate on spirituality has the effect of taking away everything that shields individuals against the physical details of living. For the first time, she does her own housework. Forbidden worldly display, she must mend and darn her clothes instead of tossing them aside. Her personal fastidiousness cannot cope with the startlingly physical life her husband lives. The Reverend Mr. Pleasant Green makes noises when eating even soft food. He always smells of sweat and stale clothing. And he keeps her so continuously pregnant that she has to learn to do without the "great ordinary things of life"--hunger and sleep.

As is true of every new experience, motherhood provokes Helga's ambivalence. Her children are precious "possessions. " They are art objects to her. She adores their "lovely bodies" which seem to be "carved out of amber. " But these feelings conflict with the ideas she has always held on the subject of children. It is the one topic on which she responds politically. She has always insisted that it is a "sin" to create more "dark bodies for mobs to lynch. " When the children are her own, they become a double symbol of bondage since she cannot leave them in order to leave the Reverend Mr. Pleasant Green. She cannot even avoid having more.

Dr. Robert Anderson is the one exception to all these situations where Helga discovers that she cannot fit in. He seems to understand her and her "search. " Like her, he is "too liberal" for Naxos and has to leave. He also comes to

Harlem, looking for a world not ruled by a "white man's god." And like her, he feels an attraction between them which is both intellectual and aesthetic.

Their depth of understanding might have made them ideal friends, if they could have come together outside of social contexts. But another quality which they share destroys this possibility. Both of them are locked into a constant struggle against one part of their own nature, and contact with each other brings that inner battle into dominance. Dr. Anderson has an "ascetic" distaste for the physical part of life, and so he is ashamed of the delight which contact with Helga brings. And Helga's pride causes her to seek ways of hurting him so she will not give in to her longing for his sympathy.

Dr. Anderson solves his identity problem through "detachment." He turns to welfare work instead of education and marries a woman who provides social companionship without stirring his senses. When he meets Helga unexpectedly in private, his passionate response breaks through, but the loss of control is only momentary. He rescues himself by launching a droning lecture on African art which forms a bitter contrast with the Copenhagen artist's opinion that Helga herself is an African art object. When they meet later, by appointment, Dr. Anderson apologizes for having kissed her.

Helga feels belittled by Dr. Anderson's easy resumption of his self control. No matter how alienating other aspects of her situation may have been, everywhere from Naxos to Copenhagen, she has always enjoyed the "primitive" power her female charm provides. When Dr. Anderson rejects her sensuality as a way of avoiding his own, she feels compelled to affirm her own wholeness by overwhelming the Reverend Mr. Pleasant Green.

Helga's pattern has always been to seek a balance by emphasizing whatever part of her personality others wish to deny, and so her response to Dr. Anderson is extraordinary only in that he should be a peer, rather than a challenge. He is himself obviously a blend of black and white, since his brown face is set off by gray eyes. The combination is "strange" and "a little frightening," yet it appeals to Helga since it implies that a genuine mixture has taken place inside him. It is an idea which gives her hope that her less visible ambivalence might be resolvable.

Helga's life has always included "two parts" which are associated with "two lands." Europe offers her "physical

freedom," while America offers her "spiritual freedom," and
she wants them both. Her problem comes from the fact that
no one around her believes in such a possibility. Her
mother's brother notifies her he must not see her again since
he has married a woman who is appalled at the thought of a
Black niece. Her Harlem friends become suspicious of her
since she has lived so long among "the enemy." And at
Helen Travenor's mixed parties, Blacks and whites identify
themselves as separate even while they dance together.

On the verge of death during childbirth, she thinks
about the people she has sought as companions in the past.
Although the qualities take different forms, she discovers
that without exception the people she has clung to have survived by being both selfish and remote. When it occurs to
her that God must fit into the same category, she feels an
"enormous disgust." Only then does she give up hope of
finding some life beyond the "quagmire," the "bog," the
"asphyxiation" of being "yoked" to "dark segregated people"
whom she has not "chosen" and to whom she does not "belong." Surrounded by "undecorated women," she longs for
the smell of "Houbigant and cigarettes." Prayed over, she
becomes convinced God does not exist.

Helga is finally as grim a sacrifice as Oroonoko was.
She cherishes the "amusing, interesting, absorbing, and en-
joyable" life available to any American of "Negro ancestry."
But she finally concludes that this life must be paid for by
the "deliberate" closing of "mental doors" on the "skeletons"
of race. She has always refused to deny any aspect of her
mind or body, and so her ambivalence finally breaks down
into an incurably divided life. She cannot copy either the
selfishness or the self-delusion of the people she has tried
to admire. And she cannot look beyond individual lives for
some larger wholeness, since the question of race seems to
divide even the concept of God.

Fiction which resolves this conflict usually relieves
the characters who suffer from it by allowing them to escape
into the companionship of friends or peers. But some writers
who deal with the topic suggest that race makes free social
choice so much more difficult that success may be impossible.

Larsen underlines this aspect of the question by allowing Helga to maintain her integrity even while she yields to
physical defeat. Helga falls into self-loathing when she is
deliberately rejected by people who should have been her true
friends. But not even despair can cause her to sacrifice her

values. She gives up hope for any life beyond her loneliness because she finally accepts the personal limitations of everyone she has ever known. But no disaster can demoralize her bitterly enough to take away her conviction that wholeness and self-acceptance are the only goals which can be right for her. The fact that she can find no one to share her values only makes her lonely. It does not make her yield.

In <u>Jubilee</u>, Margaret Walker approaches this same question in a more optimistic light. The difference does not come from a better situation or a luckier life. Vyry Dutton's difficulties are infinitely worse than Helga Crane's, in that Vyry was born a slave. Since <u>Jubilee</u> spans the Civil War, the conflict it depicts is vividly focused and includes violence as well as emotional abuse. Vyry is whipped almost to death, kept in ignorance, hated, betrayed and shamed, but her personality converts even horrors into experiences she can learn from. The result is a "doctrine" of her own.

As is usual in the novels where successful individualism is considered possible, Vyry's integrity eventually attracts to her an understanding and like-minded friend. But Walker adds an unusual element to the satisfaction with which the novel closes in that Vyry insists upon support from a community which comes to value her even though it does not understand her. The effectiveness of Vyry's "doctrine" is underscored by the fact that she gets the treatment she wants from an ignorant community which does not share her values or even really sense how totally separate her standards are. In allowing Vyry to control her relations with outsiders without the use either of power or of manipulation, Walker extends the idea of friendship groups beyond the isolation which has been an element of such situations from <u>David Simple</u> onward.

As was the case in <u>Quicksand</u>, <u>Jubilee</u> depicts far more than a simple conflict between races. On Dutton plantation, there are social divisions among both whites and Blacks. Big Missy is considered a "real lady," since she is domineering toward everyone except her children. Her husband goes to the opposite extreme, loving his slave mistress more than his wife. Though the owners share a life of luxury, the tone of their experiences is extremely different. John Dutton assumes his slaves love him and feel grateful for the orderly life they lead on his land, while his wife draws energy from the knowledge that she is hated and deserves to be.

The life of the driver, Grimes, is more like that of the slaves than it is like other whites. He lives in a house only slightly better than a slave cabin. And though he is technically free to come and go according to his own whims, the demands of his work keep him tied to the plantation as unremittingly as if he were a slave. He rises before the slaves get up, and he falls into bed at night so exhausted that the twitching of his legs interrupts his sleep. In contrast, slaves are not normally driven so hard as he drives himself, and usually they are allowed regular periods of rest which he cannot share since he must supervise all the varied activities and groups.

The range of lives and attitudes among plantation Blacks is equally great. Field hands are looked down on by everyone, including the other slaves. Many of them are not even known by name. Since house servants share in the luxurious surroundings of the plantation, they enjoy enough status to express contempt for poor whites, as well as lesser slaves. House servants have enough to eat, and their individual personalities are taken into account. Those in special situations which involve skill or trust may even be indulged and flattered. Marse John sometimes comes to the kitchen to thank the cook for special meals, for example. His son Johnny is entirely and trustingly dependent on his body servant, Jim. Miss Lillian cares more for the blessings of her slave playmate than for all the elegance and fuss plantation whites can shower upon her.

Lives outside the plantation are as clearly stratified on a different basis. Many of the poor whites are relatives of either Grimes or Dutton, but the relationship counts for no more than does the similar blood link with slaves. In the winter, poor whites come to the plantation to beg for food. In the spring, they come to beg for seed. In the summer, they beg for work. The only source of pride for them is being white, since they barely survive.

Whites who live in the nearby town have better lives since their income as well as their social identity comes from professional work. Plantation people are ready to be polite to the banker or the doctor since their status does not depend on the number of slaves they own. And town life is so completely different that professionals exist outside the subtle distinctions which rank country people from "lord" to slave.

Free Blacks bring town and country standards into clear conflict. There is only one free Black in the neighborhood Jubilee describes, and since he is both professional and rich, he should be respected and secure. However, Georgia law assigns him by race rather than by work or financial status. He pays a heavy tax for the "free papers" he is required to have. He must have a white sponsor, and he is tied to his sponsor's land, like a peasant. His personal wealth, his importance as a blacksmith, his education, and the fact that he was born free are truths which become unimportant in the context of the one detail which is crucial to his status--that he is Black.

This elaborate social web does not mean that social mobility is made easier by the many small gradations which bridge across the major gaps. When Big Missy becomes suspicious of the cook and insists on selling her, they try to retrain a field worker to fill the vacancy, but she cannot learn the new work, even for the sake of the improved life which goes with it. When the demands of munitions factories leave the plantations shorthanded during the early stages of the war, house servants cannot work in the fields.

The same inflexibility confines whites. John Dutton's aunt married a small storekeeper rather than a plantation owner. His wife feels justified in looking down on people "in trade," and so the marriage gives her a reason to despise John's aunt and his cousins on a permanent basis, though she consents to patronize them as poor relations when they visit Dutton plantation at Christmas.

The only person whose status changes in the prewar world is Grimes. He is poor white by birth, and after infinite struggle he becomes a driver. Since this difference provides neither respect nor financial advantage, it suggests that the only changes which can be achieved are those which are not accompanied by any social result.

In so confined a society, Vyry's situation is less ambiguous than her family background would otherwise suggest. Born to John Dutton's slave mistress, Vyry is a slave. Because she has inherited her father's fair skin, blond hair and blue eyes, strangers always believe her to be a twin to Dutton's legitimate daughter, who is the same age. Miss Lillian frankly calls Vyry her sister and prefers her to any other playmate, but the affection between the children makes no difference to Vyry's situation. The lesson

Vyry learns from this is that looking white does not make a person free.

Vyry's interest in herself as white turns out to be extremely temporary. While the girls are very young, they play together as if they were alike, and when Dutton brings treats to his official daughter, he always urges her to share with Vyry. But his wife really runs the plantation, and so she is the white person all the house servants have most contact with. No slave would wish to copy such a model. When Vyry is old enough to be brought to the Big House to start her training, she discovers she is a slave, rather than a playmate. She also discovers Big Missy Salina's true character. Being white is Salina's only virtue--even Miss Lillian does not pattern herself on her mother--and so Vyry turns away from white models, regardless of her skin color. She is enormously relieved when she is assigned to the cook's quarters rather than being kept in the Big House, as personal servants are. Closing the door at night and shutting out the white world where Big Missy rules is like escaping into a different life which is "grand and good."

Rejecting whiteness is a reasonable response to Vyry's discovery that neither behavior nor status is connected to color in any consistent way. However, it leaves her without any clear way of thinking about herself. Forced to accept that she is white in her skin but not in her situation, she has become sensitive enough to social ambiguity that she cannot settle quietly into the alternative. She must live as a slave, but doing so does not bring with it either the mindless submission of demoralization or the equally automatic defiance of hopeless integrity.

Still too young to set up her own categories, Vyry begins thinking about the less obvious relationships her situation surrounds her with. She has a Black as well as a white half-sister, since Dutton gave his mistress, Hetta, a Black husband in order to mask his relationship with her. Hetta's white children are placed with foster mothers because they irritate her Black husband as much as they enrage Dutton's wife. The result is that Vyry has never played with Lucy, as a childhood companion, the way she has with Miss Lillian, and so the two little girls scarcely know each other and have very few early experiences in common.

Separating them even more is the fact that each seems to have drawn her personality from her father rather than from the mother they share. John Dutton's easygoing nature emerges in Vyry's generous-spirited response to other people's problems. But Lucy copies her father Jake's sullen personal resentment of everything connected with the white man who makes use of her mother. Because of their mother's status, both girls are designated as house servants. Lucy follows her older sister Vyry into training, where her special bitterness makes her life even harder than it is for other slaves in the Big House, but Vyry has too little feeling of kinship to suggest ways for her to avoid trouble.

Knowing Lucy teaches Vyry an important lesson, even though a feeling of closeness never does grow up between the girls. Vyry discovers that Lucy shares her longing to be free. Since the slaves rarely talk about freedom, Vyry has had no way of knowing whether her yearning might be entirely personal, or whether it might result from her white ancestry. But her half-sister is entirely Black, and so Vyry comes to understand that dreams of freedom are provoked by slavery rather than by the color of the skin.

Lucy provides a second lesson, which is even more important to Vyry. A public festival is arranged around the hanging of two Black women accused of murder, and slaves in the region are forced to attend, as a warning. Under cover of the distraction, Lucy escapes. Vyry silently rejoices in her sister's freedom. However, she does not want to share in the resourceful defiance which was Lucy's means of accomplishing her aims.

This ability to hold goals in common without sharing the methods other people use to reach them becomes Vyry's unstated resource in her search for a set of beliefs which will suit her personal needs. Vyry does not even consider copying Lucy's coldly calculating ability to think only of herself in the midst of public sordidness and horror. Instead, she uses her sister's success to achieve a mental freedom for herself which is far more important to her than the simpler physical relief Lucy gains.

What Vyry learns is that ambiguity exists, even when it is specifically denied. In the past, all the free individuals Vyry has met have been born free. When Lucy is added to this group, she seems to change the rules. The insight is important because it frees Vyry from her innocent acceptance of the principle that social views are accurate even when they are neither fair nor reasonable. Though she has no one with whom she dares to discuss such defiant thoughts, Vyry begins to draw her own conclusions about her situation. As her independence develops through exercise, she begins to judge the opinions of people she likes, as well as those she deplores. The process puts her in touch with her individuality and constitutes a major turning point in her progress toward a value system of her own.

The years which follow the freeing of Vyry's mind turn into a series of tests of her commitment. Events of every kind put pressure on her will, but she is able to deal with everything from temptation to disaster by judging on her own in a way which transforms all experience into material for the refinement of her personal beliefs.

Her teenage love story is an example of how she maintains her grasp of ambiguity in the face of overwhelming odds. When Randall Ware wants her to fall in love with him, he "sparks" his eyes and "flashes" his teeth and jingles the coins in his pocket. Vyry is troubled by his "animal magnetism," but what gains his point is his talk of freedom.

Vyry insists she will not marry unless Randall finds a way to set her free. However, Miss Lillian is in love, too, and by the time Vyry has cooked for the enormous wedding which launches her white sister's future of "luck and happiness," Vyry is more tired than she has ever been. Dragged down by this weariness which springs from her depression over the painfully direct contrast between their lives, Vyry's resistance falters. Her own unofficial marriage follows quickly, partly from the same romantic love which impels Miss Lillian, and partly because lying in her "black magnet's" arms keeps her from dreaming about the hanging and the death by whipping of one of the most trusted of the house servants.

Pregnancy emphasizes Vyry's separateness rather than strengthening connections, as such an experience usually does. She thinks freedom is doubly important since it now involves her child, but Randall's response is patronizing. He goes through the slave substitute for marriage, thinking it will satisfy Vyry. With casual cruelty, he insists he would die rather than be a slave, himself, but he patronizingly assumes Vyry is concerned only about marriage and not about the law which grants freedom automatically to a woman who marries a free man. His promise to buy her if Dutton ever offers her for sale only reinforces the discrepancy in their status which he accepts so casually.

Silently recognizing that Randall will never be a route to freedom, Vyry turns to her father. Marse John is as amiable toward her as he usually is toward his slaves, assuming she has involved herself with someone else he owns. But when she explains her situation, he is shocked. Unlike Randall, he immediately understands that she is really asking for her freedom. His good nature keeps him from a cruel response, but it does not change his attitude. He tells Vyry that he owns her and he owns her children, too.

Dutton's simplistic view relieves Vyry of any hope that fatherhood may modify slavery, but she is still unprepared for Randall's attitude. Dutton's attitude can be somewhat excused since owning Vyry only gives him a second basis for controlling her choices in the way fathers treat daughters even in fully conventional relationships. But for Randall to take delight in a son who is another man's slave is a situation Vyry cannot adjust to. She realizes that her life is "bound up" with Randall as tightly as it is "claimed" by Marse John. But their patronizing unconcern with her appeals convinces her that her values are separate from theirs, regardless of their beliefs about ownership. She affirms her identity to herself by discovering that she can sing traditional slave laments in the "dark rich voice" of the Black cook who trained her. Doing so relieves her frustration without alerting the men she rebels against.

Vyry's separation of herself from these two free men becomes total when Randall asks Vyry to run away with him. For years, he has seemed content to slip into Dutton plantation after dark in order to visit Vyry and father a second child with her. He is a large property owner, and so he has not even considered leaving the area. It is only when the war to come puts free Blacks under pressure that he suggests he can help Vyry escape.

Such an attitude would be neglectful enough, in any event, but it is rendered doubly painful by Randall's insistence that she must run without her children. She affirms that she wants her freedom, but not at the cost of her children. Randall patronizes her as usual, insisting that she "trust him" and repeating that she must leave them and that she must come alone.

Vyry's loyalty to her own standards clears up her situation in several ways. Heading toward the spot where Randall is to meet her, she carries her baby and leads her son, as she has insisted she must do. Unfortunately, her boy, Jim, takes after his father. He whines every step of the way and slows her down even though it is clearly not too far for him to walk, since he trots back home without a murmur after they are captured. When Vyry does not make it to the meeting place, Randall casually assumes she has lost her nerve, and he disappears without a backward glance. Dutton is away from the plantation when Grimes punishes Vyry as a runaway by whipping her and leaving her to die, bleeding at the stake in the sun. When her father comes back and finds her half dead, he swears and raves, but he punishes no one in her defense.

The uniformity with which Vyry is betrayed by the males who matter to her might suggest that Walker's intention is the feminist political point hinted at in the explanation Vyry is given about her "womanhood." When Vyry is old enough to start having her periods, Aunt Sally soothes her fears by explaining that menstruation is a good thing since it distinguishes her from "puny-fied" men. Men are nothing but "breath and britches and trouble," and she is lucky to be different from a "no-good man," who cannot even manage to have his own children.

Within the context of the novel, this view becomes one of a wide range of simplistic judgments which Walker includes as a way of developing a large idea which contradicts any narrow assumption. Her point is not that survival and justice depend upon choosing the best among a clutter of simplistic preconceptions. Instead, she shows that any simple opinion is too incomplete. As Vyry matures in a context of judgments based on groups, she notices the damage done when no provision is made for individual differences. This insight is the basis of her increasingly subtle judgment. It helps her keep her mind clear of the casual prejudice which overcomes Blacks as well as whites as their plantation world ends.

Like every other category in the novel, freedom is not a simple idea. In Walker's use, the legal definition is no more than a small part of a concept so complex that Vyry acquires her freedom in stages as she grows up, rather than as a single legal change brought by war. When no obvious authority remains on Dutton plantation, Vyry finds herself taking responsibility because someone must. Miss Lillian has always turned to Vyry, and so it is by habit that she appeals to Vyry when Big Missy has a stroke. And when her mother dies, Miss Lillian clings to Vyry, begging not to be left alone.

Vyry is confused by Miss Lillian's treatment of her, even though it does not represent a major change from her behavior when they were little girls together. She is surprised as well as puzzled when the doctor talks to her as if she were an acknowledged member of the family. But she is uncertain of how her resentment should be focused. Is she irritated at hearing how whites talk about Blacks when only whites are present? Does she begrudge this belated designation as a family member, now that the family is only a burden and cannot be a help?

Regardless of how she is treated, Vyry maintains careful distinctions for herself. When too many deaths demoralize Miss Lillian so badly that she cannot even dress herself without being reminded, the doctor asks if Vyry can send to some part of the family who might take her in. Cautiously neutral, Vyry mentions Miss Lucy as Marse John's relation. But when Miss Lucy and her husband arrive, they casually accept their relationship to both Marse John's daughters. They are kind and attentive to Vyry in the same way they are to Lillian. They insist Vyry take keepsakes and items of value when the home is broken up, and they not only offer help for the future, but they give it willingly when Vyry eventually is driven to ask.

This unexpected new inclusion into the family by people who are perfectly aware of her complex identity allows Vyry to do some thinking before she confronts similar treatment from strangers. After she moves to Alabama, she is accepted as white, and so she gains an insider's view of how whites feel. It is an appalling world. So ignorant they think Black people have tails, whites are confident all Blacks deserve hatred. They are so sure all whites agree with these ideas that they are frank about both their ignorance and their judgment.

This information is important since it helps Vyry refine her goals. She has always insisted that reading and writing are as important as freedom. But the reason she deplored illiteracy was that it seemed to her to be the source of ignorance, and she took both to be a part of slavery. The shocking exposure to white ignorance extends her earlier conviction that qualities of mind and personality must be considered separately from any social situation. She finds that illiteracy is a handicap which takes no account of color, since the sharecropper who cheats her Black husband also cheated a white family before them in exactly the same way. She also concludes that learning to read does not in itself remove ignorance, since Klan members can read.

These conclusions are reinforced by her parallel discovery that escaping slavery does not leave her free to lead her own life. Relocating in Alabama, Vyry easily gets a job as a cook. She is kindly treated, since the family she works for is very willing to replace its lost slaves with hired equivalents. But when she gives notice that she must quit to have her child and to help her husband with the spring work on their own farm, her employer becomes angry and bitter. The Klan appears promptly to burn Vyry's farm and drive her and her family out of the area.

These new understandings of white lives are accompanied by equivalent distinctions about Black behavior patterns. Even after almost everyone has left Dutton plantation, Vyry remains since Randall said he would come back for her children, and she is sure he will come back for the property he considered more valuable than her freedom. She pretends to wait because of a promise, and she does feel a connection to Randall, in spite of his treatment of her. Yet her feelings cannot be straightforward since some aspects of Randall's behavior have always troubled her. In the prewar days when she wanted to discuss her own freedom, he hushed her up in a persistently patronizing way. When he countered by lecturing her on national and international politics, her mind wandered away from the abstractions which made other slaves angry without making them free.

The crucial nature of this value conflict is symbolized by Randall's decision to go to a political rally instead of coming home to Vyry directly after the war. Waiting around long after everyone who is able to has come home, Vyry has time to explore her feelings about Randall by comparing him to Innis Brown.

Innis Brown values the same things Vyry does. His postwar freedom is meaningless to him until he falls in love with Vyry's children and stays on the plantation to be around the first "whole seeming" Black family he has ever met. Since he was a field hand before the war, he is an enormous help to Vyry in a physical as well as intellectual way. He willingly relieves her of some of the burden of farming to support Lillian's family as well as her own. Even more important, he triggers her realization that she must fight prejudice inside her own feelings as well as find some way to deal with it in others. She has always assumed everyone looked down on field hands, but Innis farms because he likes to, and the discovery forces her to take a second look at her own thoughtlessness.

The contrast between Innis and Randall develops gradually enough to allow for realistic growth in Vyry's understanding of the forces behind events. After Vyry marries Innis and the family is settled on their own land in Alabama, Vyry's son Jim kills one of Innis' sows through neglect. Now a teenager, Jim is still whining and still actively interfering with other people's dreams. Frustrated beyond endurance, Innis whips Jim. Vyry is appalled that violence has entered her own family and reacts in rage against Innis. But then she realizes that she has behaved exactly as Innis did. Innis has expressed fury at having his dream of independence threatened, while she is ready to kill Innis for invading her dream of peace. If she rejects Innis' behavior, she must also reject her own.

This episode shows the basis of Vyry's success. She is at peace not because she lacks the lesser impulses other people must struggle with but because she thinks about what happens instead of accepting ready-made opinions. Patiently taking complexity into account, she concludes that her motherhood feelings do not relieve Jim of responsibility for his own behavior. While provocation does not make Innis' outburst less violent, it does mean she cannot automatically classify him as a deficient father. When Jim attacks Vyry by sullenly clinging to his selfishness, Vyry observes how much like Randall he has turned out to be.

By watching her family and her own reactions, Vyry realizes that single-issue judgments lead to hate rather than to clarity. This is the insight which allows her to choose between Randall and Innis when Randall arrives belatedly to claim his family. Mature enough not to be dazzled by the roll of greenbacks and the air of importance which Randall brings, Vyry now notices the other aspects of Randall's self-satisfied air. He is rude to her--giving her orders in her own home, insulting her integrity, and using vile language in front of her. Standing up to him patiently rather than angrily, Vyry demonstrates her "doctrine" at the same time she explains it. She tells Randall he is bitter and that his hate is no better than white hate.

Ethnic Alternatives / 131

Vyry tells Randall she has no time for hating, and the basis of her choice between the two men becomes clear. When he was courting Vyry, Randall admitted that he owed everything to the help of two white men. Now, he insists that every white man is "evil." Innis sides with Vyry when he mildly says that people get along all right if they tend their own land and do not bother others. Innis understands Vyry's standards, and shares them, and so Vyry's choice is easy.

Tolerance plays so crucial a part in Vyry's doctrine that it takes precedence even over motherhood. She insists she will not teach her children to hate, and she has struggled to set Jim free from the hate which is central to his personality. But when she sees hate leaping out of Randall's eyes, Vyry realizes that inheritance makes hate basic to Jim's nature, and so she releases her oldest child to Randall with her blessing and restructures her family by moving the more cheerful son she shares with Innis into the newly vacant room.

Her way of dealing with the white community takes the same form. Mistaken for a white woman as she sells farm produce door-to-door, she hears almost universal hate and distrust against Blacks. But the persistent prejudice does not keep her from helping a terrified young white woman in childbirth. The community needs a midwife and begs Vyry to accept the role. Vyry's response reveals her genuinely remarkable nature. She says she cannot make commitments to a community which hurts her feelings by hating people of her race. It is a simple statement which insists upon her own feelings without making either accusations or claims.

The structure of Vyry's statement makes a permanent peace possible. The community offers to protect her, if anyone should ever try to cause her trouble. They organize a house-raising and a quilting bee to make their welcome more emphatic. And Vyry gladly takes up the role of "granny," since her self-image is to offer help to anyone in need.

"Mutual need" is a satisfactory basis for the whole community since it is voluntary on both sides. The community declares that Vyry and Innis are good people, whatever their color may be. Vyry accepts the fact that prejudiced feelings can be ignored in individuals whenever tolerant behavior keeps lesser impulses inactive and out of sight. This "spiritual wholeness" which Vyry consciously achieves is not really understood by the community, but they value the part of her behavior which they can perceive. Tolerance from the larger community is enough for Vyry, since Innis understands her "unusual" character and gladly shares her privacy.

By using tolerance rather than ambivalence as the basis of understanding, Walker can grant happiness and peace to Vyry in a success which is not available to Helga Crane. Through a combination of inheritance, modeling, and thinking on her own, Vyry manages an eclectic doctrine which resolves both the anger produced by repressive group judgments and the more specific defiance resulting from the black or white divisions which are limiting, exclusive, and falsely absolute.

Novels like these which deal with ethnic identity in the context of a broad cultural and psychological framework succeed at releasing the social problem from the oversimplification which can make it seem so despairingly hard to modify. Patterns which focus on value systems rather than prejudices offer a way of thinking about conflicts regardless of blind spots, prejudgments and wounds. Non-patronizing understanding between equals is important enough to cause lesser ideas to fade.

Rosa Guy shows how values can accumulate ethnic overtones even in the absence of the kind of explicit pressures most of this fiction represents. Guy's Edith Jackson focuses on a teenage girl's struggle to grow up into a set of values different from the norms her background offers. The problems of becoming educated, developing independent self-respect and deferring gratification are compounded by confusion over ethnic assumptions. Edith must fight against automatic rejection of "white" values and "middle class" values in addition to the usual young person's struggle to identify personal talents and define legitimate sacrifices toward their development.

Nella Larsen's Passing also features a young woman who must deal with her early assumption that taking a stand on her ethnic identity will automatically clear up her questions about social values. In this novel, Larsen's heroine marries a man who does not realize she has a mixed heritage. Since he adores her but loathes Blacks, she is put under constant and direct pressure about her identity. She is troubled even more by the limitations she has placed on herself than she is by the effort and risk of concealment.

"Passing" successfully turns out to be defeat for her. She cannot face the loss to herself which living in a single racial context enforces, and so she restores herself to wholeness by secretly resuming her links in the Black community.

By emphasizing the absolute necessity of selecting elements from several possibilities rather than submitting to preexisting roles and values, each of these novels shows that complexity is a workable solution to the problems caused by widespread prejudice against minority groups. In the context of such a procedure, tolerance depends on patience with differences rather than on redesigning humanity to fit some universal, equalizing blend. An appreciation for variety is essential in making room for individuals who fall outside the norms for any reason. It becomes doubly important in these novels, because uniformity cannot be enforced by pretending differences do not exist when social divisions are based on something so arbitrary and visible as skin.

Note

1 Ernest A. Baker, History of the English Novel (New York: Barnes & Noble, 1929), vol. III, p. 169.

5. NEW ROLES IN OLD SOCIETIES

Charlotte Smith, The Old Manor House
Elizabeth Gaskell, Ruth
Elizabeth Stuart Phelps Ward, The Silent Partner
Toni Morrison, Sula

others:
Katherine Anne Porter, "Old Mortality"
Rebecca Harding Davis, Dr. Warrick's Daughters
Geraldine Jewsbury, Marian Withers
Margaret Drabble, The Millstone
Mary Shelley, Frankenstein
Constance Woolson, For the Major
Mary Roberts Rinehart, Miss Pinkerton

Being treated like a harmless crank is one way of being free. Novels which use this often overlooked or undervalued route to tolerated unconventionality are in some ways the most hopeful form of fiction about individuals who live outside the norms. By focusing on people who willingly accept the idea of obligations to others as a natural part of living in any community, such stories imply that conventional society will put up with different standards if they can be perceived as idealistic and therefore irrelevant rather than threatening.

This kind of difference does not cause major upheavals because everyone is likely to accept the ideals themselves, at least in theory. It is usual enough to admit that family and nationality carry obligations as well as benefits, and so a person who pays unusual attention to this side of the social bargain appears to be only excessive without seeming really wrong. Individuals who insist upon paying their social debts in unusual ways may be teased or taken advantage of or deplored as self-punishing extremists, but they are not likely to be rejected outright, since the real basis of their difference is normally misunderstood.

Such individuals willingly explain themselves to their friends and relatives. They analyze existing roles and insist on the function rather than the degenerated forms in conventional use. Since society in general rarely thinks of roles abstractly, most people can feel self-flatteringly sophisticated in contrast to the rare individual who seriously thinks about the basic social obligations which roles imply. Some normal people may wistfully admit that idealism would be lovely if reality left room for it. Excused by pragmatism, they can refuse to take exceptions seriously. Still, the gallantry of a struggle to live up to everybody's goals is usually so attractive that idealistic individuals are often valued, even while their attitudes are set aside.

Fiction which focuses on idealistic lives varies considerably, over time, but regardless of whether an eighteenth-century view of an heir is dissected or a twentieth-century conception of sisterhood is redefined, the novelistic procedure is the same. In each example, central characters work just as hard to serve others as they do to develop themselves. Since normal people would behave this way only through passivity or submissiveness, society is accidentally misled, and the mistake intensifies their problems. Perceived as unselfish, they are given no room for private needs. They cannot simply desert a society which insists they live someone else's life because it is their willingness to notice and serve the needs of the people around them which sets them apart in the first place. Their best response is to settle on the ready-made social niche which has the most potential for expansion and use it as a way of working out an individualized bargain with conventional society.

Fiction expressing such a life method can produce critical reactions which are intriguingly similar to the way society treats characters within the novels. In The Old Manor House, Charlotte Smith did justice to her hero by manipulating fictional conventions enough to annoy 200 years of critics and literary historians. For example, a contemporary reviewer was disturbed by Orlando's personality, which seemed immoral to him,[1] while twentieth-century comentators charge that characterization is more or less absent,[2] or that plot structure is violated.[3]

Such responses are triggered by the unusual nature of the social bargain Smith depicts. Her story concerns the second son in a family whose fortunes have declined. A major part of Orlando's problem is that his social niche is well defined. However, to the delight of readers and the distress of critics, he does not behave as he "should." In order to make his remarkable nature believable, Smith resorts to a procedure which was very unusual at the time--she explores the instincts and recounts the experiences which contribute to the makeup of her young paragon. And then, in order to insist that his unique charm is not a fluke, she brightens her cast of characters with some more quickly explained parallels. The resulting psychological realism is often not recognized since it is not expected in the novel of the time. The ethical complexity also may not be taken seriously since it is more idealistic than the normal range of attitude provides.

The pattern Smith uses to redefine the norms is symbolized by the selection of a profession for the novel's hero. Orlando Somerive listens anxiously as his family and friends go down the list of possibilities, examining the worldly result of every choice available. His own concern is with the function rather than the status of the life. His uncle is willing to make a merchant of him, but Orlando does not want to judge himself by the amount of money he can amass. He has the talent to be a writer, and he does write poetry for private enjoyment, but making a profession of the skill would mean writing plays, and putting his name before the public would be a breach of family dignity. While still studying at the local school, he serves as a kind of unofficial chaplain to an elderly cousin, and his brother insists Orlando's ethical sensitivity suits him for "the petticoats." But Orlando is distressed by the perfunctory behavior of the priests he knows. He has the rational ability to succeed in the law, but he is so appalled by the "legal misery" he sees around the courts that he could never submit himself to a profession whose business is to "assist men in ruining each other." He has the mind and personality to be a tutor, and he enjoys the work so much that he turns his courtship into a tutorial in reading, writing and logic. But striving to make his beloved's mind as attractive as her "form" is not at all the same as accepting the dependency which an official tutor's post would involve.

Orlando has insisted from the beginning that he would gladly be whatever his family wants to make of him, with the single stipulation that he wishes to be independent. But independence is extremely hard to accomplish in Orlando's situation. His most obvious hope had been to inherit from his eccentrically fond "ancient" cousin, and he is so successful as her half-acknowledged heir that his father jokingly accuses him of having given her a love powder to make her set aside both his father and his older brother in his own favor. Nevertheless, Orlando is unwilling to "practice the arts" of a "legacy hunter." He spends time with his elderly cousin only out of a kindly awareness of her loneliness since he is convinced that her attention does not extend beyond a little "present liking."

Orlando's own choice would be to make a farmer of himself, since his only wish beyond independence is for a quiet, rural life. But his family sets such unassuming work aside. Not only would they dislike it, themselves, but they remember that being unpretentious was what cut the Somerive branch of the family off from the Rayland estate generations before. Since Orlando is the first Somerive to catch a Rayland eye in three generations, a repetition of the originally damaging modesty of goals is rejected out of hand.

The role which most nearly answers everyone's requirements while avoiding everyone's objections is soldiering. If a commission is purchased for him, Orlando's service will be respectable enough to satisfy his family. He has the personal courage and the decisiveness under stress which soldiers need. The influence which gets him his appointment in the first place will assure him of advancement so that he will become independent eventually. And as an officer, he will come in contact with "the world" and with men in groups in a way which all the men and some of the women around him think he needs.

The only objection anyone can raise is the fact that the occupation of soldiers is to go to war. This offensive detail is underlined in his case by the fact that his intended company is fighting in America, at the moment. Orlando has reservations about a career focusing on "the art of destroying honorably our fellow-men," although even his usually humane mother considers Americans to be not men but rebels. And when the family friend who arranges for Orlando's commission insists that the rebellion was pathetic from the start, Mrs. Somerive unflinchingly rejoices in their promised prompt defeat, since it will mean that the men will be back home by the time Orlando can hope to join them. He can expect to be garrisoned in his own neighborhood, and his occupation will be recruitment.

This careful pruning of the role helps make it acceptable to Orlando's family. He is to wear a uniform like his most glorious ancestors, and so his cousin concludes that his mind will be occupied while his morals are left intact. He is to be a "safe soldier," and so his mother endures the thought of a red coat. He is to be a "soldier of peace," and so his father accepts his departure from family control.

Orlando's views are different from the start. He willingly seeks the commission since it will get him out of an intolerable situation at home and will offer at least the hope of independence at last. These personal benefits do not diminish his concern with the social implications of any work he is to perform, however. And it is not until he can turn away from the practice of killing and look at the theory that he can be wholehearted about the profession. He is able to commit himself to the abstract idea that soldiers go to war in order to protect the nation.

The protector's role comes naturally to Orlando since he has been fulfilling that function in a domestic form for months, despite his youth and situation. In fact, he fears he has become so necessary to his family that he has lost the right to think of his own wishes. Strong and athletic, he is an obvious source of physical protection, risking a duel to defend his cousin's right to preserve her game, and retrieving his older brother from drunken escapades. His performance in the more intellectual side of the role is equally automatic. He accepts an appeal for permission to court one of his sisters, he helps another sister think about conventional behavior in order to refine an ethical system of her own, and he intervenes with Mrs. Rayland's companion in an effort to gain better treatment for her ward.

Such behavior would seem remarkably selfless even in a young man who found himself suddenly head of his family through the loss of all the older males. However, Smith emphasizes her intentions by developing these traits in Orlando while he has a father and an older brother still alive. Since it is the youngest of the Somerive men whom everyone turns to for protection and advice, Smith succeeds in separating the role from the qualities implied.

Because the traditional protector's role is not vacant, Orlando should not have to accept family responsibility as he does. But Mr. Somerive's conduct as a father gradually forces Orlando to rely on his own opinion even while he behaves dutifully whenever he can. In Orlando's opinion, for example, Mr. Somerive all but sells his younger children, under the guise of establishing them in conventional ways.

He actively hurries one daughter's marriage to a rich Irish merchant who is too young to know his own mind and too much a stranger, both to the family and to England, to be sure of anything beyond his intended bride's beauty. He refuses to notice the planned ruin of a second daughter at the hands of one of his friends. And he twice tries to sell Orlando, once agreeing to give him for an apprentice-like adoption by his brother-in-law, who will make a merchant of him for the sake of family income, and later eagerly accepting the offer of a marriage, with twenty thousand down, between Orlando and a woman no one likes.

Mr. Somerive's insensitive conventionality is a problem in other ways as well. He indulges his oldest son in a "natural turn to expense" because he expects Philip to be the Rayland heir. Growing up with no checks of any kind on his naturally volatile behavior, Philip points out that firstborn sons are heirs in all "Christian countries." Believing his birth justifies his expectations, he does nothing to persuade his cousin that he is worthy to inherit from her. Instead, he toasts her death and poaches her game, feeling jealous but not feeling urged to reform by her obvious preference for his younger brother. While he waits for the inheritance he considers his by right, he behaves like his father's heir as well, stripping his immediate family not only of their entire present income but of their past savings for the daughters' dowries and the future security of the mother's marriage settlement as well.

Since Smith uses Philip's behavior to help characterize Mr. Somerive, Philip turns out to be more than simply the conventional dissolute heir. His defects are carefully accounted for as the result of an unfortunate combination of heredity and environment. Like one of his sisters, Philip inherits his father's lack of self-control. The weakness is magnified by a model who neither demonstrates nor insists upon control. As a result, what is merely ineffectiveness in the father turns into active vice in the son.

Emphasizing the contribution of environment to this tragedy, Smith provides a different outcome for the sister whose character is the same as Philip's. Since Isabella is subject to her mother's control, her inherited defect develops into no more than a tactless and wild high-spiritedness.

The lack of control which some of the younger Somerives inherit emerges in Mr. Somerive as a destructive indecisiveness. Uncertain how to act "for the best" in controlling Philip and providing for Orlando, he does nothing at all. When the sons themselves finally force him into some kind of reaction, his responses are ill-considered and frantic rather than protective and wise. He undermines his health with worry over his undeserving older son's happiness, and he alienates his dutiful younger son through fretful insults. Persuaded by Philip that Orlando has a "criminal" attachment to the niece of Mrs. Rayland's paid companion, he is disgusted by Orlando's self-indulgence. Contradicted by Monimia's real modesty and beauty, he becomes even more insulting about her. He remains abusively convinced that an unworldly marriage is more destructive than any amout of personal depravity could ever be, and so he insists that Orlando is in more danger from innocently loving a pure but unpretending young woman than Philip is from the gambling addiction which denudes him of his last shreds of self-respect.

Since his father is tyrannical when he should be admiring, weak when he should prevail, and blind when he should intervene, Orlando is forced to analyze the protector's role. He becomes convinced that a man's right to advise his family does not include permission to be unjust, and so he warns his father not to give him orders which he will have to disobey. He is sure a father's obligation to judge and correct his children's morals does not entitle him to set up worldly advantage as a substitute for integrity, and so he insists he has a right to love the woman who pleases him since he is willing to work for her.

Orlando observes his father rather than simply taking advantage of him as Philip does. It is a difference which makes his exposure to his father's defects even more dangerous than that of his brother. A father who fails on every point might seem to show that the role should be rejected. What saves Orlando is his ability to notice that there is no relationship--either negative or positive--between any role and the character of the individual in it. His brother's abusiveness, vulgarity and depravity do not keep him from being considered the Rayland heir. His father's whining and wavering do not keep him from being the nominal head of the family. On the other hand, his mother's womanhood does not keep her from being resourceful and strong.

Facing a pattern of discrepancy which shows that individuals may be better than they are called upon to be, just as they may be less than they need to be, Orlando has no trouble identifying his own pattern. He is determined to do his duty as a son and brother, regardless of his father's defects. He draws strength from the integrity of mind and character which he inherits as well as copies from his mother. When his father becomes hysterical at the realization that Orlando may be in danger, Orlando is able to insist he will not be governed by his father's fears since his mother would not wish him to be a coward. When it becomes obvious even to the younger children that one of Isabella's suitors intends to kidnap and seduce her rather than offer marriage, it is Mrs. Somerive who sensibly arranges that Isabella will never be left alone and exposed to the anticipated danger. Mr. Somerive continues an excessive and blind cordiality toward the man who plots betrayal. Used, insulted and beggared by their oldest son, Mr. Somerive worries himself into a decline and dies. Mrs. Somerive gathers what she can from the wreckage in order to protect and bring peace to the other children.

The qualities Orlando inherits from his mother make it possible for him to withstand the environment which proves so disastrous for his brother. Although playful as a child and "fascinating" as an adult, he spends all his unoccupied time reading. Constant contact with the best thoughts of the past gives him a large-mindedness which lifts him above the limitations of his father's family and encourages him to spend his time in the quiet library at Rayland Hall as an escape from the turmoil created by his brother's presence at his parents' home.

These meditative habits build upon the sensible coping skills which he inherits from his mother and produce a mental independence which is emphasized by constant use. Discovering that one of his sisters is embroiled in an elopement, he demands to know the details, and when he is sure she will not be exposed to "improper adventures," he refuses to interfere. He will protect her reputation, but he insists that her choice must remain in her own control. Discovering himself to be in love with Monimia, he arranges for assignations in the library at Rayland Hall, since they have no other way to meet. But when he gets her alone in secret, he gives her stacks of books with passages marked, and they engage in philosophical discussions intended to improve her "natural good sense" out of the ignorance her aunt intends for her. Trying to relieve her of the fearfulness of superstition, he insists he will not use his social and educational advantages to prejudice her against ghosts but instead will show her the evidence he has used to free his own mind and ask her to judge for herself. When she is terrified at the separation soldiering will bring, he points out that she can be as brave as he is by drawing courage from the same sources he uses, and he adds to her reading list.

Although many of his experiences are undesirable in themselves, they do allow him to test his theories, and he has the satisfaction of observing that his way of life is more practical as well as more idealistic than his father's way. By giving the appearance of being a protector rather than a martinet, he gains access to Isabella's elopement plans, which remain utterly unknown to her dithering and blustering father. In contrast to his sister's exposure while under her father's eye, he protects Monimia even in his absence by teaching her to judge for herself rather than depending upon what she hears from self-interested people, including him.

By the time he is to protect the nation, he has both theory and practice to convince him that a protector has no right to judge for others by forcing his preferences on them. Instead, the only real protection comes from fostering the development of the protected individual's best nature while demonstrating ways to keep evil influences at bay as much as possible. Such a definition of a protector is different in every detail from what his father says and does, but it is seconded by the practical dignity his mother demonstrates and by the integrity and independence he sees developing in both his favorite sister and his fiancée.

Orlando refines his ideas in the relative protection of a rural community and in the company of women, but Smith does not suggest that their usefulness is limited to such environments. She provides him with a variety of near parallels during his life as a soldier, in order to show how his idealism functions among worldly men and in a battle zone.

Warwick, his first companion, is as handsome as Orlando is and as "humane, generous and candid." But unlike Orlando, he has the additional social charm of some "acquired imperfections" which make him agreeable to men and women alike. His liveliness is as appealing to Orlando as it is to readers, but Orlando is not charmed away from his own more rigorous standards, despite the novelty of Warwick's literary cultivation and conversational skills. In an amusing episode during which the two young men tour the sin spots of London, searching for Philip, Warwick cannot hold himself back from engaging in whatever activity is going on. While Orlando is interested in the possibilities displayed, he stays

clear of temptation by considering the irony of losing himself
when his intention was to find his brother.

A less cultivated companion, Fleming, helps Orlando
clarify his thinking about the function of a soldier. As they
embark for America, Fleming is torn between helping the
men under him and comforting the wife and young children
he must leave undefended. So obvious a conflict between the
claims of country and family causes Orlando to wonder what
war is for. Fleming tries to help him by explaining that a
soldier's job is to fight, not think. Such a view shocks Orlando instead of persuading him. He has been taught that
England's strength comes from the belief of her people in the
rightness of her government, and the demonstration that England is strong because her people believe they should not
think for themselves violates his interpretation of national integrity.

Hoping his reaction is unjustified, he struggles to put
war into a larger context. He runs through literary representations in his mind, beginning with the classics, and reminds himself how battle is always presented in terms of
glory. But as he looks at actual battlefields, he sadly admits
that the violence is really for money and for usurped authority. He questions American prisoners, and their answers reveal intelligence and strength of character which persuade him
that they are right to defend their homes and families. Firsthand experience shows him that English troops are not protecting their own nation, they are destroying the life of the
American countryside, depopulating whole areas and depriving
stragglers of their humanity.

Orlando's exposure to the truth of war continues when
he is captured by the Indians. Although he has been taught
to think of Indians as savages, he discovers that the ones he
meets have been betrayed, rather than betraying. The English have promised to pay them for killing settlers, but when
no pay appears, the Indians turn against the lying English.
Wolf-hunter, an Indian of "more open countenance" and "more
gentle manners," befriends Orlando, and during the winter of
his captivity, the two men share the "secret sympathy" which
attracts "generous minds" regardless of race or nation.

* Orlando responds to these experiences in the same way
he reacted to his father's personal defects. He never falters
in his conviction that people in danger must be protected.
But he has decided that politics and governments do not serve

this purpose. In a rare display of bitterness, he decides that the abstract reason for war is the "revenge of monarchs," while the practical result is widespread suffering which he can do nothing to relieve. Summarizing the case for soldiers, Smith brings Orlando into contact with an honest but beggared old man who has lost his leg in the service of "what is called his country." The irony of this decent man's having been "deprived of his leg to preserve the balance of Europe" helps Orlando get rid of any lingering belief in politics while preserving his sense of duty.

Carefully distinguishing between war and the men who fight it, Smith shows soldiers and sailors helping Orlando when he is finally repatriated. They respond simply because they see that he needs help and not because he is a fellow soldier--his hair has been shaved like an Iroquois and he is dressed in castoff French clothing, so he looks at least like a thug and perhaps like a spy or smuggler. In the context of generosity from individual soldiers, Orlando's sale of his commission is established as a rejection of the government which hired him and not of the men who were his companions.

The aid Orlando receives on his way home is important to his understanding in another way, as well. Since he is able to maintain his dignity even when he is helpless, he attracts the generosity he needs, and he knows how to accept help without losing his integrity. It is a skill which he has ample opportunity to exercise since he arrives home to find his father's house sold and Rayland Hall in the hands of the church. A young lawyer helps him recover the inheritance of the Rayland estate which has been stolen from him, and a neighbor helps him locate the scattered remains of his family which his brother has abandoned.

Since all the assistance he receives springs from simple decency, it contrasts vividly with the behavior of people on whom Orlando has a conventional claim. The country lawyer who handled the Somerive estate denies that any son other than Philip exists. Mrs. Somerive's rich London brother denies that he has any nephews. When Orlando locates his brother in prison for debt, Philip laughingly addresses him as "Sir Knight," says he thought Orlando was dead and asks him to pay his debts so he will be free to go back to his gaming.

The problem is a domestic parallel to the governmental abuses which Orlando separated from the personal generosity of soldiers. When either national or personal authority and rank are seen in terms of power, the result is selfishness, neglect and cruelty. The basic function of either version of the protector's role will not be served except by individuals who offer help where it is needed.

Smith uses the conventional vehicle of the happy ending to show that such behavior can exist inside families, just as it can occur between soldiers, even when governments try to interfere. Orlando and Monimia marry without waiting for him to find some new way of supporting his family, and his reward for having helped her to cultivate her "natural good sense" is that she quietly applies for piece work at a large linen warehouse in the neighborhood as a way of contributing to their support. She does her sewing perfectly openly as they sit together in the evenings, and so her activity does not involve her in either manipulation or concealment. And since Orlando's view of a husband's rights does not include the authority to approve or disapprove of every choice his wife makes, he does not comment on her activity and so escapes any shock to either his "tenderness or his pride."

Such financial desperation is temporary since Mrs. Rayland's having taken Orlando as her heir is well-known among the local people, who can testify to the existence of a will later than the one which is offered at her death. When the true will is found and Orlando comes into possession of the Rayland estate, he uses his wealth to establish his family in comfort at Rayland Hall, and he rewards all those who have helped him selflessly, without any expectation that he would ever be anything but poor. On the other hand, he does not seek punishment for the people who have defrauded him, since regaining his ability to provide for his family is his only goal.

Such an outcome is a final validation of Orlando's theory. Both financial and emotional rewards come to him as a result of his conviction that the best way to protect is to teach and serve, rather than to overpower. His steadfast kindness to his old cousin results in an inheritance such as normal second sons cannot expect. His boyhood willingness to be a tutor rather than a seducer earns him a successful marriage to a woman conventional advisors have forbidden him to see. His brotherly defense of his sisters' rights to their own integrity gains for him their enduring devotion.

In order to show that the essentially domestic nature of Orlando's concern is an attribute of the protector's role rather than simply a personal quirk of this particular hero, Smith includes a second example of the interaction between heredity and environment by introducing Fleming's son. Adopted by a relative upon his father's death, young Fleming is made into a sailor, but he has not been in that career long enough to become indifferent to "moral evil." In addition, he was well-educated before he was ordered to sea. Even more important, he "delighted" in reading romances as a balance to the classics he was required to study. The result is a remarkably well-trained sensitivity which allows him to protect Monimia disinterestedly, without expecting the usual return demanded from a beautiful and defenseless young woman. Monimia's gratitude to the son, together with Orlando's affectionate memory of the less well-educated father, adds young Fleming to the family as an appropriately unusual husband for Orlando's favorite sister.

By the time Smith has defined Orlando's character and placed it in a context where it develops a rationality of its own, she has taken the protector's role out of its conventional abuses and revealed it as it ideally is. Both the public form--soldiers and sailors--and the domestic version--husbands and fathers--benefit from her attention to the real function as distinct from unthinking habit and the exploitation of power. Even though the phrase is originally used for selfish and deceptive purposes, Orlando truly is a "soldier of peace" in that he defends everyone who needs his protection, as a soldier should, and he does so without tyranny in a domestic environment, as is appropriate to peace.

Since these are not the conventional forms of these roles, Smith adds to the remarkable content of her novel by developing a theory about the effect of early environment on character. Instead of the procedure usual at the time, which was to assign the personalities of characters and then describe their lives, Smith patiently exposes her developing characters to both good and bad training and good and bad examples. Then she can show that their reaction to experience builds on inherited traits in a pattern sufficiently intricate to produce the kind of originality her theme requires.

Smith's unusual characters consciously evaluate their situation in terms of their experiences and their abilities. Therefore, they do not need to withdraw from society or reject their apparent roles. Instead, they live by views which make sense to them, and since their opinions grow partly out of their relationships with other people, some kind of social role is automatically implied. The result is the unusually hopeful belief that a tolerance for individuality springs from the half-unwilling flexibility which is universal to humanity except for these unfortunate individuals who have both heredity and environment against them.

The interplay between heredity and environment is a crucial element in Elizabeth Gaskell's Ruth, as well. Ruth is a fallen woman, but she is also a folk saint. The categories normally are mutually exclusive, in the opinion of "the world." But when the subject is an individual young woman rather than a pair of abstractions, even clear-cut roles such as these may turn out to have causes and results which are quite different from what is usually believed.

Arguing that anyone who falls into "youthful follies" should have a chance at "self-redemption," Gaskell focuses her book on a woman whose childlike frankness makes her too trusting to survive unprotected in a neglectful and manipulative society. Ruth's development is accompanied by an account of her seducer's later life. Their environments are as different as are their reasons for falling into "youthful folly." In addition, the way both adjust to change in their situations contributes to an understanding of their basic natures and possibilities of reform. As their lives develop along the lines of their very different responses to their early mistake, they become case studies of the way situation and character interact to form adult roles.

Ruth's basic nature is so extremely loving that she is almost childishly dependent in her feelings, when she is young. Her honesty is equally naive. She is so completely lacking in conventional pretense that she will not say she has worked hard when she has not. Almost entirely unselfconscious, she has none of the instincts of a flirt. She knows she is pretty because people tell her so, and she does not understand that everyone thinks she ought to pretend not to know what they mean. She looks "straight and innocently" at men because it is the way she looks at women, and she does not know everyone will be led astray by her directness. Confused by the hidden motives of others, she unguardedly appeals to them for help, even while they are betraying her.

Ruth's inability to figure out what other people are going to do comes partly from the fact that her mother died while she was young. This situation crops up continuously in Gaskell's work. Losing a mother's influence sometimes allows young women to make social mistakes, as it does in Mary Barton, because Mary's father is too absorbed in his own trouble to be carefully enough aware of Mary's growing independence of mind and spirit. Wives and Daughter's Molly Gibson is more fortunate, in that her father's protection limits the amount of damage which judging for herself can do.

Balancing the tendency to break social rules is the fact that motherless girls are free to develop their own judgment and to cultivate a self-reliance far beyond the norm. Mary Barton, for example, saves herself from downfall by allowing commonsense to outweigh either social fear or social shallowness and empty snobbery. And Molly Gibson's unassuming combination of sweetness and moral strength enables her to withstand even constant exposure to her stepmother's manipulative conventionality.

Ruth's situation incorporates parts of both these patterns. Her mother died before warning Ruth about "the subject of a woman's life." Her father also died before courtship could raise the question in a different form. Her guardian is a complete stranger and therefore takes only financial responsibility. A kindly old man who remembers her as a child does try to give her advice when he suspects she is in danger from the man who seduces her. But the only thing he can think of as an explanation is to remind her that "the devil goeth about as a roaring lion." Since her seducer looks like a "handsome young man," rather than either a lion or a devil, Ruth gains nothing from such a delicately Biblical warning.

The dressmaker to whom Ruth is apprenticed is the one person who is unmistakably obligated to help, but she is too sunk into self-interested sophistry to do her real duty. Rather than protecting Ruth from temptation, she self-righteously cancels Ruth's apprenticeship when she sees Ruth in the company of a young man who cannot intend to marry her. Satisfied to assume that any such assocation must indicate fully accomplished sin, the dressmaker does not even ask how far the relationship has gone.

Almost worse than clear neglect and abuse is the fact that Ruth is left with no one to love and be loved by. Because tenderness is central to her nature, she automatically responds to the one person who listens to her and seems to care about her. Mr. Bellingham calls himself her brother. He delights in her company and spends time with her. He urges her to use her own judgment about situations she faces. Her innocence makes it impossible for her to believe that anyone could plan to ruin the life of someone they like. Therefore, she takes Mr. Bellingham at face value. She has no reason to be wary when he insists he cannot leave her homeless after her apprenticeship is so violently broken off.

Even after she is leading the life of a kept woman, Ruth has no idea what society thinks her situation is. In her own eyes, Ruth is a young woman blissfully in love with a handsome, charming, and cultivated man who also loves her. Not noticing that Mr. Bellingham is travelling in out-of-the-way places to avoid scandal and discovery, Ruth is innocently delighted with the new world he opens up to her. The wild beauty of Wales stirs a new sense for her. She does not dream that her gentleness and her obvious love for Mr. Bellingham warn everyone they meet that she is not a wife.

Even living in sin, Ruth's sweetness is unblemished. One woman apologizes for being unable to show the "proper contempt" for her while another laments that Ruth makes it impossible to avoid being kind. Ruth is shocked when she finally discovers society's attitude as a "new idea." Her innate nature emerges clearly in her reaction. She assumes Mr. Bellingham's love is as innocent as hers is, and so she does not mention her discovery, for fear that he might think less well of her, if he found out how other people react. Also, she will not give the slightest hint of complaining against pain which he has caused. Instead, she makes up her mind that her highest duty is to make him happy, regardless of society.

Being deserted confirms Ruth's strengths. The life of prostitution which society expects as her next stage does not even cross her mind. Instead, she decides to kill herself, on the perfectly reasonable basis that it is against her nature to live without love, and her parents, as the only other people who have loved her, are already dead.

The bad luck of Ruth's losing all her protectors is balanced by her good fortune in becoming the subject of a social experiment designed by a Dissenting minister who has witnessed her gradual awakening to society's views. Ruth's sweetness and beauty first attract his attention, and her obvious innocence arouses his pity. When he is sure that Bellingham has deserted her, he decides to see if it is possible to reeducate young women who unknowingly fall into vice.

Mr. Benson's faith in Ruth's basic goodness is affirmed before his experiment has had time to take conscious form. She runs away from him when he finds her crying hopelessly as Mr. Bellingham's coach disappears from view. He tries to follow her, but he is a cripple, and so he cannot keep up and finally falls. His involuntary groan stops Ruth. Even on her way to her death in the river, she turns back to help someone in distress and need.

Gaskell develops this reclamation project in realistically small stages. Mr. Benson takes Ruth into his own home, where she can witness another new idea--the unassuming consideration which springs from kindness and tolerance. She willingly shares the housework, but she is so full of sighs over her lost love that the maid finally delivers a kindly and humorous lecture on the virtues of work.

This speech is an important transition for Ruth since it calls her out of herself. Her absorption in her grief is another form of the lack of social awareness which made it possible for Mr. Bellingham to deceive her in the first place. The same quality also maintained her innocence in love by keeping her from noticing that she had become an "object of remark."

Being socially unaware is a kind of protection from the pressures of a bad environment, but the same quality shuts out the influence of good surroundings just as effectively, and so it turns out to be a disadvantage, when Ruth's companions change. Her extravagant grief has almost the same effect on her relationships that egotism would have, and it is selfishness which the servant's lecture warns against. But the quality which actually is at the heart of Ruth's response is a kind of deficiency of egotism--she has not learned to think of herself as having any influence on the lives of others. Because of her innate sweetness, all she needs is a homey reminder that her gloom spreads distress around her. She instantly determines that her private suffering will not be a burden on people who have befriended her. At first by strength of will, and then by habit, she steadfastly copies the cheerfulness and unselfishness with which the Benson household surrounds her.

The birth of her child triggers additional growth for

Ruth. Not realizing that society thinks she ought to hate an illegitimate baby, she begins to participate actively in her own redemption in order to do a better job of raising her boy. Planning to teach Leonard herself, she begins her own education and discovers that she enjoys using her mind. She eagerly embraces work as a nursery governess in order to be more independent, even though it means being away from Leonard most of the day.

After Ruth learns what she is in society's view, her innocence takes a new form. As loving and as direct as always, she replaces her old spontaneous dependency with a self-control which makes it possible for her to be sure that her behavior fits her values. Vividly aware of the harm that impulse and self-indulgence can do, she is gently firm with the children she teaches. Discovering selfishness by seeing its opposite in Mr. Benson and his sister, she modifies her lingering love for her seducer by realizing that his nature would be a bad influence on her son.

Mr. Benson and his sister provide the shelter that Ruth's early life lacked, giving her room to develop the strength of will and the integrity which her affectionate nature partially masked, while she was very young and defenseless. But even so wholesome an environment is not without its defects. Knowing that he is wandering into "labyrinths of social ethics," Mr. Benson begins his experiment by accepting his sister's suggestion that Ruth be transformed into a widow. The lie is necessary since it allows society to judge her on the basis of her conduct rather than to reject her blindly on the basis of her one mistake. Still, it makes her role a lie, and so she is still vulnerable to the slightest gossip about her past, regardless of all the growth and goodness which come after.

It is a major turning point for Ruth when she is confronted by society's unwillingness to forgive and inability to forget. She is relieved to have faced the worst, in spite of the fact that she loses her job and endures casual insult whenever she goes outdoors. Since she has lost the respect and even the patronizing courtesy of society, she is free to govern herself entirely on the basis of her own values. The result is that she emerges from this new disaster of discovery intellectually and morally independent even of the Bensons.

Ruth's relieved resolution to adhere strictly to the truth is tested immediately. On discovering that she has become an object of vicious gossip, her first task is to tell the truth to her son. In a scene which is touchingly parallel to her young fear that her seducer might think less of her if he discovered what society calls her, she decides she will tell her son all the vile words he is going to hear about her and about himself. Her motive is to soften them by having them come to him, the first time, in a context of love.

Thinking of love reminds Ruth that there is more than one way of judging, and so she turns aside from her first harsh plan. She tells her son the facts of their situation. She then tells him how the world will judge them and points out the differences between how men judge and how God judges. She promises him that he cannot suffer for her sin, except at the hands of society. She insists that God judges "more tenderly than men," and that though people "never forgive," the opinions of men are not the most important thing.

Ruth's response to the loss of her job is similarly independent of the opinions of the world. She applies for any work she is qualified for and is consistently turned down. After months of patiently endured rebuffs, she is finally called in as a sick nurse among people who are too poor to risk being self-righteous about her past. One of her friends protests that she is too well-educated to do such lowly work, but Ruth defends her education by pointing out that being able to read Latin means she can read the prescriptions.

Her willingness to take any job society will allow to her is typical of her mature integrity. Her frankness emerges in her delight at living her own role without deceptions. Her loving nature is exercised in her service to the suffering poor. She is at peace with herself at last, and this composure adds to her growing reputation until finally she is so much in demand that she can choose her cases. Typical of the distaste she has always felt for being patronized, she refuses invalids who can be served by expensive nurses and dedicates herself to those whose need and helplessness allow her to make use of her best qualities. Eventually, her attitude toward herself and toward her work earns her the respect of even the "roughest boys," who would normally sling insults at a person known to have a past like hers. By the time an outbreak of typhus terrifies even medical personnel, she has enough faith in the trust of the poor to believe that she will not be rebuffed when she volunteers as matron for the fever ward.

Her faith that the town has begun to judge her as she is, rather than simply in terms of her one mistake, turns

out to be justified. As matron, she saves lives and receives
official commendations. But more important than these personal
rewards is a scene outside the hospital walls during the
height of the fear. Townspeople are gossiping about her.
One says she has been a "great sinner" who is courting death
as her penance. Another answers that a person like her
could not have been a great sinner and that she works not for
herself but for the love of God.

As the conversation wanders on to document that Ruth
has become an unofficial, living saint in the minds of the
townspeople, her son overhears. Hesitantly proud for the
first time since their pasts became known, he steps forward
to claim her as his mother. His tentative courage is rewarded
when all the people crowd around to call down blessings
on him and to add more and more stories of his mother's
goodness, gentleness, selflessness and courage.

Ruth's rehabilitation would not have been possible without
her strength and determination. But regardless of how
saintly she might be within herself, she could not have functioned
socially without a change of heart in the people around
her. Gaskell was convinced that, given a chance to live up
to its best nature, society is as capable of growth and "self-redemption"
as individual sinners are. She may have been too
optimistic--her novel was publicly burned in a ritual of outrage.[4]
But within the book, forgiveness is a social possibility.

The revolution in social attitude comes in highly individual
ways. Ruth's close friends find it easy to look within
themselves and remember that they have been less than
perfect. Mr. Benson has lied about Ruth's past, for example,
and so he is humbly aware of how tempting it is to try to
control the result of an act rather than to think of the rightness
of the act in itself. A young neighbor woman generously
insists that she has fallen to as many temptations as have
been available, in her extremely sheltered situation. The
realization gives her the strength to sympathize with Ruth's
struggle rather than think only of her fall.

People for whom love and friendship are not the basis
of social connection have a harder time. Mr. Bradshaw is
not conscious of ever having made even so much as a mistake,
much less a sin, until he involves himself in an election
where bribes are used. During the excitement of the
campaign, he satisfies his conscience by remembering that
he has not offered the bribe money in person. But after the

election is won, he begins to realize that the townspeople know he must be involved. The thought is so galling that he flings himself into tirades against Ruth with extra vigor, hoping to prove his own high standards by the extravagant display.

Mr. Bradshaw is forced to admit the real impact of his self-righteous tendency to judge inflexibly when his son is exposed as a thief. Mr. Bradshaw has always bragged that Richard has never had his "own way" in his life, and he fails to notice that his son's apparent submissiveness is no more than the self-protective hypocrisy of a character lacking in "moral courage." Since the community knows what Richard has had to face, they counteract Mr. Bradshaw's violence when the crime is revealed. The man Richard has defrauded refuses to press charges, since Richard's crime has been an individual act, rather than a pattern. And Mr. Bradshaw's business partner separates Richard from his father "permanently," since he is convinced that the son can be rehabilitated if he is allowed to live in a more wholesome environment.

The primary sinner is, of course, Mr. Bellingham. Even in a context of egotism, he stands out as self-absorbed. He runs for Parliament not from any vision of public service but simply because he is tired of yachting and travelling. When Ruth meets him accidentally in the course of his campaign, she is at first overwhelmed by her long-cherished love for him. However, they both have changed. She has developed a higher standard of "what people ought to be" and he has allowed his "worse self" to "become permanent." He laments that she is so beautiful and demands that she return to their old arrangement. Ruth points out that going into keeping knowingly is an entirely different act from being tricked into it as almost a child. Since he hates to have an impulse thwarted, Mr. Bellingham offers marriage, and Ruth finally defends herself against his appeals and her own painfully continuing love by explaining her real views. She can stand up to anything for the sake of her son, and a person of Mr. Bellingham's character would be an evil influence on a boy whose nature is as frank and warm as her own.

Redemption is not a possibility for a character who never thinks beyond himself. Mr. Bellingham changes his name in order to inherit additional property. He cares only for Ruth's external, physical beauty. He is flattered to have so fine a son. When Ruth catches his fever while she is nursing him in his delirium, he regrets that she has died "of her love of me." He casually identifies himself as her seducer, but Ruth's friends are far from casual. Mr. Benson grimly warns that men may judge Mr. Bellingham lightly but God will not. He reinforces the implied threat by vowing that Ruth's son will never face the "shame" of knowing who his father is.

To counteract the selfishness which makes Mr. Bellingham unredeemable, and the excessive tendency to trust which made Ruth vulnerable as a girl, Ruth's son is raised to be "self-dependent." This is the conscious direction of his education, as planned by Mr. Benson. It is also the unconscious pattern of his life model, as lived by Ruth. Because of the strength of his early background, he is able to withstand the shock of discovery. He becomes reclusive for a while, and struggles pitiably in his dreams. But his values do not give way in the face of his trouble. He makes up his mind to be a "law unto himself," in the best sense of the phrase. Young as he is, he takes up the "great questions of ethics" which the "majority of the world" have long since "settled." He refines his values in abstract discussions with Mr. Benson, and he puts his beliefs into practice by cherishing his mother.

His gallantry contrasts sharply with the moral helplessness of Mr. Bradshaw's son and shows the superiority of learning over obedience. Blind submission to unquestionable authority forces children to grow up weak, sullen, angry and sly. The difference mental independence makes in childhood is a foreshadowing of the flexibility needed by adults, if they are to look beyond the rigid, simplistic, thoughtless judgments of "the world."

Gaskell does not suggest that the moral and social rescues of Ruth and her son are unique. As head of the fever hospital, Dr. Davis befriends Ruth. He asks to take her son as his apprentice, with the idea of making him a partner and eventually turning his practice over to the boy. When Ruth hesitates, he explains his motives. He has been impressed with both Ruth and her child, but his most important interest comes from being illegitimate himself. He knows how vicious gossip feels, but he also knows that being socially useful is possible even for outcasts, because he has transformed himself into a valued and respected member of the community.

Ruth dies of the fever which brings her social rehabilitation into public view, but the book ends affirmatively, nevertheless. Exceptional individuals cluster around each other, around Ruth and her memory, sharing the sense of having made social rejection temporary by refusing to be degraded when they were cast out.

Gaskell begins her novel with a direct statement of her project. She defines acculturation in a characteristically unassuming way. She explains that people are "absorbed into "daily life" before they are aware of the "chains" which most people do not have the "moral strength" to "despise." "Daily domestic habit" forms the "natural leading strings" which most people do not grow beyond. Still, there is the "one in a hundred" who can break such bonds when an "independent" "inward necessity" takes precedence over "outward conventionalities."

Both the rule and the exception are documented by the book. Acculturation does usually apply, and so Ruth constitutes a plea for caution in designing and maintaining the attitudes which will be "leading strings" for most people. But the novel also shows that social conventionalities can be set aside by those who are highly enough motivated. When the "right time" comes, such individuals can move even the opinion of "the world." A "fallen woman" can turn into a "great sinner" and finally become an object of "reverence." An "illegitimate son" can become a "pleasure," a "dear object of love," a person to be "blessed." If even the "roughest boys" can learn to show respect for people whose nature is totally out of keeping with the role which is assigned to them, then more comfortably situated social groups can surely bring themselves to cling less mindlessly to the blind and blanket prejudgments of "the world."

Elizabeth Stuart Phelps Ward also suggests that even the most acute of society's problems can be coped with by revising social attitudes and rethinking the actual function of traditionally assigned roles. In her American "factory novel," The Silent Partner, Ward depicts the impact of the factory system on all the different kinds of lives it touches. She does not deny the differences in wealth, cultivation and status which conventionally divide factory classes. But she does question the importance of these convenient categories by calling attention to other ways of grouping characters. More concerned with personality than with income, she shows that passive or satisfied individuals in all standard groups scarcely think of their role, while a few improve their lives, and others vaguely wish for something better without achieving any change.

Judging on the basis of personality rather than on social labels produces a kind of fiction which can leave its unusual characters in place while still allowing them to develop an identity which suits themselves. Unlike Trollope, who provided both social and academic education for her factory people in order to bring them together outside the factory world, Ward arranges friendships across the conventional barrier between owners and workers without calling for so much as a change of clothes.

The difference is deliberate. Ward is as likely to refer to her characters by their function as she is to call them by their names. Perley is an "indexical" person whose every gesture is instructive because it is symbolic. She is the essence of a "young lady," to her friends as well as to her fiancé, and even after they know her as as individual, she is still "the young leddy" to the factory hands. Maverick Hale is "the junior partner," his father is the "senior partner," Perley's father is the "managing partner," and Perley becomes the "silent partner" when she insists on being something other than merely the junior partner's fiancée.

Categories also apply to the "hands." Sip is a "factory girl," Dirk is "the young watchman," Stephen Garrick is the confidential clerk and a "self-made man," Catty is "the type" of the factory poor.

All these characters are vividly individual when they are talking, yet Ward insists upon their identity as types by referring to their factory designation in narrative passages. Her method underlines the dual nature of her concept of identity. Her unusual characters manage to explore their own personal potential at the same time that they consciously and willingly remain within their existing social framework. They are individuals who decide to set convention aside in order to live up to their highest possibilities. This means that they reject only the easy and normal shortcomings of carelessness and selfishness. They do not reject their social assignment.

Of the three individuals in the novel who move beyond the conventions for their role, Perley Kelso is the most immediately intriguing. Her situation would seem to leave her nothing to wish for. She fulfills her obligations by being amiable and beautiful. As a result, her father pampers her, her fiancé adores her and her friends admire and flatter her. She is so surrounded by money and by luxury-minded people that her idea of taking trouble is to have all the padding removed from her carriage when she wishes to change its scent.

Some aspects of her personality, however, tend to unfit her for this idle role. She has a "weakness for an occupation," and she is curious about the details of lives which are different from her own. It is these qualities, rather than changes in her situation, which bring about her transformation. She begins as a person who cannot understand what the term "miserable" means. But after some investigation, she realizes her own luxury can never make her happy again, after she finds out that factory girls are subject to "the cotton cough."

Perley's differences from her protected peers become the center of her personality as a result of a series of educational experiences. Sitting in her carriage, she is attracted by the color of the street life she watches. The evening is stormy enough that she has dreaded even walking to her carriage, and her own reluctance causes her to notice how little difference the weather seems to make to the factory people who are out in it. As if attending a play, she watches Sip Garth resisting the wind like a "desperate prize-fighter." But finally she wonders if it is "odd" for her to sit warm, dry and pampered inside a scented carriage while other people struggle.

Perley's protected status receives another shock when she talks to the factory girl on a whim. Sip insists there is no difference between working class entertainment at "the Blue Plum" and the operas Perley attends. She warns Perley that the topics are the same, though the opera "plates over" behavior which is treated frankly at the Blue Plum. Perley defends herself by launching into an elaborate statement of her artistic theory.

This impulse to treat Sip as an intellectual and emotional equal produces a major change in attitude in both young women. Perley is politely vague, and hesitant in a well-bred way, while Sip is blunt and harsh. Yet their awkwardly mismatched conversation reveals a shared impulse to protect each other and to explain themselves, regardless of the norms.

The cocoon of privilege which shelters Perley is further invaded when her father is crushed to death on the factory shipping dock. His death makes little difference to her daily details, but missing him causes her to realize that she is "not accustomed to feeling at all." This new vulnerability leaves her ill prepared for the additional shock which her fiancé's reaction causes. Her contact with Sip has triggered her interest in the factories, and so she asks to inherit her father's partnership, along with his money. The elder Mr. Hayle hides behind the conventionally patronizing explanation that she is not qualified for such a position, but Perley refuses to cooperate with the evasion, asking to be allowed to qualify herself. More direct, Maverick claims to be charmed by the originality of her "kink," but he is frank enough to state that he is the "last man upon earth" to go into business with his wife. She is to be content with a "woman's influence," like other women. Maverick's treatment of Perley during the conversation is more convincing than his arguments--he thinks about having an artist do a formal painting of her hand as it rests on her tea table, and he entertains himself by sketching little faces on her fingernails.

Perley sees this situation as a major turning point. She is willing to leave her property in the hands of Maverick and his father because they are successful businessmen, but she will not trust "her people" to them, since they are so inconsiderate. Both the awareness of the factory hands as "hers" and the consciousness of them as "people" are "eccentricities." Predictably, Maverick and his father answer "gallantly" rather than reasonably. Their behavior leaves Perley without any recourse. She has not been educated well enough to out-argue Mr. Hayle, and she is "too fond" of Maverick to win against him. Their contempt for everything except her beauty is clear in their reminder that she can work at the Sunday school if she wishes to be busy among the "hands." She submits to the rebuff with a graciousness which allows them to think they have prevailed. But she also makes up her mind to help the factory people in her own way.

Perley's service project is at first no more acceptable to the hands than it is to her social peers. Determined to find out how the workers live in order to understand what their lives lack, Perley wanders around town after the mills have closed down for the night. Bub Mell, an eight-year-old street tough steals her glove. Rather than scolding or threatening, she escorts him home in order to find out why he works in her mill instead of going to school, as the law requires. Bub's father is so resistant to questioning that she explains herself, in the hope that he may sympathize, once he understands that seeing and hearing how factory people live has become her "job."

Her interest moves beyond a straightforward desire to know when Sip insists on escorting her home. Perley is puzzled that anyone could imagine she might be in danger, since she assumes her position protects her. Sip bluntly asks what Perley imagines she has done to justify any "special interest or respect" from the hands. By the time Perley has finished answering this question, she has completely changed her attitude toward her life.

Perley's new role is not easy to establish, but she is committed enough to continue in her own way, regardless of the almost universal resistence which she meets at first. She is a constant presence in the factory slums, where she helps the sick and encourages the despairing. Her concern is gradually accepted as genuine, and everyone begins to count on her self-assigned role. Bub Mell is caught by his rags while trying to steal tobacco from a fellow worker and dies mangled in the machinery he works beside. The active partners cannot bring themselves to go to Bub's parents, but Perley sets off to bring what comfort she can almost before they have finished asking for her help. When Dirk falls asleep and fails to ring the watchman's bell at midnight, Perley gets out of bed and goes to the mill to wake him in the hope of saving his job. Bijah Mudge is fired for testifying before a state investigation into factory conditions and is blackballed throughout the region. As a result, he ends up in the poorhouse. Still, his bitterness against the management of the Hayle and Kelso Mills does not prevent him from appreciating Perley's helpless but human and soothing visit.

A major part of Perley's effectiveness with the workers is this willingness to enter into their lives. When a strike call threatens the mill, and none of the partners has any idea of how to respond, Perley is able to point out that she knows "these men" better than the Hayles do. She insists that the workers will not strike if they are "trusted" with an explanation of the need for the wage reduction which has provoked the strike. Maverick and his father refuse such an innovation, both for its own sake and because of the precedent it seems to establish. But the new managing partner, Stephen Garrick, has been "in the dressing room" himself. Because of his experience, he suspects Perley's idea is worth trying and agrees to make a statement to the angry mob of workers outside the mill. The workers hear Stephen, but they accept his statement only after "the young leddy" is sent out to them. Perley stands among them in the rain, as helpless as they are to change the decisions of the partners, and it is obvious to everyone that, by now, she has earned their special respect.

If Perley had been willing to let the matter rest with such activities among the workers and at the mill, her change in habits might have passed almost unnoticed among her idle social friends, who avoid such situations. But she is determined to enrich the workers' lives as well as soften their discomforts. Instead of using her money for expensive drapes and impractical clothing, as she used to do, she turns her home into a kind of cultural center. She buys paintings which will interest her new "friends" and hires musicians and lecturers who will give them something to think about while they work.

Society is predictably stunned. Perley gives a party for thirty of her factory friends and a handful of the society types who used to be her most constant companions. Her special friend from the past, Fly, sincerely tries to understand. She even defends Perley when Mrs. Silver says that Perley should have been literary, in order to excuse so much "eccentricity." Perley's preference for spending most of her social time with the workers, even to the extent of attending their chapel, seems "morbid" to Mrs. Silver. In social conversation, Fly loyally protests that Perley does not "rust" and seems to enjoy herself. But even Fly admits privately that it bothers her to see how much the "dreary work" seems to suit Perley.

Social discipline in this novel is more a matter of conversation than of enforcement, and so Perley is not shunned, even though "Society" complains. Mrs. Silver protests that "poor Perley" has forgotten her "duties to Society" and insists that Society has rights which any lady must respect. Nevertheless, her lament that Perley is "dead and buried" turns out to be a matter of opinion rather than fact. Perley goes to the usual social functions only a third as often as she used to, and her old friends miss her. Far from being cast out, she arranges her withdrawal over the protests of her friends.

Perley rearranges love on the same basis that she uses to reorganize friendship. Maverick entertains himself one morning by using a fiancé's privilege to decorate her with a shawl in various arrangements, ignoring her warnings not to treat her like a "lay figure." To Maverick she is an art object, and any other basis for a relationship is too absurd to be taken seriously. Perley's own view of her role has changed too much for them to find any common ground, and so she breaks the engagement. Maverick protests that she will miss him, but Perley insists that she will miss him only in the way she would miss the piano, if it were to be removed. Their views of her function are now so different that she "loves" him only in her moments of weakness--when she is tired, has the blues, or suffers from boredom. She is sure that the part of her she considers to be her "self" does not love him.

Perley's definitions of love and marriage are validated by outcomes. Maverick's first reaction is to watch her new life with a "sense of puzzled loss." But eventually, he takes her at her word and decides to marry her old friend, Fly, who explains herself as a "little, foolish, good-for-nothing girl" who will be conventional enough to make him happy.

Fly is as right about herself and Maverick as Perley is about the kind of relationship which her love requires. It is more appropriate for her to fall in love with Stephen Garrick, who shares her concern for the factory people and who meets her constantly on the missions of mercy which call both of them out among the hopeless and poor. Still, she believes that even suitable love does not imply anything beyond the emotion itself. If she were to marry even an understanding man, she could not continue to live the "public" life she prefers. Stephen sadly agrees that her nature makes her a "priestess in a waterproof" rather than a wife. Honest and analytical as always, she points out that she does not "need" Stephen for the usual reasons--she is not lonely, homeless, miserable or afraid of growing old. Her discussion of a partnership with the Hayles has proved to her that marriage forces a woman to "invest in" the life which her husband "conducts." She prefers "a business of my own."

A marriage between Stephen and Perley would have been a traditional resolution of the novel's problem, since it would unite Perley's privileged class with the factory class from which Stephen has raised himself and thereby suggest a kind of classless future. But Ward's point is not the usual reformer's idea of gradually solving social problems by erasing social differences. Instead, she uses both these characters to show that individuals can live up to unselfish ideals regardless of their situation. Society forgives Stephen for his "fanatical benevolence" since he has risen out of the mills and is "naturally" concerned. But the workers disagree, believing that such a man traditionally makes a "hard master." These contradicting opinions suggest how easily his behavior will be misinterpreted. He tells Perley that his goal has been to bring others "out of the mud" as fast as he can get out himself. They both know this is not easy, but Stephen has a right to insist that it is possible, since he has done it. Still, he admits that he is an "unpopular master" since workers who give up the attempt to copy him ease their feelings by blaming him for being unfeeling toward the "wounded part of the world."

Such a reaction comes from the fact that Stephen is not able to make major changes in policy, any more than Perley can. Like Perley, he is limited to the type of partnership which Hayle and Kelso offers him. He recognizes that neither he nor Perley is in an "easy position." She uses her silent partnership as a basis for visiting "her" workers in their homes and using her own home as a recreational alternative to the Blue Plum. His managing partnership occasionally allows Stephen to intervene directly. He transfers "Irish Jim" to an area where only men and boys work, intending to limit the seductive damage done by Jim's exceptional grace and black mustache. Knowing that Dirk Burdock hopes to "be something," he gives the young watchman a second chance instead of firing him as he is supposed to do when Dirk falls asleep on the job.

Even if Perley and Stephen were less limited by the nature of their "partnerships," they would not be able to change other people's lives for them, as Perley discovers by experiment. Since Sip Garth has become her good friend, Perley tries to take Sip out of the mills and find other kinds of work for her. Perley gets Sip a job as a cook, and Sip burns the soup. She has to quit a job as a nanny for fear she will shake a child who cries incessantly. She speaks back to the housekeeper at a hotel where she works briefly. Her skills are too minimal for her to do even plain sewing for pay. Sip would try almost anything to please her friend, but Perley's experience is so different from her own that Perley's suggestions for change simply do not apply. Sip finally gives it up and "asks in" again at the mill, which is her world.

Like Perley, Sip changes her life by revising rather than rejecting her role. One of the things about Sip which first interested Perley was the factory girl's conviction that she could perform better than the entertainers at the Blue

Plum. Perley encourages this side of Sip's personality by arranging for her to do presentations in the lecture series at her home. Sip is extremely popular with the worker audiences, and Perley agrees that she is "more than Siddons." But it is not until her pathetic sister dies that Sip finds a way to use this talent to move beyond the limitations of her life. Catty's death relieves Sip of family responsibility, and she is free to become a "very happy woman" by admitting that she is "not other folks." She is not willing to marry and create more factory children, and she has already learned that she cannot fit herself into anything other than factory work. Her version of Perley's and Stephen's combination of integrity and acceptance is to turn herself into a doorstep preacher, speaking in her own harshly effective way about what she calls "poor folks' religion" made up of a blend of "God's words" and "Catty's words."

Catty needs someone to speak for her, since she does not have words in the usual sense. Born deaf because of the noise of the mills and her father's alcoholism, and going blind because of the wool disease, Catty is ugly, retarded, "miserable" even in her dreams, "wicked" and uncouth. Sip takes all these difficulties together--both what Catty does and what is done to her--and insists "it's never her fault." Meeting Perley, Catty strips the rings from her fingers, not to play with them or steal them, as convention would interpret the gesture, but simply to remove the hard clutter from Perley's otherwise soft hand. Fond of Sip, Catty promises not to walk the streets, but the boredom of waiting at home in the complete idleness of deafness and increasing blindness drives her to break her promise. In her helpless limitation, she becomes the symbol of the "deaf, dumb, blind, doomed" world of the "laboring poor." She embodies their "confident" habit of "stepping to their own destruction" when she wanders unknowingly into danger at the mill and is drowned while all the hands watch helplessly. By transfiguring Catty into a "poor folks'" Christ for Sip to preach about, Ward emphasizes her idea that all kinds of people must find their own niche inside their limitations.

The helplessness of even self-sacrificing people to change other people's lives for them emerges against a background pattern of individuals who neither escape nor transcend their role. The labor agitator, Bijah Mudge, has a savings account, for a while, and he gives each of his five sons first a trade and then a handsome coffin. But Bijah ends up in the poorhouse, despite these aspiring moments. The young watchman, Dirk Burdock, starts out thinking the empty mills at night seem almost a "churchly place." But eventually Dirk decides he is not "getting on" in the mills, regardless of his early hopes and Stephen Garrick's quiet encouragement. Self-acceptingly, he turns to a woman who will marry him in his present state, and he feels almost content. The junior partner, Maverick Hayle, admires Perley's "strength" and "helpfulness," but he shrugs his shoulders at her "oddness" and never even considers changing any aspect of his own behavior.

Personalities such as these help define the assigned roles which so few people modify even when they feel hampered by them. Any standard rebellion almost guarantees failure since it is based on the hope that rejecting conventional restrictions will bring more or less unlimited freedom. Bijah Mudge, for example, plans to change the world with his labor agitation, and so unrealistic a demand defeats him. Dirk expects to rise off the factory floor, as Stephen did, but he continues to divert his energy into conventional courtship activities and so provokes his own shortfall.

Those who escape the confines of their roles follow a quite different procedure. They change the way they see their role, rather than trying to change the world. Perley gives up the private luxury of her lady's role, but she also refuses to think of herself as a reformer, insisting instead that "the world" occasionally "gets into the dark" and needs people like her for "groping purposes." Stephen knows his background makes him an "unpopular master" and does not hold the judgment against the workers. He also does not use their rejection of him as an excuse to stop helping them. In love, he laments that he has no way to court Perley since the conventions of her world would require him to "tie up flowers" for her or "sing little songs," whereas he is a worker and will not pretend to have become a gentleman. Sip tolerates oil and dirt because factory work is the only job she can put up with. She even accepts the cotton cough, because the roughened voice it causes is appropriate to the way she wants to use her dramatic skills.

These three characters succeed in very different ways, as they should, since their situations and backgrounds are so different. Nevertheless, the basis of their success is identical. They honestly analyze their own abilities in order to understand their limitations and their preferences. They explore their situations in order to discover what can be changed. They submit without comment to situations which they recognize as beyond their control. They put their energies into sacrifices which take the form of self-control--a method of dealing with their surroundings which allows them to escape the mindless and self-destructive activity which Catty symbolizes.

This way of dealing with their personal needs allows all three to maintain their social connection by remaining within tolerated limits of their roles. Perley is an "eccentric young lady," Stephen is a self-made man and therefore is "naturally" a "fanatic," and Sip has "nothing saintly" about her as she preaches from doorsteps in the foulest alleys. Such descriptions minimize differences from the norms and show that society is willing to try to accommodate "eccentricity."

At the same time, tolerance which comes from glossing over differences tends to emphasize the abnormality of individuals who behave as these three do. Since the normal people around them insist on brushing aside the quality which they themselves consider their most important feature, their dedication to an ideal of service would leave them painfully isolated if each of them really were as unique as a less-aspiring norm would like to pretend.

Fortunately, the same unusual awareness which sets them slightly apart from conventional people also allows them to recognize each other as like-minded friends without regard to discrepancies in social situation. All three of them accept that their primary dedication is to their "own" work. But they are glad to notice that their work brings them together constantly. Following different paths toward the same goal, they can offer each other the "right hand of fellowship" as a way of softening the isolation which otherwise comes from insisting on individual lives.

Appropriately to its sixties context, Toni Morrison's Sula places sisterhood at the center of social connection. In a community where unemployment is the norm, and women routinely raise children alone, neither work nor family duty can play a major role. Men are lovers, brothers, sons, drifters, and sometimes short-term husbands. It is the women who organize the community since they are the ones who take responsibility.

Such an arrangement might produce a matriarchy, and it is true that the Peace family traces its characteristics through the generations of its women, almost without regard to the occasional and temporary presence of a biologically necessary male. But the Peace women are not the kind of family which could ever become a "norm," since each of them is too remarkable as an individual. Their presence in "the Bottom" is balanced by the Wright family, a conventional two-parent household which offers the community a reminder about lives which are considered standard, even though they are not statistically usual for this group.

In this community where theoretically conventional behavior is no more statistically commonplace than eccentricity is, social bonds confront a daunting network of barriers, from the generation gap and motherhood to racism and sexual politics. Out of the entanglement, the social and personal relationship of "girlfriends" emerges as the most enduring and satisfying possibility.

Focusing on social rather than biological "sisterhood," Morrison brings together two children who have no siblings. Nel Wright and Sula Peace are ready for their friendship before they meet. Both are solitary little girls who daydream of a truly understanding companion. Nel imagines "smiling, sympathetic eyes" watching her pre-sexual subordination to a "fiery prince," and Sula visualizes a watcher who shares her delight in a wild gallop on a beautiful horse while "tasting sugar" and smelling roses. The differences in their daydreams are as significant as the similarity is. Both long for someone who will sympathize and share their life. But Nel cannot move beyond the conventional and passive, even in imagination, while Sula's chaotic household encourages more independent, personal, sensual dreams.

Nel's yearning to be "wonderful" lacks details since the "oppressive neatness" of her home rules out creativity along with disorder. Painstaking pressure from her parents wears down what little "sparkle and splutter" she shows. The conventionality which results is deceptive. Nel's grandmother was a prostitute, and so the tidy home and adoring husband Nel's mother achieves are a carefully assumed pattern rather than being the casual result of instinct, modeling or habit. Nor does social pressure help establish such a theoretically standard way of life. When Nel is married in an aggressively traditional ceremony, the experience is unique to the community, since most of the couples in The Bottom simply go to the courthouse or, at most, ask a preacher to "say a few words."

Such carefully controlled behavior by the Wright family helps establish the discrepancy between an idealized standard and daily, statistical norms. The gap between the two is large enough to make room even for individuals like the Peace women, who almost automatically challenge any preexisting pattern of shared lives. For three generations, Sula's family has lived in the community without feeling bound by its rules. Both their roles and their freedom force the rest of the community to think about the way they live. Their air of certainty, together with their uniqueness, help less introspective people see the difference between the way they react and the way they assume they ought to feel.

Conventional patriarchal forms are challenged by the Peace women, who remain the center of the family even while they take on a variety of roles. Sula's grandmother, Eva, represents a fairly routine type of household head, in a female version. The children who give her head-of-household status result from a brief marriage to a man significantly named "BoyBoy." When BoyBoy walks out, Eva's struggle becomes grimly essential. She is determined not to accept the abject poverty which is normal in such situations, and so she leaves her children with a neighbor and does not come back until she has the ten thousand dollars which will make their lives tolerable, even though getting it costs her a leg.

Eva accepts the responsibility to help her children grow up with as vigorous and independent a spirit as she brought to the problem of survival. When her only son, Plum, returns from the war, he is hopelessly addicted to drugs. It seems like a defeat that this "big man" wants nothing except to be "a baby all wrapped up inside his mamma." Reasonably, Eva points out that he would "suffocate" even if it were possible for him to "scrunch" himself up again inside her womb. Suffocating inside a woman is not a man's death. Since she has already done everything else she can to help him mature, she rescues him one last time by holding him "real close" and rocking him for a while. Then she soaks him in kerosene and sets him afire so he can die "like a man."

Disappointment with the male roles of husband and son does not drive Eva into the conventional response of blame or hatred. To her, men are not differentiated enough to come out of their category and turn into individuals. BoyBoy made an exception of himself by being a burden, and so she keeps herself "alive and happy" by hating him. When Plum shows that he intends to copy his father and become a burden, too, she solves the problem. When she is free of his interference, she can take care of her own feelings by continuing to love her "Baby Boy" in memory.

Eva loves "all men," unless they call attention to themselves as individuals. After she is old enough to refuse the "act" of love, she is still surrounded by teasing, "pecking," and laughing "flocks of gentlemen callers." She enjoys their company and leaves "her men" feeling that they have been "in combat with a worthy, if amiable, foe."

Perhaps because her life is easier, "manlove" in Eva's daughter, Hannah, takes a different form. She is widowed rather than deserted, and so she has no urge to hate even one man, as Eva hates BoyBoy. Hannah makes no demands of any kind and leaves all men feeling that they are "complete and wonderful" as they are and "don't need fixing." She is extraordinarily beautiful, which means she does not have to make any concessions in order to attract men. Since she finds sex pleasant while trust is impossible, she becomes a casual, "daylight" lover who never feels unreserved and committed enough to sleep with a man.

The responsiveness of the Peace women seems delightful and inclusive to the men, but it really comes from a complete impersonality. Except for BoyBoy and Plum, males have too little individuality for the Peace women to see them as anything other than simply men. The Deweys show how this idea works. Homeless children are occasionally dropped by Eva's house and left in her somewhat impersonal care. The first little boy Eva names Dewey is black and has the "golden eyes of chronic jaundice." She calls a second boy Dewey, too, even though he is younger and light-skinned, with red hair and freckles. When the neighbors remind her that she called the first one Dewey, she simply points out that this boy is "another." The third little boy is still younger and looks different from either of the other two, having "chocolate skin and black bangs." Nevertheless, Eva names him Dewey. The neighbors object that it will be impossible to tell them apart if they all have the same name. Eva agrees and adds that no one needs to tell them apart because they are "all Deweys."

Eva's labelling has a mixed result. One of the mothers eventually returns, but leaves again alone, since she cannot tell which Dewey is hers. Eva sends them all to school at the same time, regardless of the discrepancy in their ages, and the teacher cannot tell them apart, either. It turns out not to matter, since they speak "with one voice" and think with "one mind." Their uniformity contents them. Their favorite game is to tie their laces into each other's shoes as a way of playing "chain gang." And they never finish growing up--physically or mentally.

The problem of the Deweys shows that maturity is not available to examples of a category who do not differentiate themselves enough to seem individual even to their mothers and their teachers. It is a kind of limitation which is common to the men. In addition to Eva's BoyBoy and Baby Boy, who become noticeable by turning into individual burdens, there is Nel's husband. Jude wants to be a road builder, for the sense of camaraderie the "road men" enjoy. He dreams of having his foot smashed with the sledge hammer so that people will ask why he limps and he can enjoy answering that he "got that building the New Road."

Shadrack's results are sightly different since he succeeds at what Jude only dreams of. Shadrack actually does enter the male world by going to war. However, his experience on the battlefield is so appallingly different in reality from his expectations that he loses faith in his own existence. If thriving on war is being a man, then, like Plum, Shadrack is not one. Not until he finds a toilet bowl in which to see his reflection can he be reassured--seeing the blackness of his face affirms one of his categories, even if he is not a "man." The partial identity is enough to help him go on as a "madman" and even assume a position of leadership. He brings enough of the war back home with him to found Suicide Day as a way of making death manageable, and eventually he leads a major portion of the male population to its death in the river tunnel which collapses and buries them instead of generating the men's jobs they idealize.

Morrison uses male destructiveness as a background which helps to define what it means to be "girlfriends." Sula and Nel become best friends partly for intellectual reasons. They "discover" that they are "neither white nor male," and so they "create" something else to be. Together, they can set aside all outside views and concentrate on their own "perceptions of things." Working up their thoughts together, conversing with each other as if with themselves, they satisfy each other's need for "intimacy."

Since they never quarrel or compete, as girls, their sense of each other is strengthened by the experiences they go through together as they grow up. Walking together in front of girl-watching loungers, they are drawn to each other instead of to the men whose lust and kindness they provoke. Threatened by a gang of teenage "hunkies" who block their road, they run together, and then they make a stand together. Interrupted by a wandering boy as they play together silently in the woods, they briefly include him in talking games and then, roughhousing, accidentally drown him. The shock of the drowning, the decision not to tell, the alienating funeral, all bind them closer together.

Only a lapse into conventionality can pull them apart. Nel is able to ignore her mother's disapproval of Sula as a girlfriend, but their friendship cannot withstand the divisiveness of marriage. When Jude gives up hope of becoming a "road man" and decides to settle for becoming a "head of household," Nel responds to his anger at having to take the lesser role. Accustomed to being thought of as Sula's friend, she is intrigued that Jude seems to see her "singly."

The way in which Jude sees Nel singly is not the one she imagines, however. He is so diminished by his sense of being denied a man's work that he decides it will take the two of them together to make "one Jude." Married, he will have the dignity of being "pinned" to an unsatisfactory job out of necessity--he will not be just another bachelor waiter hanging around a kitchen "like a woman."

Nel is "selected away" from Sula without really understanding the implications of the convention she has fitted herself into. But Sula seems to understand that marriage contradicts friendship. She does not comment or protest, but she leaves The Bottom at the end of Nel's very traditional wedding. Hoping to find some alternative to the girlfriend she has lost, Sula spends ten years wandering through every section of the country, investigating every kind of man, and even going to college. She does not come back until she has tried everything else.

There are several stages to Sula's search for a mature form of the old intimacy of girlfriends. In the first place, she comes up Nel's front walk dressed like a "movie star," but she tells jokes and memories like a friend. When Jude comes home, full of a "whiney tale" about how hard it is to be a "Negro man" in "this world," Sula does not wait for Nel to "excrete" the "milkwarm commiseration" he expects. Like her grandmother Eva, she has more adult ideas. She substitutes an elaborately ironic explanation that Black men are the "envy of the world" because everyone fears, adores, copies, dreads or envies them. Jude is intrigued enough to decide that Sula has "an odd way of looking at things" which "stirred a man's mind." Accustomed to Nel's unchallenging response, he assumes his body is not "stirred" by Sula's wit. But eventually Sula explores her friend's marriage by standing in for Nel in Jude's bed.

Jude and Nel interpret this episode in terms of their own conventional personalities, evidently forgetting what it means that Sula is involved. Jude assumes he has left Nel "for" Sula, and Nel accuses Sula of "taking" Jude.

However, nothing Sula does relates to norms in any way. Her interest in Jude does not outlast his marriage, since it is friendship with Nel she is looking for. She asks Nel why she "can't get over it" since they were "such good friends." This reaction shows what her real motives are. She wants to share Nel's experience at the same time that she reveals to all three of them how strongly committed girlfriends are.

Sula is satisfied that Jude's response proves the weakness of conventional bonds such as marriage. Even in the midst of her grief and shock, Nel recognizes that the loss of Jude is not the most saddening part of the episode. What makes it all "too much" is not being able to "talk things over." Miserably, she discovers that the worst of losing Jude to Sula is the conventional rule which tells her she must be cut off from her girlfriend.

Sula's exploration of her friend's life does not end with taking Nel's own place in the wife role. Doing so proves very little, since Jude's weaknesses have made her friend's marriage dubious from the beginning. Only by involving herself in a serious relationship with a man who is not defective can Sula discover what Nel thinks marriage is.

Ajax provides Sula with insights which neither Jude nor Nel can give. He is not like other men. He loves his mother because her "life is her own," and so he does not look for replacement nurturing from his women. Unlike Jude, he steals quart bottles from a porch when he wants milk. His "idea of bliss" is to soak in a hot bath. And airplanes are his most profound excitement. These preferences free him from the usual dependencies, and independence makes his "beauty" seem "sinister," to most women, even while it invites them.

For Sula, his charm is that he talks to her and refuses to "baby or protect" her. He assumes they are well matched, both being "tough and wise." She also senses that they share thoughts and traits of personality as well as sexual excitement. Half hoping that tradition might be right, after all, and that this particular man might become as complete a friend as Nel was during childhood, Sula puts a ribbon in her hair, cleans the house meticulously, and suggests that Ajax "lean on" her when she discovers he has had a brush with the police.

Ajax is surprised by the change, which carries the "scent of the nest." He believed Sula was independent, like his mother. He thought she was different from "all her sisters." It was her "delicious indifference" which attracted him. These are the qualities which Sula has revealed in her dealings with men in the past, but they come from contempt rather than being goals. Respect for Ajax allows her dream of friendship to emerge, but any kind of reliable involvement is anathema to Ajax. He leaves town, feeling a "mild and momentary regret" over the conventional end of what had been an unusual relationship.

Sula's reaction echoes his in a way which shows how basically impossible it is for minds and spirits to meet across the division between the sexes. After Ajax is gone, Sula discovers that she did not even know his name. His driver's license identifies him as Albert Jacks. A. Jacks, not Ajax. So basic a misunderstanding reveals their division even more totally than his departure does.

Having proved the uselessness of marriage as a route to shared experience, Sula lapses into loneliness. She explicitly refuses to try the alternatives The Bottom seems to recommend. She will not consent to being a mother because the only person she wants to "make" is herself. She will not cling to a man for the sake of having a "job." In an echo of the frankness they used to share, Nel confronts Sula about being different. But Sula rejects her advice by insisting that Nel suffers from a "secondhand lonely." Someone else forced Nel to be alone, whereas Sula's "lonely is mine."

For them to quarrel over loneliness is appropriate, since Sula is dying. She is reconciled to death because she has "sung all the songs there are." Still, her responses to Nel make it obvious that she has given up hope for "any new songs" only because her girlfriend is helpless to escape from adult conventionality in order to keep her company.

In spite of Nel's attempts at denial, the bond between these girlfriends is more lasting than any other relationship in the book. Sula asks Nel to get her pain prescription filled and assumes Nel will pay for it as a matter of course. Nel feels used instead of loved and turns away in conventional irritation. But Sula never does give up. She calls, "Hey, girl," as if they had never stopped being the best of unquestioningly loyal friends. And when death turns out not to hurt, her last thought is the automatic intimacy of girlfriends: "Wait'll I tell Nel."

In contrast to the vividness of Sula's life "in this world," Nel's adulthood has been "empty and dead." Married, she lives in Jude. Deserted, she lives in her children. Deprived of her friend, she visits Sula's grandmother in the rest home where Sula has confined her. Such behavior is dictated by conventional ideas about "virtue," but Sula has insisted that if only one of them is "good," the "good" one is not Nel. After Sula's death, Nel finally begins to agree. Both the "energetically mad" former soldier, Shadrack, and the now-senile Eva Peace mistake Nel for Sula. The reminder of her past intensifies her unexpected sense of sorrow which helps her set aside the role she has put on in the belief that it is the only one available for adults. Like Jude, she has settled for second best. But everything is "explained" when she remembers that she and Sula were "girls together." All the time she has thought she was missing Jude, it is really Sula whom she missed.

Expanding Sula's role beyond the intensely personal relationship with Nel, Morrison develops a similar pattern of reaction in the community at large. When Sula comes back to The Bottom, looking like a movie star, the community decides she is the personification of evil, since a normal person would have gotten fat or lost some of her teeth. The men remember that mosquitos never bit Sula, at picnics, and she could drink beer without belching.

The women see her as a challenge and a threat. Sula's scorn for motherhood forces them to affirm the value of their role by taking better care of their children. They begin to "cherish" their husbands out of a need to justify their own judgment of the men Sula sleeps with only once and then discards. They keep their houses clean to establish the appeal of domesticity.

Sula's power is demonstrated by the time span of these reforms. Most women feel threatened by Sula's ability to be "independent-like," as if she were a man. Her existence seems to imply that everyone could escape convention if they wanted to. The idea that a new way of living might be "good" rather than "evil" is so demanding that they fit themselves eagerly into the most traditional form of the woman's role. But what they gain is simply safety, not satisfaction. And so, as soon as Sula dies, they go back to being neglectful mothers, bad housekeepers, angry lovers and careless daughters.

This social function is summarized by Sula'a funeral. The Black community is so determined to reject her life that they refuse to bury her. However, insurance provides an "elegant" ceremony, even without the help of loving neighbors. Some members of the community participate, since they will not let a "strange woman" separate them from "their God." In fact, Sula makes them more religious since her life justifies the structure of their belief. For this community, God has a "fourth face," which "explains" Sula. The additional "face" belongs to the "brother" who "hadn't spared God's son."

Talking religion, as becomes the additional face of God, Sula insists that permanence is what makes Hell so bad. Like the rest of the community, Nel organizes her thoughts by reacting against everything Sula believes. Therefore she insists that change is what Hell really is and tries to prove her point by clinging to traditional roles that already have fallen out of phase with daily actuality. Regardless of conventional resistance, the sixties come, and things are "so much better" as old roles break down too completely to be argued over. Though she is not alive to see it, Sula proves right in the end.

Sula's function for The Bottom is to challenge unthinking tradition and assumptions about permanence which are based on roles instead of personalities. The cliché vision of housewifery is out of date, since women are failing to live according to its rules. Men are really "pool haunts" and "bachelors," in spite of what they say "a man" is. In a community of "Deweys" and mothers, Sula's fierce independence forces everyone to be aware of change, even though most of them react against it.

It is a thankless role to remind normal people that they neglect the rules they say they live by, and so Sula's ending is not happy, even though it is affirmative. Sula's "brilliance" attracts the "genuine" companionship of rare individuals, like Ajax, who value "indifference to established habits." But permanence is a trap, to Ajax, just as it is Hell to Sula, and so they cannot be "comrades." Similarly, only little girls can be "girlfriends," in Nel's mind, and so adult "sisterhood" is beyond her reach.

But being girlfriends is by no means so temporary as Nel imagines. It is the one relationship which does continue after death, as Sula's power shows. Sula has been dead for twenty-five years before Nel figures out how the term applies. Finally understanding her real loss, she begins to grieve. And since there is no date on the friendship of girlfriends, she endorses Sula's vision, at last.

Women's roles are very commonly a target for revision in this way. It is a topic which seems to grow most easily out of Southern writing, in America. Katherine Anne Porter, for example, routinely includes some form of feminism among the traditions she uses to help her heroines develop an independent sense of self. In "Old Mortality," the usual family recollections cluster around the beauty, grace and charm of one ancestor who seems to have been a traditional belle. Even as a girl, the heroine insists upon a more complicated view. Her drive toward developing a fully rounded personality is nurtured by a less-discussed but equally important awareness of a grim, awkward and spinsterish ancestor who helped secure the vote for women.

Rebecca Harding Davis also makes use of regional attitudes as background for her unusual views. In Dr. Warrick's Daughters, Davis follows the careers of women who explore both Northern and Southern ways of life as they set their individual goals. Travel outside their birth region allows these women to come into contact with contradictory traditions about the woman's role. This variety changes the usually narrow view into a spectrum of possibilities elastic enough to include a besotting addiction to money as well as a manipulator who pushes her ordinary husband toward a greatness which is more her value than his. There is even room for a contented heroine who chooses not to exploit her extraordinary personal charisma. Bystanders are puzzled by her preference for living quietly with an equally unconventional husband in a world of nature, but they tolerate this oddness since it is clearly right for her.

Comparable English novels often suggest a more aggressive break with convention. Geraldine Jewsbury's Marian Withers, for example, analyzes the dilemma of a young woman who wishes to be "good" in a way which will satisfy the people around her. After exploring the usual possibilities, which do not make room for her real generosity of spirit, she finally emerges as an unofficial social worker among the neighborhood factories. Unlike Perley Kelso, she sees no reason why the conventional role of marriage cannot be expanded to include this larger function. She therefore marries a service-oriented young manager who encourages her in her unusual work. In this outcome, Jewsbury goes a step beyond Ward, since she protects her heroine from the traditional self-sacrificing choice between private happiness and public responsibility.

Margaret Drabble also challenges the division between public and private roles, which is traditionally treated as absolute, if it is a choice to be made by a woman. In The Millstone, Drabble follows the career of an academically talented young woman who has a child without automatically electing to have a husband. Her research, her writing, her teaching, her motherhood, her friendships with men and with women, as well as her function as a daughter and sister, all receive separate attention as parts of her life which impinge upon but do not automatically restrict other possibilities. Not intentionally a social innovator, the heroine amusingly displays her acculturation by reminding herself of what she "should" do, each time she makes one of the modestly flamboyant choices which reflect her independence.

An intriguing group of novels within this category are those depicting the possibility that some abnormal people deliberately learn the conventional role as a skill, rather than unconsciously absorbing it as a cultural given. In such works, an appearance of normality may be deliberately planned for by someone whom it does not fit at all.

A remarkably overt example of this process is Mary Shelley's Frankenstein. Shelley's man-made adult is pathetically lacking in the social connection which babyhood and juvenile charm solicit for more conventionally produced beings. In the novel, Frankenstein's creature tries to learn language by eavesdropping, tries to gain acceptance through sweetness, and tries to claim a companion on the basis of pity. His attempt to construct both a social and a personal role for himself offers Shelley a basis for reexamining functions which are usually assumed unthinkingly. The result is a critique both of the acculturation process and of social roles.

Shelley's decision to place this process in a frankly surrealistic mode may have been as important as her famous name in keeping her novel alive. Constance Woolson is equally concerned with analyzing cultural function, but her realistic approach to dispassionate social analysis allows standard historians to see her as a "tourist"[5] rather than a social commentator.

In For the Major, Woolson analyzes the conventional role for women by depicting the strategies of a wife who deliberately maintains herself in the situation which is her husband's ideal. Discovering that he married her because she is small and blonde and therefore can be mistaken as winsomely innocent, she keeps her youth by coloring her hair and softening the light in her drawing room. She conceals her past, when she finds out that he assumes she has none. And she exists in the community as a shyly perfect hostess for "the Major." Only after he dies does she allow her wrinkles and gray hair to show. And with the touches of reality comes a relieved display of the sophisticated intelligence which suffering and subterfuge have cultivated in her.

Not all such lives result in grief. Mary Roberts Rinehart offers a cheerful version of this strategy in her novels about Miss Pinkerton. Miss Pinkerton uses the conventional role of nurse as a cover for her detective activities. Wearing a white uniform and primly knitting, Miss Pinkerton is able to spy on people who are clever enough to baffle the police but are not intelligent enough to look beneath the surface of the woman's role. Her masquerade is so convincing that she is able to solve case after baffling case. The only person who understands her is the policeman with whom she works. His reaction to each of her solutions is to offer himself in marriage. She always rejects the offer, but his appreciative persistence is a charming affirmation of a personal as well as social value for female complexity.

Notes

1. Anne Henry Ehrenpreis, "Introduction," The Old Manor House (London: Oxford University Press, 1969), p. xiv.

2. Ernest A. Baker, The History of the English Novel (New York: Barnes & Noble, 1929), vol. V, p. 191.

3. Ehrenpreis, p. xiv.

4. The Letters of Mrs. Gaskell, ed. J. A. V. Chapple and Arthur Pollard (Cambridge: Harvard University Press, 1967), p. 223.

5. Robert E. Spiller, et al., ed., The Literary History of the United States (New York: Macmillan, 1953), p. 868.

6. THE ECCENTRIC ROLE

George Eliot, <u>Daniel Deronda</u>
Elizabeth Gaskell, <u>Wives and Daughters</u>
Elizabeth Gundy, <u>Bliss</u>

others:
Zelda Fitzgerald, <u>Save Me the Waltz</u>
Sarah Orne Jewett, <u>A Country Doctor</u>
Elizabeth Stuart Phelps Ward, <u>Dr. Zay</u>
Charlotte Lennox, <u>The Female Quixote</u>
Diane Johnson, <u>Loving Hands at Home</u>
Muriel Spark, <u>The Prime of Miss Jean Brodie</u>
Elizabeth Gaskell, <u>Cousin Phillis</u>

A tolerant observer may decide that society does not always drive its misfits away. Nonstandard behavior is sometimes made manageable, instead. It can be called eccentricity if it is tied to a specific role, as in the case of artists, scientists, professors, and gurus, who are expected to be at least a little strange. Society benefits because the variety is interesting and because unconventional people lead the way toward growth and change. And since some unusual people want to keep in touch with normal society, individuals are helped, as well.

The limits to this social structure are obvious and sometimes cruel. Individuals cannot set aside the norms simply by wishing to be different. They must be talented or intellectual enough to live up to the other demands of the role, since even escape involves standard rules, in this structured form.

Novels which focus on social roles where eccentricity is expected usually include this dark side. Emerging from the normal mass are two kinds of people. There are the talented individuals who struggle to find ways of overcoming their helpless eccentricity, since they recognize it as a social handicap. By contrast, there are the people of normal skills who wish to be treated as exceptions but have nothing special to offer society as a way of justifying their claim.

Fiction depicting this situation is easy to misjudge. When some characters want to be eccentric but cannot accomplish it, their defeated submission to the norms may absorb so much attention that the successful eccentricity of other individuals is set aside. Readers may not notice what they have done to the work as a whole by overly involving themselves with defeat. But even when they know that the triumph of norms is only a part of the action, they may try to dismiss the leftover element by calling it a flaw.

George Eliot's last novel is an unusually well-documented case. F. R. Leavis suggested changing its name to "Gwendolyn Harleth,"[1] insisting that it was a kind of mini-Middlemarch, pulled partly out of shape by "Zionist" padding. This has proved to be an easy first opinion, since Daniel Deronda does include the English country world whose values Eliot represented with varying degrees of tolerance and affection throughout her writing career. Still, a novelist at the height of her powers is unlikely to have forgotten what she was doing to the extent of misunderstanding a third of her own book, and it is important to remember that Eliot flatly rejected efforts to read Daniel Deronda as a collection of disconnected parts.[2]

A reader's reward for letting the author make her own point is the discovery that Gwendolyn Harleth's story is completely interwoven into Daniel Deronda's novel. Topics, events and characterizations are meshed so completely that Eliot is proved right in thinking she had a single story to tell. She needed to offer a pair of central characters rather than a single hero because her theme includes male as well as female experience and ranges from "English country people" to the "far off shore" of Jewish culture.

As paired individuals, Gwendolyn and Daniel face many of the same situations. In the beginning, both of them judge and are judged on the basis of the usual English country standards. Later on, both are changed by the Jewish lives they encounter. In addition, both are involved with a third value system, which places artists in a "caste" above other people. As they struggle to make their lives meaningful and pleasant, Daniel and Gwendolyn serve as a living critique of all three ways of judging.

Eliot begins with the most typical of the three "worlds" her novel concerns. Standard English society emerges in the early sequences of the novel where money is used as the constant reference. Money is the topic of conversation, the basis of judging, the source of interest, the social glue. An heiress must consider herself "an appendage" to her fortune. An heir has at his back the "ghostly army" of a public which automatically approves of him. On the other hand, even a "splendid girl" without funds must admit her helpless disadvantage. And no matter how "unusually agreeable" a young man without an income may be, he cannot expect his love to be returned.

Eliot does not imply that money is a solely English fascination. Daniel's first private contact with the Jewish world is through a pawnbroker and his family. Here, as well as among the English, money is at least as much an idea as it is a livelihood. One of the children in the pawnbroker's family is far too young to be concerned with incomes, and so his reason for being a sharp trader is the simple joy of winning at business transactions.

This parallel makes clear that Eliot did not intend for <u>Daniel Deronda</u> to be simply a conventional complaint about the materialism of English society. Other populations suffer vividly from the same fascination, and so money in itself cannot be the basic English problem.

The "national taste" for coldness which accompanies the counting house personality is the real source of trouble for the English in this novel. Gwendolyn's triumphant marriage reveals the true nature of the "national type." Marriage is forced on Gwendolyn as her only means of self-support, but it is Grandcourt's emotional remoteness which intrigues and reassures her. After marriage, Gwendolyn and Grandcourt are able to maintain the appearance of glamor in their English context, since they share a commitment to frigidly correct behavior. Nevertheless, in private, the domestic emotions they offer are fear, dread, disgust, and a rivalry of wills.

Such soul-destroying "correctness" comes from being English rather than from wanting money, as Eliot shows by developing Jewish family life in fervid and passional contrast behind an equally financial surface. Jewish children bask in doting affection. Jewish fathers are adored as well as loved. Friends are woven into the Jewish family so sympathetically their lack of blood relationship is masked and set aside.

The frank emotional heat of Jewish family life is at first appalling to Daniel, who has been raised as an Englishman. When a stranger grips him by the arm to question him about his parentage, he recoils from a gesture which seems insultingly familiar to him. In addition, he is shocked by the open reference to a dilemma which he has always considered too private to discuss even with his loved and trusted guardian. He emphasizes the difference between their standards of behavior by answering "coldly" that he is an "Englishman."

When he later approaches the Jewish world voluntarily, Daniel still reflects the coolness and detachment of his English upbringing. He decides to study the Hebrew language and ponder Jewish history and theology. Such an intellectualizing scheme contrasts pointedly with the acculturation methods usual in the Jewish community. Young Jacob Cohen, for example, stands between his teacher's knees to mimic the sound of poetry which may become meaningful to him eventually, though he does not understand it as he learns it. When his attention wanders, he is not held to the task. Mirah was more dutiful as a child, but the result is not more profound. Her adult sense of herself as Jewish is a matter of lullabies and lisping--it has to do with her feelings only. She never thinks of her identity as a "set of propositions."

These contrasts show the extent to which Daniel's upbringing has modified his identity by birth. His parents were Jewish, though his mother wants him not to know it, and so he spends an anxious childhood wondering who he is and doubting even his own legitimacy. In love with a Jewish woman, he depends upon his reading Hebrew in her family as a way for her to get to know him. Fervid by nature, he is overwhelmed by his feelings as both a son and a lover. And yet, in an "English" way, he remains touchingly convinced that only his mind can help him toward satisfaction in either relationship.

English "correctness" comes out in Daniel as a sensitive self-repression somewhat masking the emotional nature which prevents him from being altogether an "Englishman." His good-natured guardian's way of pointing out how differently Daniel behaves is to ask him to stop flirting. Daniel is affronted at the accusation, innocently insisting he never flirts. An amused Sir Hugo explains that any English woman is inevitably overcome by a handsome young man who is so extraordinary as to listen to her remarks sympathetically, look at her tenderly, and talk to her in a "Jesuitical way." In other words, Daniel is sensitively "reserved" in his feelings, but the light in his eyes is so untypically warm that he racks English female hearts by accident.

This exchange between Daniel and his guardian is amusing, but it grows from the book's most serious idea. Daniel cannot help "flirting," since his misleading charm comes from what he is, not from what he does. His experience shows that the most attractive personality is one which blends worlds rather than unthinkingly accepting "the herd" assigned by birth.

Gwendolyn's relationship with Daniel underlines this point. Her stake in confronting both worlds is closely parallel to Daniel's. From their first meeting she accepts him as an emotional mentor and moral guide. Her submission to his judgment makes him so large a part of her imagination that she is stunned when he abruptly reveals his new identity to her. His discovery has changed him by giving him a new self-confidence. Without Gwendolyn realizing it, he has become far less yielding and sympathetic. Cruelly, he forgets his own first recoiling reaction to the Jewish world and greets Gwendolyn's floundering frustration with silent anger. When she assures him he is not changed personally by his discovery of his parentage, Daniel is offended again.

By being unfair to Gwendolyn, Daniel shows how unable they both are to bring about a genuine bonding between two worlds. For Gwendolyn, it is an automatic response to assume he will not become "a Jew," since his failure to be "an Englishman" was what attracted her in the first place. But Daniel is right in rejecting this response since he knows he has changed. His rigidness with Gwendolyn fits an emerging pattern of which she is unaware. When Daniel meets his mother at last, he is sullenly accusing toward her in a spontaneous way which is startlingly uncharacteristic of the man he used to be. Enraged by her concealment of his Jewishness, he begins to talk in terms of "my people." Still, like Gwendolyn, he prefers a combination of English and Jewish values, and so he hopes to keep what he sees as good in his English childhood. He tells himself he will work for a union between the two worlds which combine in him without in either case fully including him.

Eliot expands this thematic element beyond the central

characters, since they are such special cases. Providing for a more general view, she allows both the most attractive Englishmen in the novel to fall painfully in love with Jewish women. Hans, Daniel's friend from school, reveals his passionate admiration by using Mirah as a painter's model who transforms traditional female lives into a "ladies version" which is more beautiful and more pure than the original. His reaction to her Jewish identity is more accepting and less egoist than Gwendolyn's reaction to Daniel--he jokes about learning to ape Jewish rituals. Since his version of English coolness is to joke about everything, including his own feelings, his humor is not in bad taste. Nevertheless, Daniel is offended. It is a touchy subject, not only because they are rivals, but because Daniel is soberly attempting the transformation Hans sees as a target for self-deprecating wit. Daniel's way of healing his own wounds is to urge Hans to deepen their manly friendship by joining with him in the half-tragic enjoyment of a shared and hopeless love.

Daniel's appeal symbolizes a crucially un-English emotional structure, just as Hans' behavior reveals him to be centrally English. It is Hans' nature to be amusing rather than morbid about his emotions, and since he makes her laugh, Mirah's mind responds to his wit without her emotions being stirred. Hans' reaction to his own defeat and Daniel's triumph further emphasizes the gulf between their natures. Hans' only change is a slightly irritable tendency toward a grimmer humor. Even in his own deepest suffering, he does not display the suffocating emotion which Daniel offers almost casually and universally.

Sir Hugo's love for Daniel's mother shows still a different aspect of the question of cultural identity. "The Princess" is herself rejecting her Jewish role, and so Sir Hugo's passionate involvement is parallel to the situation Gwendolyn hoped for from Daniel. "English" to the core, Sir Hugo does not contemplate Jewish culture even to the playful extent that Hans does. In fact, he embodies English remoteness by accepting a child when it is a wife he has asked for and by casually removing Daniel from his Jewish birthright.

Sir Hugo turns out to be an attentive foster father to the child of his lost beloved, and it would be easy to respond simply to the sweetness of his behavior to Daniel. Yet Eliot shows a growing resentment in Daniel in order to emphasize the hidden significance of Sir Hugo's actions. Sir Hugo knows gossip credits him with being Daniel's natural father, and since he has no son, he enjoys the companionship of the exceptionally attractive and intensely dutiful young man he has raised so indulgently. Eliot deals kindly with Sir Hugo--his love for Daniel is one of the more charming elements of the novel. Still, Daniel refuses to separate that love from a self-serving wish to have the appearance of a son where none was given.

Sir Hugo never explicitly rejects Jewish culture because Daniel's mother did that for him, but he symbolizes English narrowness of vision by allowing Daniel to suffer under the English assumption that his inevitable difference comes from an illicit birth rather than from a Jewish ancestry. Since even so attractive an Englishman as Sir Hugo turns out to be essentially self-seeking, Daniel learns to value the self-unaware passion available almost everywhere in the Jewish world.

Daniel is determined not to choose between his worlds, but his growing disapproval of Sir Hugo shows how helpless he is to avoid making choices. Everyone else takes it for granted that he will have to live in one world or the other. When he tries to fit himself into the Cohen family scene, Jacob identifies him as a "swell." By long habit, he lives in Sir Hugo's family, but Sir Hugo's wife complains that Daniel has "gone mad."

Innocently blurting opinions other people are too tactful to state, these naive characters show the reaction of society to such purely personal roles as Daniel believes he has constructed. Though he may feel he can set aside individual reactions, he cannot shrug off the impersonal fact that public rituals are tied to a specific social world. When Gwendolyn asks, "<u>Can</u> you marry?" she emphasizes this difficulty. If he is going to marry, he will have to choose a rite in which to do it.

In other words, Eliot is emphatic that simply wishing to escape is not enough to release individuals from the "herd" into which they were born. Gwendolyn's difficulties reinforce this point. Throughout the early stages of Gwendolyn's development, Eliot describes her character in masculine terms. The force of her will is like a man's. She has a man's need to dominate. She wishes to control her own life, as a man does. Like a man, she defines her highest happiness in terms of being thoughtless, strong and free.

But Gwendolyn is not a man, she is a "splendid girl," and the meaning of this difference is taught to her in grimly unyielding ways. Marriage is the only resource available to a woman like her. Since she is unwilling to marry, she is left to face the "labyrinth of life" without a "clue." When Gwendolyn is made helpless by sudden poverty, Eliot changes the narrative in order to surround Gwendolyn with feminine adjectives. Finally submitting to an engagement, Gwendolyn escapes into the brief "woman's paradise" of having every whim uncontradicted. After marriage deprives her of every smallest shred of independence, she is described totally as an object, "wrapped" in beautiful clothes, "her ears pierced for gems."

When she would like to reclaim her individuality, her only hope seems to be to run away from Grandcourt and the "distorting male standard" which guarantees his total triumph over her. But even so violent an act would not provide escape, as she realizes when she thinks of Grandcourt's mistress, Mrs. Glasher. Mrs. Glasher seems to be "a woman's life." She is a warning, a victim of "manslaughter," an image of the uselessness and degradation facing a woman who lacks a husband and therefore lacks a social niche. When Gwendolyn appeals to Daniel for help in escaping the sickening "dance" of a life composed of "what every one else does," he uncomfortingly advises her to submit, as men submit to "maiming." She is to accept her woman's situation as men accept an "incurable disease."

Daniel might have been more sympathetic since he has the same mixture of sex-role tied traits. In the beginning, he shows the sensitivity of a "bright girl" and the tenderness of a woman. But the social result is simply that he is an "unusual young man" in a "usual world." He visualizes the suffering of others more than is comfortable for him, but he is not confronted with horrifying warnings about a man's life. When noticed at all, Daniel's mixed personality is no more than a perfectly tolerable "moral" eccentricity. And as is the case with her characterization of Gwendolyn, Eliot gradually shifts Daniel's personality toward the traditional role for his sex, allowing him to become more controllingly aggressive and dominating. His mother marks the turnover point by observing that he had better marry a submissive woman since he would never consent to "merge" himself with a wife.

Both central characters are most appealing when they are androgynous, and they are most hopeful while they imagine they can combine national identities as well. Yet neither succeeds in avoiding the limits of sex and nation, in spite of their yearnings and struggles. Their inability to escape from social categories forms a background for the one role which rises above divisions of every kind.

In Eliot's world, only artists can take themselves outside of social roles. They are not tied down by financial questions since their dedication is to art. They escape the "subjection" of love without having to give up love, itself. They avoid the "bondage" of marriage without having to relinquish marriage. Merely social rules do not concern them since they recognize each other across any chasm of class or background, and they categorize anyone outside their "freemasonry" in a single, nonartistic grouping.

People within the artist "caste" escape the norms in a variety of ways. For example, Daniel's beloved, Mirah, can support herself as an artist, though no other young woman could maintain her sweetness and modesty while parading herself for hire. In her role as a musician, Mirah is admired and courted in the elegant homes where she would never dare to go in the guise of a normal person for fear of being snubbed, even by the servants.

Daniel's mother also turns to art to escape the narrowness of a woman's life. She is gloriously successful--adored, obeyed, almost worshipped. Yet her triumphant refusal to be the same thing other women are comes to a jolting end when she loses her nerve. Having given Daniel away rather than live as a mother during her time of glamor, she allows a temporary illness to sap her courage. The resulting defeat is total. Dying, years later, and agonized by guilt, she has no way to defend herself against Daniel's unyielding resentment except to admit her greater subjection--she has been engulfed by the five children inflicted upon her by a second marriage of despair.

Such a dreadful end for "The Princess" is not meant to show that female artists always come to grief. Mirah marries Daniel because she genuinely wishes to, and he is himself gifted, so he will know how to appreciate her talent in his household. In addition, escape from the public aspect of an artist's life is a relief to Mirah, since her father was so exploitive of her childhood talent.

Miss Arrowpoint, too, is a "thorough musician," whose soul has "more ears" than the souls of other people. But she is genuinely content to study, rather than perform. She finds an outlet for the social aspect of her artistic nature by helping other artists. And she benefits personally because her independence of judgment gives her the confidence to set aside conventional questions about how a lady and an heiress "must" behave. Knowing her own mind, she is not embarrassed to offer herself to Klesmer, a musician who loves her and will cultivate her talent.

In marrying off both Mirah and Miss Arrowpoint, Eliot underscores her idea that artists do not simply escape into an anarchy where they can be free of all restraining expectations. Instead, artists take up a different set of duties which normal society uneasily accepts as a substitute for what is usually required.

Klesmer's situation is a case in point. He is welcome everywhere because of his genius, even though he is always personally inconvenient. He is too passionate for the county society where he meets Gwendolyn and too large for the drawing room where he meets Mirah. Nevertheless, Miss Arrowpoint insists that genius is always "en règle," and her conventional parents support her in this view. The entire society may silently believe that greatness such as Klesmer's ought to die and get rid of the inconvenient "outward man," but no one thinks of rejecting him in his role as musician.

The situation changes when he steps outside his role. What may be excusable eccentricity in a genius is not to be borne when the same man presents himself in the clear-cut social role of prospective son-in-law. The enraged Arrowpoint parents order him out of the house and disinherit their daughter for allowing him to offer himself in such a guise. When Miss Arrowpoint insists she was the one who made the offer, they merely renew their outrage and blame.

Son-in-law is a lesser category than artist, however, and ultimately, true priorities prevail. It is only very briefly that the Arrowpoints try to force their daughter to do as other people do. Even before the marriage, they accept Klesmer, outward man and all.

The happiness of this marriage summarizes Eliot's point. Art provides a public role which makes room for eccentricity and self-assertion. But artists are women and men, as well as talents, and so they need a marriage of entangling sympathies for private satisfaction. Klesmer was admired during his days as a bachelor musician, but he is not a happy genius until he finds himself in a marriage of equal talents.

In the case of artists, even marriage does not invoke the normal social rules. Daniel's marriage to Mirah encourages conventional speculation about the beauty of the children they will produce. But Klesmer and Miss Arrowpoint are not submerged into biological process. Instead, they, themselves, are the focus of their joined existence, and they surround themselves with individuals selected from both English and Jewish groups on the single basis of respect for ability and dedication to art. Once they have established their right to each other, the Klesmers are granted independence from the "usual world" by the world itself.

Some readers object to Eliot's acceptance of marriage as fulfilling,[3] and others find Daniel Deronda "strange."[4] But for Eliot, anyone who tries to escape all regulation from all outside sources is essentially a person without a "clue." Her reality requires some kind of dependable social connection. And, given the limitations of society, such contact can take place only within a formal role. Therefore, a higher duty to art is the only escape from the ordinary "yoke" of the "herd."

Eliot's subjects in Daniel Deronda were traditional--the arts, faith, county society--but her imagery is drawn from the scientific discussions of her day. She explained hesitancy in terms of blind worms, for example, and compared idle travellers to vacuums. The contrast between tone and topic is appropriate since it gives a modern air to her new look at old questions. Still, she left it to her remarkable contemporary, Elizabeth Gaskell, to take up the social role of science explicitly.

Gaskell had Charles Darwin in mind as she planned Wives and Daughters.[5] Her young hero, Roger Hamley, is a scientist, even as a child. He borrows books from the community doctor instead of satisfying himself with his family's very traditional library, and this abnormal taste gives the impression that he is "not much of a reader." His preoccupation with looking closely at scientific subjects makes him seem at best "not brilliant," and as a little boy at school, he is teased unmercifully for being "slow."

Roger's lack of concern with poetry and the classics is obvious in his outdoor life, as well. When he looks at a

pond, he does not see a pool of tranquil loveliness, he sees
a possible source for the "treasures of nastiness" which fill
his net. Walking about the estate with his father, he fails
to respond with a feudal eye to views of timber and bog. Instead, he keeps a sharp lookout for undiscovered plants as
speciments for his collections.

Even to sympathetic eyes, Roger's interests are handicaps. His father ruefully admits they would need to give
honors in natural history before Roger could be "safe" at
Cambridge. His mother insists he is so full of "messes"
such as natural history and comparative anatomy that he
couldn't fall in love "with Venus herself." His fiancée considers him hard to talk to, as well as plain and awkward.

Less indulgent commentators find even more to complain of. He talks too loudly.... His face is too expressive....
He has no profile.... His idea of sympathizing is to offer "philosophizing comfort." Finally he goes so far as to grow a
flowing beard.

To show how important all these defects are, Gaskell
holds up Roger's older brother as an ideal example of everything traditional society admires. The heir to an entailed
estate, he is beautiful, perfectly dressed, fastidious, distinguished in manner, amiable, graceful, amusing, brilliant, a
genius, and a poet. The social value of his perfectly finished
manner makes clear that a gentleman's surface is everything.
He might as well not have personal defects, since no one
mentions them.

The community the boys grow up in never even considers the possibility that they might not look like what they
are. Osborne looks aesthetic and so he is accepted as being
a poet. It is a bewildering puzzle when his poetry proves to
be unpublishable, whereas Roger's writing is praised in the
scientific community. Osborne looks educated and so he is
called a genius. As it turns out, he barely passes his degree, and it is Roger, instead, who becomes senior wrangler
and fellow at Trinity. Once out of school, Osborne declares
himself willing to earn his way if someone will suggest anything he could do, but it is Roger who is actually able to find
a position which pays well enough to support both brothers.

An heir might support himself by making a brilliant
marriage, but Osborne is already married to a servant in
secret. His only way of behaving like an heir is to borrow
against the estate. When Roger finds out that their father's

life has been estimated, along with the timber, he is able to rescue his father's dignity by borrowing against the salary he will earn as a scientist.

Such clear evidence about personal worth sometimes rearranges community opinion, at least briefly, but no "mere facts" change people's minds in basic ways. After Roger is undeniably famous in London's scientific circles, his fiancée begins describing him as "too learned and clever." She continues to point out that she likes pretty people, and he is not "pretty" in either looks or manner. Roger's mother-in-law-to-be starts flattering and encouraging him, but her sudden thaw turns out to come from her hopes that Osborne may die and leave Roger as the heir. When Osborne produces a son, Roger again has nothing to offer beyond his personal merits and fame. Therefore Mrs. Gibson returns at once to her original attitude. In social terms, Roger can't "add," even if he is a mathematical genius. The best Mrs. Gibson can say of him is that "uncouthness" may be appropriate to a "scientific traveller."

The views of society are echoed in Roger's family, despite the constant contradiction his behavior offers. Osborne loves him and occasionally defends him as a person of "solid worth." Still, he will accept only sympathy and money from his younger brother. He admits Roger's intelligence in an abstract way, but he absolutely ignores Roger's opinions and rejects his efforts at advice. Their mother reacts in a similar way. Just before she dies, she confesses that Roger may not have "received justice" from them all, but her revised sense of her sons' worth does not prevent her from yearning only for Osborne, at the end.

Squire Hamley's responses are the clearest illustration of the way social norms overwhelm private views. Roger resembles his father physically, and Squire Hamley knows he does not look the part of a man who can count his descent straight from "nobody knows where," or at least from King Alfred. His face is red, his hands and feet are big, and his figure is thick. These are not the attributes of a gentleman. In the same way, he announces that Roger is too "red-brown" and big boned to be of "gentle blood." Nevertheless, they are Hamleys of Hamley. It is Osborne who looks the part, and yet he resembles his mother, who "couldn't tell her great-grandfather from Adam." The contradiction puzzles the Squire, but it does not influence him. He is so sure Osborne's worth is equal to his appearance that he daydreams impossible and brilliant marriages for him. He is equally sure Roger's value echoes his appearance. He tells Roger he is "slow," even after Roger has become senior wrangler. He values Roger's instantaneous, submissive obedience, since it is appropriate behavior in an unimportant, second son. But when Roger tries to insist that he can rescue the estate which Osborne's debts have jeopardized, the Squire doubtingly asks how he will get the money. Roger is driven to call himself a "fine fellow" and mention his "wonderful merits." He tries to soften the statement by joking and by quoting a review of his scientific work, but the problem remains. Even though it is in his father's service, he has praised himself--an ungentlemanly act. Squire Hamley responds with a complaint against Roger's use of French, with its dubious overtones of Waterloo, in his writing. He admits the written praise of his clumsy younger son has pleased him, but it clearly has not changed his way of judging.

The same resistance to contradiction occurs in Osborne's case. Long before she meets him, Molly, his young neighbor, has learned he is a hero. Since her doctor father has trained her to be observant, Molly starts by noticing a discrepancy between her ideal and the real man actually presented to her. She had expected a powerful and agile person, but Osborne seems effeminate. She anticipated an eagle eye and is surprised to find his blue eyes are cold and weary. She had looked for the vitality of extremes--either a Homeric appetite or an endurance of long fasting--but Osborne is "dainty" at the table. She had assumed a grand individual who would be larger than life, but he gives the impression only of "mentally squinting" at her as his audience. Nevertheless, by the time their first meeting is over, she notices only his beauty and his grace and feels ashamed of having questioned his right to "idolatry."

When Osborne's near failure at school forces a new look at his merits, the outcome is similar. Mrs. Gibson thinks briefly that he is less agreeable, but the difference does not seem worth mentioning. His mother admits he has caused much grief and suffering in the family, but when Molly tries to soften the criticism, Mrs. Hamley protests against Molly's making him sound weak instead of wicked. Her own solution is to push both possibilities aside and recall what an adorable little boy he was, before his actual character showed.

As was true in Roger's case, Squire Hamley's attitude sums up the social dilemma Osborne's adult behavior produces. When Osborne leaves school almost disgraced, his father suddenly sees his debts as extravagance and criticizes his elegance as fitting him for nothing but a dancing-master. Even more disappointing is the discovery that Osborne is unloving, now that he is grown. Yet, after his first outrage, the Squire deals with these discrepancies in the same way his wife did. He turns away from the evidence and comforts himself with bittersweet memories of Osborne's childhood, when there could be no question that he was an adorable, promising and loving little heir.

This attitude is not a simple illustration of tenderness in fathers. When he sorts through a lifetime of evidence in order to find a way to keep on loving his son, the Squire is illustrating Gaskell's concern with the way belief overrules evidence. As mouthpiece for community opinion, Miss Browning states this principle in its most extreme form. Losing an argument with Mr. Gibson, Miss Browning shuts him up by insisting that she will yield anything "sooner than be reasoned with." She makes it clear that neither reasoning nor yielding will have any effect on her beliefs.

With this range of behavior as a background, Gaskell can expand her point beyond the usual. Fathers and neighborhood gossips are expected to edit information. But Roger certainly has good reason to ignore social judgments, partly because he has a habit of observation and also because he suffers so constantly from mistaken social views. Both his sweet nature and his brilliant mind are persistently set aside. He is too warmhearted to resent this fact, but he certainly knows it. And so, if logic had any influence on behavior, he could be expected not to make the same mistake himself. In fact he is attentive to the minds of men outside the family, attaching himself to the scientists in the community without regard to rank or social ease.

Nevertheless, his emotional life takes place in the same arena that society provides for any young man. Men of all ages and conditions are bewitched by Molly's stepsister, Cynthia, and Roger falls "most prone and abject," regardless of his abilities in every other context. Guaranteed an income as long as he does not marry, he nevertheless "feeds his passion" in every possible way, like an "unreasoning child." Besottedly in love, he admits he knows too little of Cynthia to understand her virtues, but he insists he could not be "deceived in that face."

In other words, the habit of scientific observation

influences his reading, his male companionship, his conversation and his professional future, but he behaves like everyone else about female beauty. Because of his own discrepancies, he knows absolutely that a person's inner character does not necessarily match the outer form, but he sets that fact aside when responding to women, and he rejects contradiction even when it is proved. During a dinner party at the Gibsons, Roger talks to his host about comparative osteology instead of making himself agreeable to either Molly or Cynthia, as he "should." But while he devotes his mind to Mr. Gibson in an exceedingly interested way, he gazes at Cynthia. It is her face which absorbs him, together with the fond imaginings her beauty triggers. In fact, Cynthia is ignoring the conversation and admits it so charmingly that Roger's standards are as undone as his heart. He fails to contradict Mrs. Gibson's assertion that even polite interest might besmirch a lady with the dreaded label of bluestocking. After their engagement, when Cynthia's letters show she has not even taken the trouble to read his before answering, he pushes the knowledge into the realm of hurt feelings without drawing the obvious conclusions about the shallowness of both her nature and her attachment. And when she finally jilts him, he is as resistant as if there had been no warning pattern.

Because of these discrepancies in Roger, Mr. Gibson feels entitled to be satirical when Roger finally subdues his commonplace young man's longing for a beautiful "grand" woman who will be his "empress" and asks for permission to offer himself to Mr. Gibson's daughter, Molly. Mr. Gibson insists that a "wise man of science in love" beats all other men in "folly." He is in a position to know, since his own second marriage exceeds in folly even Roger's situation, without the excuse of love.

Mr. Gibson's love story, as he calls it, expands Gaskell's theme beyond the relatively simple problem of personal attractiveness. If Roger were the only scientist in the novel, he might seem to be caught in a crossfire too unusual to offer any insight into humanity at large. Even in isolation, his character is intriguing, since it is not usual to link either intellectual seriousness or physical plainness with persistently attentive domestic sweetness. The combination of the three qualities is astonishing enough to turn the novel into a charming tribute to the social holocaust created by the intelligence and sensitivity of Gaskell's model, Charles Darwin.

The Eccentric Role / 197

But Wives and Daughters treats of far more than simply the individual case. Even though he is wholeheartedly a scientist himself, Lord Hollingford wonders whether science can be called a profession. He can afford to speculate, since he has a social position guaranteed him as a "Lord." Mr. Gibson also gains his social footing on a basis other than his identity as a scientist. It is his sympathy, more than his pills, which earns him a welcome everywhere. And though Molly starts out loving him for himself, after she is old enough to discover social rules, she falls into a new respect for him as a handsome man. He thinks his doctoring should speak for itself, and so he does not discuss his background. But it is really his personal elegance which appeals to the community. Lacking other information, the gossips explain his charm as resulting from an unacknowledged link with nobility. For him to be a high-born bastard is entirely satisfying. His view of himself as scientific has no impact on his role as doctor.

Gaskell does not rest her case with men. Molly has been raised to be "rude"--that is, Mr. Gibson objects to her being taught the usual things for fear of diluting her "mother wit." He insists on self-control and uses his ironic conversational habits to train her in logic. Roger strengthens this pattern unknowingly when he tries to comfort Molly over her father's second marriage. He invites her to use his microscope and lends her books so new knowledge can lead her interests away from useless weeping and wounds.

Attention to her mind becomes Molly's lifeline. Even as a small child, she turns to images of death when she is swamped in an undiluted social role. The first time she is alone in conventional society, she becomes faint and ill. Later she protests to her father that she felt like a lighted candle as the extinguisher approaches. Her father deals with the self-pity by asking how she knows the feelings of candles. Roger uses a similar procedure when he insists she should think of someone besides herself. As her father's daughter, she responds rationally, protesting that doing as others like will be the same as killing herself. Still, she appreciates Roger's "roughness" and does begin to notice her father's needs, in addition to her own.

Molly's growth as a clear-eyed observer is fostered both by her father's frank inclusion of death as an aspect of life and by Roger's interest in distinguishing among the cells of different kinds of bees. Their training builds on the scientific personality she inherited, so that, by the time she is an adult, she can defend her own judgment even against her father, when he tries to protect her from gossip. Confidence in her rational ability and her moral judgment enables her to refuse to justify herself. She insists that Mr. Gibson accept her situation as she sees it, and since logic is a value with him, he does not feel the need to insist on obedience as the highest good between them.

Although Molly's behavior is limited to a social context, she clearly displays a "scientific" personality. Self-confident in a modest way, rational, observant, intensely sympathetic, she is comfortable in the company of other such minds--her father, Roger, Lord Hollingford. Bored and "extinguished" in conventional settings, she maintains her integrity by becoming a "diplomatist" and returning social answers which will satisfy normal listeners without in fact embracing restricting ideas.

Except for the scientific men who value her unusual nature, reactions to Molly are predictable. Osborne discovers her to be a beauty in the making. Cynthia also sees her neglected attractiveness and tries to improve her wardrobe sense. Squire Hamley responds to her frank sweetness and adopts her as a comforting daughter. The Brownings value her modesty and submissiveness. Her stepmother complains about her lack of finish.

In order to comment on Molly's function as a female version of the scientific role, Gaskell introduces a character who appreciates scientists without being one herself. Lady Harriet exists primarily as a fond sister, an affectionate daughter, and an intelligently "condescending" titled member of the community. Still, growing up with a scientific brother and sister taught her the meaning of their type of unusual behavior and so she recognizes it in Molly. She calls Molly her "mentor" and her "famous little truthteller" and treats her like an equal. This relationship is the final element of Molly's acceptance into the scientific realm which supersedes mere social rank. Love might delude Mr. Gibson and Roger, and young beauty might distract Lord Hollingford, but Lady Harriet has no motive beyond simple respect. Her disinterested attachment proves there is more to Molly than merely her social role.

Since her scientists have to find their place in conventional society, Gaskell creates a foil for them by defining their opposite--a socially charismatic individual. Cynthia's "physical charms of expression" beguile women as well as men. She is beautiful but unconcerned about her own beauty. She is poised as a wild animal is. At first, she is alluringly passive. But she begins to chatter, under pressure, and then she is adored for her wit. She "likes to be liked" and captivates newcomers as innocently as a small child does. She flatters the vanity of all men, from lord to gardener, but she also bestirs herself for women when they will allow her to, winning a depth of loyalty from Molly which takes precedence over even her love for Roger and her father.

On the surface, Cynthia is exactly what everyone believes they value. Her helpfulness at parties seems like selflessness. Her playful responsiveness looks like innocence. Her assurance becomes dignity. Her concealment of her thoughts is perceived as yielding sweetness. Her acceptance of adoration is understood as tender feeling.

But these are social skills rather than moral values, to Cynthia. She grew up with no goal beyond pleasingness, and she is surprised to find a "higher standard" when she comes to live in the Gibson household. She is at first attracted, not by the moral code but by Mr. Gibson, who is the "most charming man" she knows. Briefly, she toys with the idea of being made into a "good woman" by association with him and Molly, both of whom are "good." In fact, the influence flows the other way. Molly sets aside moral ways of judging when she thinks of Cynthia. And Mr. Gibson is quick to explain away Cynthia's defects, even when she brings trouble down on Molly, who is the emotional center of his life.

Cynthia's irresistable charm comes from her perfect social responsiveness, not from personal intensity. She admits she wants a lot of love "widely spread about." She wants worship instead of discriminating judgment. And she wants these things in a conventional, social way, even while she admits the existence of other values. She takes Molly as her protector because she must, but she loves Molly as a beautiful girl who needs help with her wardrobe. She accepts rebukes and money from Mr. Gibson because he expects her to, but she admires him as a witty man at ease in any society.

This attitude pattern emphasizes Roger's situation. Since he lacks the social appeals of the Gibsons, the integrity he shares with them is only repellent to Cynthia. He is not handsome, and so she dislikes his "goodness" as well as his learning. She accepts judgment from Mr. Gibson, but she will not let awkward Roger judge her on the same standard, which was not made for her. She lets Molly forgive her, but she is disgusted at the thought of Roger presuming to do so. His personal ugliness makes a total difference in her moral view.

Since Cynthia's function in the novel is her social attractiveness, Gaskell does not make her a villain, despite the grief she brings. Her enormous appeal might have spoiled her, but Cynthia manages to be neither egotistical nor cruel. Instead, her avoidance of deep feeling is understandable in a girl whose mother has rejected her from infancy and whose early friends have made use of her. Unlike Molly and Roger, whose moral and intellectual training is overseen by an affectionate mentor, Cynthia grows up without guidance and so learns to respond only to society's views. The result of exclusively social training is adaptiveness rather than integrity, as Cynthia's adult nature proves.

By appealing to the Gibsons and to Roger against their better judgment, Cynthia focuses the social dilemma of the scientific personality. Anyone who likes to pretend that reason is "lord of all" is even more vulnerable than other people when emotions have to be involved.

Gaskell highlights this idea by showing her scientists at ease only when they are associating with their peers. Her scientists frankly seek each other out in the midst of other kinds of social groupings. For example, parties at the Towers usually involve "dancing men," but "useless scientific men" are also sometimes there, and at last, Molly is included, too. At the Gibsons', Obsorne and Mrs. Gibson carry on the polite part of the conversation, while Cynthia meaninglessly dazzles all the men. In counterpoint, Roger and Mr. Gibson are scientific instead of polite, and it is their conversation which Molly understands.

When they cannot escape into each other's company, the scientists in Wives and Daughters try to manage some kind of social courtesy, though their struggles are often pathetic. Lord Hollingford, for example, longs for a handbook of small talk from which he would be overjoyed to memorize phrases for common use. Mr. Gibson defends himself from boredom with satiric rejoinders in normal conversation and then is ashamed of the confusion he causes.

Molly's frank and speculative gaze is rude, and her tendency to have opinions is pretentious in a person of her age and class.

When the scientific offender can be judged on some other basis, social tolerance is guaranteed. Almost anything can be forgiven a title, and so Lord Hollingford escapes the social punishment his ineptitude at "capering" would bring down on him if he were a commoner. Mr. Gibson is elegant and physically charming, so his abrupt way of talking is ignored. Molly is unfailingly sweet, so her tendency to observe can be explained as an awkwardly attentive sympathy.

But not all scientists can be fitted into a conventional social niche, even by a society willing to make allowances for individual quirks. Roger has no social position since he is a second son. Big, red and awkward, he has no physical appeal. Philosophical even in sympathy, he lacks conversational fluency and grace. Intense rather than elegant, his emotions are cumbersome in a drawing room. Lacking all conventional assets, he sums up the scientist in a social role. He has nothing else to offer, and so "poor old" Roger must resort to fame.

Sometimes poignantly, often amusingly, Gaskell shows how doggedly society struggles to redesign nonstandard individuals into traditional molds. Any scrap of a routine explanation will seem better than accepting something new. Still, Gaskell evidently had Darwin in mind for her theme as well as her hero. She provides Roger with a position in the normal community in addition to his reputation among his scientific peers, thereby suggesting that society will accept new roles, even if only as a last resort. This willingness is useful to everyone, since special people need to feel they have a social use beyond the intellectual companionship they give each other. Society needs to tolerate such people as interesting, if it is to avoid being left behind by change.

Roger Hamley's plight occurs in a twentieth-century female form in Elizabeth Gundy's Bliss. What does society offer a woman who is 6'1", hopelessly clumsy, and stricken with homeliness in her bone marrow? In Bliss, such a woman is treated to casual rape followed by "sex-starved spinsterhood," with dispassionate labels ranging from "big bird" to "giant" scattered along the way.

Does it help if her intelligence is as outsized as her

body is? At first, being bright seems to be just another
handicap for Gundy's Leona de Vos, since her Ph. D. qualifies her to compare the trivial conversation of her living
colleagues with the minds and emotions of the "great dead
men" she studies and respects. As a specialist in Rennaissance love lyrics, she has written a book about Herrick which
manages to be dull in a proper academic way. But she lives
in a "Shakespearean" cottage, and John Donne, in the form
of his <u>Songs and Sonnets</u>, keeps her company in the faculty
lunchroom.

  She is not shunned by her fellow faculty members, but
their persistently cynical attitude repels her. In tune with
Donne's celebrations of love and sex, she has no taste for
the satire which absorbs their conversation. She can "defend
herself" with "barbs and cleverness," as they do, but she
sees no reason for it. She is sickened by herself when she
falls into their kind of academic patter and dreads the possibility that she will end up fitting into their world, not because she wants to, but because she can.

  "The world of Associate Professor de Vos," as Leona
calls it, is worse because she is a woman. Some of the men
she works with are as socially awkward as she is--they are
"dwarfs," or boring--but that does not keep them from marrying. Thinking about the discrepancy, she concludes that
her size and intelligence would be more suitable to a man--
she seems like a "harmless" man to her students. But she
does not want to be a man.

  Over drinks and party sandwiches, she watches faculty
wives and speculates about how it would feel to be like other
women and "give pleasure to the world" in a completely
passive way. Wives know they have done enough when they
just "exist."

  In contrast, Leona always feels she must earn even
harsh forms of attention. She minds her manners, even with
her rapist, apologizing for slapping him and then answering
politely when questioned. Feeling "more normal" because a
later seducer has helped her enjoy sex, she hopes to show
appreciation by doing anything no one else would do for him.
She thinks she is offering some specific, physical gesture.
But he is her thesis advisor, and so it turns out that she
lives up to her bargain in an academically ironic form. Dedicating herself to his sensations during office conferences, she
becomes a "six-foot-one-inch geisha." Deserting Shakespeare
at his insistence, she ends as an expert on an "eighteenth

century madman" whom no one reads. When she leaves school as his "finest joke" in both body and mind, her isolation is severe.

As is typical in this kind of novel, Leona begins by wishing she could find a place for herself in the normal world. The academy accepts her, professionally, because of her mind, but she can take small comfort from a social context which considers everything so "ludicrous" that she fits in as a joke. Her academic lover believes he has been affectionate when he calls her a "lonely whooping crane." With the perpetual detachment of irony, he critiques her words of love instead of responding to them. His idea of a lover's murmur is to analyze Latin labels for the physical services she performs.

Clutching Donne, who did not consider the mind to be a defect in a lover, Leona tries to imagine other possibilities. She watches the maintenance crew and daydreams of packing her "good man's" lunch pail, patching his pants, diapering his kids. She likes the thought.

However, longing to perform normal acts is very different from actually being normal. Gundy works out the contrasts by interleaving Leona's story with chapters depicting Hazel, the typical wife who really does supply lunch and kids to the campus handyman Leona daydreams about.

By describing the lives of these two women in alternation, Gundy is able to establish parallels without the need to comment unduly upon her point. Hazel is a stunningly persuasive portrait of a conventional housewife. She watches lurid soap operas for the same reason Leona absorbs love poets. Hazel wins prizes for her baking in the same way Leona gains recognition for academic writing. Hazel drops by the bank, hoping to catch the eye of the money order clerk, while Leona assesses the availability of guests at cocktail parties. Hazel's surrender to the beauty of stores decorated for Christmas shoppers is similar to Leona's response to the world of nature--the scents of spring, the release of storms, the nostalgia of flowers scattered through an overgrown lawn.

At first, the two women seem too different for the parallels to have much meaning. But Leona falls in love with Hazel's husband, Bliss, and this connection causes their lives gradually to converge. Bliss and Leona begin to understand each other as he does odd jobs around her house. His sixth grade education saves him from academic irony, but his human responsiveness shows him how different Leona is from Hazel. In his frank way, he draws comparisons. When Leona envies his wife because he gathers mayflowers for her, Bliss points out that Hazel prefers plastic flowers. When he installs a fireplace for Leona, and she imagines him enjoying his fireplace with his wife, Bliss says they do not have time to watch a fireplace because of the TV.

Once the novel's pattern is established, it is a simple matter to carry judgment into areas not obvious to Bliss. Leona finds a worm on some vegetables she is cleaning and carries it outside rather than killing it. By contrast, Hazel makes her horrified little daughter watch while a hyena lengthily kills a wildebeest on TV. Bliss confidently drives out to a u-pick farm, knowing Leona will have gone out there in unspoken understanding that he "felt like a feed of corn." But Hazel bakes for her family only when she feels like it. Leona dreams about the daily routines they will set up when they marry and both go to work on the campus--she to teach and Bliss to work at maintenance. Hazel, who never leaves home except to shop or gossip, nevertheless refers to how "me and Bliss" work on the campus. While Leona fantasizes about love with Bliss, Hazel really is in bed with him, but his tender efforts do not distract her from her fantasies about the money order clerk and about new bedroom purchases from Sears.

A pair of ironies worthy of the most satiric professor emerge from the novel's understated details. A wife is normally thought of in terms of her husband--Leona thinks of the role in that way, too--and yet Hazel, as an actual conventional wife, evaluates every part of her world in terms of herself. Bliss is a source of income and a sexual tool to help her with her fantasies. Her children are mantraps to lock Bliss into this role. Wanting a new dress for herself, Hazel tells Bliss it will be a treat for Janie to have new mother and daughter dresses made for them. And when Bliss asks for a divorce, Hazel hauls Janie out of sleep to scare her into a convulsion as a way of making Bliss obey.

Such behavior is normal. Hazel fits smoothly into her social context, is well thought of by her peers, and feels good about her success in dealing with Bliss' behavior problems. Though she expands from a size 16 to a size 20 in the course of the novel, fat is not the handicap height is. She ends the book as self-satisfied as she began.

Hazel's attitude is justified by the reactions of society. Eavesdropping as usual on her party line, Hazel hears a description of the whole affair. At first, her friends and neighbors assure each other that Bliss beats Leona. Then, since they have never seen him be anything but gentle, they decide that he does not care enough about Hazel to beat her. And even though they know to the last detail how much Hazel overspends Bliss' income, they "know" Bliss is supporting both women.

They are conventional women gossiping about one of their own, so the response is not surprising. But Gundy's point is a larger one which becomes clear when the academic world gossips in the same way. Like Hazel's peers, the academics believe Bliss beats Leona. They also assume money is a part of illicit sex, though they have a better grasp of campus salaries, and so they decide Leona is supporting Bliss' family to buy his loyalty.

These groups could not be more unlike, in external ways. Still, they concoct an almost identical story, and so make Gundy's point clear. Brilliance in a woman makes an on-the-job difference. But in her privacy, she is "a woman" like other women. For all their education and their irony, academics do not know how to fill in the unknown details in any way beyond the single role.

Something is added to the women's role by both sets of gossips, however. The faculty busybodies are curious and fascinated, but they are also tolerant, as they would be with another man. And Hazel's friends easily accept the idea that Bliss' feeling for Leona is profound. They understand that Leona's looks are not important, since she has other qualities to offer.

Leona's special category is made clear at the Snodgrass Fair, which she attends in order to see Bliss in his own world. She gets directions from a man she thinks must be an "idiot," an irony which turns her into the freakshow, in her own mind. But Bliss' friends recognize her from her picture in the paper and treat her with kindly respect.

Her academic role does more than protect her. It makes her love story possible. Well paid, she can hire Bliss as a handyman. Used to dominating a class, she is able to take the initiative in love. Trained to analyze language, she learns how to talk with Bliss, setting aside faculty patter and speaking directly and honestly. When she realizes she has answered a simple question from him by sounding fashionably weary about Europe, she backtracks and admits that travelling "makes me lonely." Bogging down in the carefully fine distinctions she starts to make about her sensations when she sees him unexpectedly on campus, she tells him that he "looked nice."

Her new language is not a sign that her perceptions have been dulled by association with Bliss' sixth-grade speech. Leona's reveries and internal monologues remain Donnean in their meticulous celebrations. The difference between thought and speech emphasizes how much alike Leona and Bliss are, in the realm of feeling. Both are solicitous lovers. Both commit themselves totally. They both feel "greedy" about love. The same things make them happy. Both are compassionate. They wish for the same things. When an issue of conscience arises, they give up trying to decide which of their two consciences it is, or which of them has a complaint.

This emotional likeness allows Gundy to point out the special privileges offered by the academic role. People who are sensitive and individual have trouble in any social context. But when Leona goes to the faculty party where her story ends, she is folded into the group with the same automatic and shallow warmth they offer anyone. She is accepted casually, as always, with no invasive emphasis on her hesitations, her grieving, sensual memories, her excess physical and mental size, her clumsiness.

Bliss also is hesitant, grieving, sensual and clumsy, but he lacks the academic escape. Having no way to justify special treatment he is forced back into the conventional role which amputates his unusual sweetness. Hazel resumes her consumerism, "working on" a color TV as if nothing had happened. Bliss tries to maintain his sense of himself by living only as a paycheck and a father. But Hazel feels good about herself and is sure all she has to do is wait in order to prevail completely.

By using the literary convention of the love triangle, Gundy shows that the personality and value of individuals really have very little to do with their social situation. Society affirms normal behavior by cramming individuals into roles. Hazel is a consumer, Bliss is a paycheck and Leona is an academic. If someone is unusual, it makes no difference to society, since people will be seen and talked about in terms of roles, regardless of how they act and feel.

The movie version of this novel turns out to be a demonstration of how this social process works. The novel converts easily to the screen because Gundy's writing is visual and dramatic and her dialog is spare. Since the movie is able to follow the book closely, when it wants to, changes to plot and character can be taken as deliberate and therefore meaningful. Comparison shows that the movie rewrites the book just enough to swamp the characterizations and normalize the theme.

The pattern of change is inclusive. Hazel becomes a "mother" instead of a "consumer," putting her children first in sociological clichés which keep Bliss home. But in the novel, Hazel screams accusations so persistently that Bliss cannot even hear the doctor he has called to handle Janie's seizure, brought on by Hazel's violence. The movie's confrontation scene shows Hazel sweetly stroking Janie's head as she reasons with Bliss. But in the book, Hazel clops Janie on the ear whenever she shows signs of copying her mother's self-interestedness. When one such assault caused Janie to drop an armload of dishes, Hazel sends Janie to her room to give herself the peace to enjoy thinking about buying a new table service to replace the dishes she made Janie break.

The movie makes Leona more conventional by blending her characterization with Hazel's. The rewritten Bliss takes Leona to a wrestling match--an activity associated with Hazel, in the book. The movie shows Bliss urging Leona to wear her prettiest clothes on their date, but the original Bliss valued Leona for her inner qualities. He defended her right to chop off her hair, when it annoyed her, and to slather herself with lotion for sunburn rather than fuss over a clown-like look. In their last interview, the novel shows Bliss pleading with Leona to fight him about his decision not to see her again. She answers that she does not know how to fight. The movie erases her gentleness by borrowing from Hazel to make her fight. The revised Leona pounds on Bliss and kicks him. All trace of her academic identity disappears when she becomes inarticulate and screams mere noises at him.

Overall, the result of such changes is to deprive the central characters of what they offer in the book. The movie fits Leona into the "other woman" role of failed homebreaker.

Bliss is changed into the wandering husband who comes to his senses and humbly goes home and is grateful to be forgiven. Hazel is glamorized into the forgiving wife and patient mother.

People so conventional could never be used in a story that turns out as Gundy's does, and so the movie has to change the ending to fit the recast characters. In the novel, Leona is ignored by her students even when she is dismissing the class. But in the movie, she receives adoring goodbyes as she leaves town. The movie Leona embraces this normalized public role by pontificating. In the book, her sensitivity is shaped by the intense privacy of Renaissance love lyricists, but the movie cancels all that and makes her quote Emerson instead of Donne. She lectures herself as well as her students by saying, "when half-gods go, the gods arrive." The point is heavy-handed normality. Bliss, with his sixth-grade education, is no more than a half-god. He has gone back to Hazel, so Leona is free to resign from this small-town college, where the men are not better than she is. She must get a job in a big city university where she can find "gods"--men bright enough to overshadow her into the appropriate role.

In case the quotation is not enough, the movie's casting underlines the point. Leona is to go back to her professor-seducer. In the novel, Clem is persistently remote, satiric rather than emotional, and no more than "half" loving even when they are having "conferences" four times a week. But in the movie, Clem is played by Stacy Keach--a man so full of charm as to be appealing even when he plays villainous roles. Clearly, "the gods" do "arrive" when Stacy Keach appears, and the rewriting is complete.

In the movie, academics are public figures and objects of respect. Profound feelings are not part of that role. If Leona is going to violate her academic identity by falling in love, then she will automatically be transformed into "a woman." A woman must not make more money and must not be brighter, since those are the qualities of a man. Neither can she offer sensitivity, since women make demands. It takes a Hazel to relate correctly to a man like Bliss. Leona is going to have to search out Stacy Keach--a man who can overshadow her in the socially approved way.

The movie turns into a kind of case study in illustration of Bliss's theme. Socially normal minds really do rewrite character and ignore the quality of individual personality. They are not cruel on purpose--obviously, somebody admired Bliss enough to option it for the movies. Trouble comes from the fact that normal people look at roles and simply do not see any other way to think. Sensitivity is not a role. Gundy allows Leona and Bliss to recognize each other, much as Gaskell's scientists find each other in the midst of other kinds of groups. But the movie is the normal treatment of such people, and both are forced to disappear into whatever role is handiest.

This demonstration of the power of norms makes the movie valuable. Of course the mutilation of Gundy's extraordinary people is painful to watch. But the final contrast with the novel is a vivid display of the treatment unusual individuals receive at normal hands.

Though these three novels are so different, they have a basic point in common. Each focuses on the struggle of unconventional people to find some way of belonging to a society which is puzzled by them. In each case, unusual characters are in emotional trouble unless they can find the fellowship of unconventional peers. But even when they do find others like themselves, they still need a role so that society can deal with them.

Most examples of this kind of fiction resemble one of these three novels in either topic or approach. The role of the artist is specifically recommended as a way of rescuing eccentrics, in Zelda Fitzgerald's Save Me the Waltz. Fitzgerald's unusual heroine is bombarded by normalizing advice. Her social contacts remind her that she has a marriage and a child to justify her existence and fill her time. However, one of her friends recognizes her helpless eccentricity and suggests she cultivate some talent, since "an art would explain" her personality.

The choice of a "man's" profession by a woman is a frequently used device, since it sets up an automatically nonstandard situation for a woman without destroying the social connections already established for the role itself. Nineteenth-century American writers seem to have been particularly intrigued by women doctors. For example, Sarah Orne Jewett's A Country Doctor shows the development of a medical vocation in a young girl who is different from the start, and who inherits difference from her mother. The mother became an alcoholic because she found no social connection which would allow her to be herself. But Jewett's heroine escapes such a fate by modeling herself on the understanding male mentor who raises her. The novel is a study of the problems faced by the young girl, by her guardian, and by the community which has to put up with her abnormal tastes.

Elizabeth Stuart Phelps Ward was more interested in the adult phase of these questions. She rejects Jewett's assumption that love has to be set aside when women decide to develop their talents. Ward's Dr. Zay is a love story, showing what kinds of stresses social views of marriage put on independent women, what kind of man can win the love and trust of a professional woman, and how such a man should go about his courting.

When a woman seeks a man's role rather than his profession, the outcome is more chaotic. Even though she had no realistic resolutions in mind, Charlotte Lennox wanted to approach this topic. Satire solved her literary problem in The Female Quixote, though nothing solves the problem of a heroine who expects current society to deal with her according to the heroic standards of the chivalric past.

Diane Johnson's "guru" in Loving Hands at Home is equally disruptive. She is wealthy enough to gain the awe of people around her. She uses her social position to insist upon new definitions for topics such as love and marriage. Money has nothing to do with such ideas, really, as she admits privately. Still, she benefits from social acceptance, no matter how irrelevant the basis.

The female form of the guru role is an interesting topic in this kind of fiction. Muriel Spark's approach in The Prime of Miss Jean Brodie is very different from Diane Johnson's treatment. Jean Brodie deliberately hides behind the conventional role of schoolteacher while modeling herself on various dictators, especially Mussolini.

Brodie's impact is profound. Her students turn into a "group" while in direct contact with her. And some never escape her influence, even as adults. Her power is revealed in a political form when one of her disciples goes to war and is killed. Her spiritual dominance is revealed when her most successful follower substitutes Brodie for Calvinism, as a child. And when she tries to free herself from both these systems by converting to Roman Catholicism, not even a convent can exclude Brodie from her adult mind.

Intelligent women who lack Brodie's flair are Elizabeth Gaskell's concern in Cousin Phillis. Phillis is as addicted to learning as any man. This behavior is accepted by her parents, but it causes problems with outsiders. Even though he admits she is attractive, her cousin refuses to marry her because he does not want a wife who is smarter as well as taller than he is. The engineer her cousin works for is attracted to Phillis, but he is called to Canada and finds himself an equally attractive young woman there. This outcome shows that intelligence is not a crucial lover's quality, even to a man who appreciates it. For anyone else, it is a handicap. The wandering engineer is a "delightful fellow," and so he finds acceptance everywhere. But Phillis is not charismatic and does not know how to mask her intellect enough to marry. Since her only link to her community is as her parents' child, she makes up her mind to fit herself back into that role. Phillis' resignation shows how essential social connection is in this kind of novel.

Notes

1 "George Eliot's Zionist Novel," Commentary, vol. XXX (1960), p. 318.

2 The George Eliot Letters, ed. Gordon S. Haight (New Haven: Yale University Press, 1954-5), vol. VI, p. 290.

3 Zelda Austen, "Why Feminist Critics Are Angry with George Eliot," College English, vol. XXXVII (1976), p. 549.

4 Ruby V. Redinger, George Eliot: The Emergent Self (New York: Knopf, 1975), p. 472.

5 The Letters of Mrs. Gaskell, ed. J. A. V. Chapple and Arthur Pollard (Cambridge: Harvard University Press, 1967), p. 732.

7. ESCAPES

Henry Handel Richardson, The Fortunes of Richard Mahony
Barbara Pym, A Few Green Leaves
Diane Johnson, The Shadow Knows

others:
Diane Johnson, Burning
Elizabeth Gundy, Cat on a Leash
Elizabeth Wilson, Love and Salt Water
Elizabeth Hailey, A Woman of Independent Means
Nina Bawden, The Afternoon of a Good Woman
Elizabeth Jane Howard, Odd Girl Out
Firth Haring, A Perfect Stranger
Zane Kotker, Bodies in Motion
Victoria Mary Sackville-West, All Passion Spent
Doris Lessing, The Summer Before the Dark

It has become conventional to discuss the twentieth century in terms of social change. Everything from space flight to the sexual revolution is given credit for moving society itself across an irreversible dividing line. Normally, the change is described as being total, in the expectation that new values and new ways of living will entirely replace traditional forms. However, the conviction that people must fit in survives each transition, since only the specific pattern, rather than the idea that there is a correct way, is subjected to discussion and change. As a result of this convention, norms and roles continue, even though they are phrased in terms of temporary stages, as if international culture had been transformed into a preschool child.

Even if new roles are promptly offered, the sense of being in transition makes it possible for individuals to fall into separate patterns which are entirely undescribed. When official social goals are subject to change over short periods of time, individuals may find themselves choosing among the varying sets of rules insisted upon within their memory. Value structures may be identified by decades, and otherwise socially passive individuals who do not clearly fit into the general patterns for their brief generation may have an opportunity to choose. Society may be so involved in its web of contradictions that norms and values are questioned instead of being handed on.

Fiction growing out of this dilemma has developed several forms. In some cases, traditional values may be challenged so effectively that they appear to collapse everywhere at once. When the reasons for the breakdowns are diverse, a coherent new pattern may seem to be out of reach. In novels where change continues, people may protect themselves by following rules from the past even when they obviously fit neither the present situation nor the people in it. On the other hand, otherwise accepting individuals may find themselves going their own way in pursuit of a personal goal when society loses its power to advise them.

Social upheaval will usually not be interpreted as a breakdown if it comes from a specific event. When changes can be considered temporary, the people involved usually think in terms of growth or progress without noticing how different basic values have become. And by the time the community is able to settle back into a well-defined pattern which is considered stable, the people involved have become so accustomed to their new rules that they fail to notice the difference overall. Only when habits are compared to some unchanging group outside the community is it possible to see what changes have occurred.

Novels depicting this type of change may see the mystique of the frontier as a source of new values rather than as the more conventional escape into the anarchy of solitude. Gold fields in particular attract individuals from a variety of old worlds and from every conceivable social background. In an environment where even keeping clean is impossible, no existing social structure greets them. Each new arrival brings a different set of inherited values with him, so no patterns fall into place through being held in common. The result is a special kind of chaos, where individuals quietly maintain the convictions they think appropriate but also accept a public situation where no beliefs apply in general.

Because of the special problems generated by the literary history of the frontier in American fiction, it is necessary to look elsewhere for a novel which treats the frontier as a social process. Henry Handel Richardson's trilogy about Australia suggests its epic intentions by focusing on place and condition in the titles of its individual volumes.[1] When published as a whole, the work became The Fortunes of Richard Mahony, even though, like Jewsbury's Zoe, The Fortunes of Richard Mahony is really the story of two lives.

Appropriately to the individual titles, Richardson's three novels make vivid the struggle of a young country which offers nothing beyond the unremittingly physical life of men who do not think beyond gold. However, crowding and revulsion invade the monomania, and a fumbling society begins. By the time Melbourne is no longer impossibly remote, and Ballarat has turned from a district into a town, social order is established, and the frontier moves on or disappears.

With this group process as a background, Richardson follows the adventures of a man who refuses to leave his inherited values behind, even while he longs for the opportunity and freedom only a frontier gives. Richard Mahony begins life as an upper-class Irishman. He violates his family's values by training as a doctor--a kind of work so distressingly physical it barely counts as a profession, in the minds of his elegant peers. Drawn to the even more physical gold fields on Ballarat, he rejects doctoring, though he tells himself his reasons are not the traditional ones. As if to prove that snobbery is not involved, he sinks still lower, according to his family's standards--he opens a general store rather than get down in the mud where the gold is.

As a storekeeper, Mahony reveals the qualities he shares with his community. Like most of the miners, he remembers a more gracious former life, even though, typically, his sense of being above the rest does not invade his habit of drifting through the days and years. He prefers impulse and reaction to self-discipline and to making plans. While he dreams of golden futures, he is satisfied with being in luck's hands.

Mahony's elegant passivity would not have been revealed so clearly if he had stayed within the restrictions of the traditional society to which he was born, but the freedom of the frontier gives it room to reveal itself unchecked. The same trait in the working miners settles into their tendency to nurse large, sullen grievances while dreaming of enormous nuggets lying on top the ground. Similarly, Mahony sits in his shack and whiles away his time by resenting the lack of intellectual companionship and dreaming of writing brilliantly for medical journals, as a way of entering into the international community of minds.

Not recognizing his areas of affinity, Mahony identifies only qualities which offend him, in order to recoil into their opposites. With a bachelor's traditional contempt for a man who consults his wife, he marries a girl who is not through growing. What he values is the sixteen-year-old stage of mind and character, rather than the person. He hopes Polly will remain childlike forever and persists in treating her as if she were naive and helpless. Improvident as usual, however, he refuses to take on the kind of total responsibility which might have the effect of retarding her growth and keeping her in dependency.

Living in a country where gold is everything, Mahony cannot discipline himself even to keep reasonable accounts so that he can remain solvent. When luck comes from investments arranged by a friend, he assumes he is free to develop his impulsiveness to the fullest. He devotes himself to spiritualism, in reaction against the materialism which has released him from economic duty. He decides to travel like the gentleman his family background would imply, whimsically leaving his fortune in the hands of a dubious agent. Inevitably defrauded, he can barely force himself back to work.

He remains an excellent diagnostician when he is not paid for his opinion, but the work of doctoring has always seemed distressingly physical to him, and the responsibility even of diagnosis is unwelcome, when it is hired. With nothing to check his nervous distaste for work, for money, and for people whose lives are struggles, he gradually degenerates into a public spectacle.

Even when he is confined as a madman, he does not relinquish his views. True to his family, who are starving elegantly in Dublin, he throws his food at his attendants rather than eat it off a tin plate. His wife finally becomes his keeper so that he can die at home of well-fed apoplexy rather than of malnutrition in the strait jacket of a public institution.

If he had stayed within the rigid, upper-class poverty

to which he was born, Mahony might never have discovered what his true character was. It is only when he goes back much later to visit his mother and sisters that he can see what his life by birth would have been. He recoils from his family's self-repressive retirement without analyzing the traits of character which make it necessary. Tradition and social pressure keep the family personality in check in Dublin, but Australia's social tolerance gives it the necessary room to develop as it is.

Recoiling from Dublin, where he is no longer suited, and from England, which also turns out not to be "home," he returns to Australia, where the frontier tendency not to interfere means that no one but his wife puts pressure on his nervous irritability, his unrestrained impulsiveness, his refusal to accommodate even to circumstances he has chosen for himself, his snobbishness, and his distaste for everything practical. If it were not for the freedom of the gold fields, he would not have discovered these to be his traits. He would have remained simply "a gentleman."

Mahony's history is accompanied by parallel portraits which lift it beyond the merely personal and allow Richardson to show how demoralizing a frontier can be. Individuals who spontaneously embody the standards of the society into which they were born may not survive when traditional supports are removed, either through travel or through social change. For example, one of the Mahonys' friends becomes an alcoholic, while another drifts aimlessly in rags toward each new strike. Older relatives become willing and even surly dependents. Teenagers strip their family home of its money and abscond.

In the absence of social regulation, people are free to explain their behavior in any way they choose. There is no accepted legal and moral presence. A protesting relative or friend counts for nothing, since one person's opinion is as good as another's in an environment where no one expresses agreed-upon interpretations. The result is a society where weak characters are able to flourish in glorious triviality because they are adept at finding high-minded justifications for every new failure and whim.

Frontier freedom is not inevitably demoralizing in Richardson's view. Emerging from Mahony's wreckage is the very different pattern of his wife. As her story begins, Polly is so shy that Mahony takes pity on her sensitivity and does not even kiss her when she agrees to marry him. She ends as the "tartar of G. G.," having become notorious for insisting on her rights. So total a transformation would be incredible in most contexts. But on the frontier, where strength as well as weakness can be fully exercised, Polly's life makes sense as Richardson follows the inevitable stages of her unpretentious growth.

It does not occur to Mahony that Polly even has a character in the beginning. During their courtship, she writes letters which carefully agree with every opinion he expresses and encourage him to explain himself and his convictions without volunteering judgments in exchange.

This might have gone no farther than seeming a conventional womanly willingness to hold her husband's opinions and second his values, if Mahony had been a stronger character, but events reveal it to be a more genuine adaptability. When marriage deposits Polly in a spider-infested shack on the gold fields, she cries, like the child she is, but she also gets to work. Horrified by Mahony's bachelor dirt, she cleans fanatically. Isolated in the exclusively male community, she makes friends of the men.

Her ability to adjust herself to surrounding reality goes beyond such personal and wifely gestures when Mahony's business falls into disaster. His customers drift to other stores after he parades his enduring snobbishness at a public meeting. Pragmatically, Polly concludes that it will be easier to change Mahony's relationship to Ballarat society than it would be to change his personality. Therefore, she urges him to return to a profession which has status on the frontier. If people are dependent upon him for survival, they will put up with his eccentricities.

Polly's assessment of both her husband and Australian society proves to be correct. Faultlessly optimistic, she sees the best in people, as well as situations, and this social skill collects a flourishing practice for Mahony. Confronted with a man whose alcoholism is destroying his family, she emphasizes how gracious he is when sober. When her brother's wife dies, and his unbearable grief causes him to recoil from the children who resemble her, Polly takes them into her own home as a blessing to herself, since she is childless.

When behavior cannot be transformed by looking on the bright side, Polly copes through a sympathizing emphasis on extenuating circumstances. Her sister makes a laughing stock of herself by appearing on Ballarat in a hoop skirt, but Polly responds to Mahony's scornful laughter by reminding him that her sister has always been in the forefront of fashion trends which everyone copies later on. When her best friend from girlhood becomes loud and crass, Polly sees the change as a side effect of the woman's generous willingness to work in a tavern as a means of supporting her bankrupt family.

When neither hope nor sympathy seems to be enough, Polly calmly develops an attitude of her own by placing kindliness above fastidious judgment. It is a shock to discover that one of her friends has "forgotten herself," but she decides that no one could think of such a sweet and gentle person as "bad." She does not tell Mahony what she knows, partly because he would be affronted and partly because of his conventional preference that she be ignorant in this area for the same reason that he tries to keep her from knowing anything about their finances. She realizes "books" take a very different attitude, but she sets literature aside by deciding that "life and books" have "nothing in common." In "books," her friend's behavior would always be condemned. This helps her see how little value books have since, in life, she could never reject her friend.

Polly's ability to take a fresh look at actuality and to accept it on the most favorable level possible is the basis of her success on Ballarat. By the time her brother John goes into politics, she has turned into a "remarkably handsome woman" whom no one but Mahony attempts to patronize. John turns to Polly for help with his campaign. Her political advice proves to be as sound as her help to Mahony was in establishing his medical career.

The difference in the way the two men react to Polly's growing social importance is a key both to their different destinies and to Polly's genius. John frankly seeks her help and follows her advice, thereby launching a career for which the only setback is death. In contrast, Mahony persistently patronizes her. He objects when she changes her name to Mary, as more suitable to her adult status. And he perceives her only as the "prettiest woman on Ballarat," rather than admitting how influential she has become. Increasingly pettish as the slightly controlling pressure of poverty disappears, he resents Mary's careful efforts to help him even while he admits how skillful she is with people. Although his fastidious ego demands the support of public respect, he shrinks from community involvement, even after Mary's efforts have gained tolerance for him as a person of importance. No sooner has she secured their position in the now flourishing life of the town than he insists on leaving Ballarat. Their return to England is the first of the impulsive moves which plunge them into ruin.

As it turns out, there are limits to Mary's adaptiveness. She accepts Mahony's character defects when she is not able to talk him out of his "faddiness," but she cannot adjust to the ancient and deadening gradations of English society. To her, English snobbery is "fudge," and Mahony realizes she will never adjust to English society since she meets everyone's eyes too "frankly," her gestures are too "spacious," her voice too "resonant," her warmheartedness too "innovative," her opinions too "blunt."

Mary can be of no help whatsoever in so alien a world. Her lack of contact with the community leaves Mahony entirely free to make his own mistakes, since he is "presentable," by English standards. Believing that medical work will be more tolerable in England, he purchases a practice which is flourishing, by English standards, only to discover that Australia has influenced his views of what an adequate income is. In his usual impulsive recoil, Mahony laments that he refused to take Mary's advice about Ballarat. Silently agreeing, Mary grimly promises herself that he will never have the opportunity for such regrets again. She vows to prevail, in future, regardless of the cost.

Mary's decision to assume control of her life makes it possible for her to disentangle herself from Mahony's inevitable downfall, although the changes are at first a matter of attitude rather than action. As long as their mutual income is provided effortlessly through intelligent investments arranged by a friend, Mary contents herself by beginning to live her own life. She fills the house with constant society, and when late-arriving children interrupt her life as a hostess, she still keeps in active touch with her closer circles of friends and family. Mahony emphasizes the change in Mary's attitude by angrily withdrawing into an addiction to spiritualism. Increasingly frank about her inflexibly pragmatic view, Mary scoffs at his gullibility, thereby letting him feel justified in turning toward the traditionally self-effacing and mindlessly soothing femininity of a neighbor who lives apart from her husband.

Since their investment income does not depend on Mahony's behavior, Mary is satisfied with protecting him from an absolute recognition of how badly he is behaving, just as she protected a similarly wandering friend in the past by refusing to mention the question of fastidiousness or sin. But when he takes control of their investments himself and impulsively ruins them, Mary can no longer afford to ignore his increasing capriciousness.

Both Mary and Mahony have trouble accepting the idea that he must start earning their living again. Mary rebels against existing like "hermit crabs" and sneaks visits from her friends while he is out of the house. Mahony violently resists her efforts to advise him since he remains convinced that women are by definition inexperienced and therefore helpless in business matters.

So long as Mahony provides even a subsistence income, he is able to defeat Mary because she continues to operate within the framework of traditional marriage roles. He sells their homes without telling her, and she submits. He insults his patients and becomes hysterical at her protests, and she has no way to protect him. He transforms himself into the village idiot by maundering in unfinished sentences to strangers, and she can do nothing beyond closing her mind to his half-concealed aberrations. Only when he entirely stops working and burns the few papers which remain of their investment portfolio does she feel justified in setting aside convention absolutely and taking charge in an open way.

Mary's coping procedures are very different from Mahony's. She calls for help from old friends who have had enough self-control to prosper, and these contacts gain her an appointment in the post office. It is in her professionalism that her personal qualities come into their most vivid contrast with Mahony's. She faces the same distasteful work situations which have always troubled him, but her determination is uniformly strengthened by details which provoked him to weaken eagerly into defeat. Living on wages and becoming a government agent means the end of her social position, but she does not hesitate. Working to someone else's schedule is humiliating, but she refuses to be distracted by the self-pity of her previously overindulged children, who whine for her to stay home and entertain them. Serving strangers turns her into a public curiosity, but she maintains the courage to face them by reminding herself that she is supporting her family reliably and using her own skills to do it. Posted to Gymgurra, she is horrified by a crossroads so remote that there are no lights, no trees, and only broken cans and bottles for gardens and grounds. Nevertheless, she goes.

Even after her transformation into a worker beyond the edge of civilization, she continues to receive the rewards she always has attracted. When pleas are not enough, she demands help from now highly placed former friends. The new role gains admiration for her as a "loyal advocate" and a "great fighter." Having to compete without special privilege against people who are young and male, she becomes "unblushing" in her official statements. The habit of outspokenness leads to an increasing readiness to insist that she is grateful to be "not a man." Assertiveness turns her into a "by-word," but it also results in her being admired as a "pair of eyes" and as a "dam fine woman."

Mary's reaction is far from typical, even on the frontier. One of her sisters-in-law responds to an incompetent husband by clinging to her children and taking money from anyone who will support her. Another sister-in-law defrauds her stepchildren in order to keep more money for herself. One of her friends hides inherited money in the hope of outlasting her wasteful and improvident husband. Another turns to drink to escape an unhappy marriage.

Mary could have followed any of these patterns if she had wanted to. Or, if her energy made rank dependency impossible, she could have used a conventional woman's way of sustaining them in poverty by working as a governess, fostering children, or running a boarding house. She has done all these things socially, raising other people's children, teaching them along with her own, and taking in a constant parade of family and friends.

Any of these standard possibilities would guarantee a kind of respectability, and Mary does consider each of them since she has always enjoyed society. But she likes her friends for themselves, not because of the status they provide. And respectability for its own sake has never influenced her, since the abstract fastidiousness which has governed Mahony's life scarcely even registers on her value system. In addition, none of the obvious solutions would relieve her of the aspects of wifehood which most madden her. She would remain dependent upon other people's whims and she would never become financially secure.

Having gradually learned to analyze and judge behavior and to act on what she sees, Mary makes her choice on the basis of values which make sense to her. She rejects any role which will not relieve her of dependency. Neither the understanding nor the choice could exist in the more traditional society of England. But since she has transplanted herself to a frontier, she is able to become independent, when she decides to be.

That her choice is as free as Mahony's is shown by her last stage. In conventional terms, everything about her situation ought to divide her from society. She has voluntarily moved beyond the outer edge of civilization. She commits herself with an unwomanly wholeheartedness to nonstandard work. She demands the right to be a madman's keeper. Such behavior is possible in Gymgurra since, there, it is not analyzed in the usual way.

On a frontier, courage and resourcefulness are what count. Anyone can see that these qualities are central to Mary's personality. Therefore, even after she has broken all the rules, she still receives the only social reward she really cares about. She lives her own way, she pays her own bills, and she is still able to "marvel" that, in spite of everything, new friends "spring up" everywhere around her.

Twentieth-century England seems the embodiment of everything inflexible and dead, in Richardson's use. Nevertheless, its structure can be interpreted in an entirely different way when its function is not limited to forming a contrast with more recently established social worlds. In A Few Green Leaves, Barbara Pym looks behind the well-behaved surface of a "typical" English village in order to suggest that late twentieth-century English society is in a state of continuous revision which would do justice to the most dynamic frontier.

At first glance, Pym's novel is deceptively absorbed in the structures of the past. The narrative is filled with the terminology of tradition, the characters are identified by role, in a medieval way, and ancient rules of precedence are not only present but discussed, in an effort to guarantee that they apply.

These qualities make the book seem almost a period piece, until their implications have been analyzed. The "villagers" know all the conventions and speculate constantly about how their present activities fit in. These discussions show everyone's willingness to perform expected roles. They also emphasize the gap between the past, current views of the past, and the present situation.

The result is not at all what the villagers intend. They are constantly puzzled as to how traditions can be applied, and they frequently startle themselves through haphazard references to rules from the past which contemporary situations show up as long dead and sometimes foolish to begin with. Since Pym's characters have such decent intentions, their difficulties are amusing, rather than tormented, and so her treatment of perpetual cultural discrepancy has an unexpectedly cheerful outcome. Maintaining a cultural tradition outside its context in time turns out to be reassuringly impossible. As a result, failure turns out to influence individual lives in a casual rather than heroic way.

Pym makes the problem vivid by organizing almost all voluntary action around some symbolic involvement with the past. Both local and academic history are enormously important in daily conversation. For example, the fact that the manor house has been empty for years does not cause local gossip to die out. It only confines the usual stories about the family to the repetition of long-remembered details. The rector disappears even farther into the past by searching for the ruins of a deserted medieval village and pondering seventeenth-century burial rites. The young doctor might seem to break this pattern since he specialized when he was in medical school. His specialty is geriatrics, however, and so he, too, is primarily involved with the old.

Even the novel's central character has a deceptive surface involvement with tradition and with the past. A new arrival in the village, Emma watches carefully to see how others act, and she writes to a former lover instead of putting her energy into making new friends. This behavior can be interpreted conventionally, although in Emma's case, it springs from an entirely different source. The old friend she writes to is more a colleague than a lover, and one of her reasons for feeling lonely in the village is the lack of anyone who accepts her in her professional role. As an anthropologist, she is "supposed" to maintain detachment and observe only from a distance. On the same basis, her absorption in almost tribal roles results from scientific training rather than from the obedience to tradition which troubles the rest of the community.

Using an anthropologist as her main character allows Pym to add a modern touch to the identification of characters by their functions rather than their names. In a purely literary context, this procedure must always seem Chaucerian. But Pym's addition of a newer science which uses the same labeling technique demonstrates the simultaneous truths that change is inevitable and that social forms persist.

If only the surface level is inspected, Pym's labeling does seem to create a static world. Concealing their personalities behind their social niches, and dealing with other people as functions rather than as individuals, everyone, including Emma, recites a litany of rules and tries to think of ways they can be made to apply. It is traditional to walk through the manor park on Low Sunday, and so the "villagers" turn out obediently. Spotting a flash of purple in the undergrowth, they dutifully discuss violets. Watching them assemble, Emma uses the "time honored" method of pulling her curtain slightly aside to make room for gossipy peeking. Miss Vereker, who used to live at the manor house, is held in "superstitious veneration" as the "favorite sister of her nephew's dead mother." Daphne, the rector's sister, "comes running to do her duty" as hostess and housekeeper for Tom when his wife dies.

Despite this universal willingness to fulfill conventions, each category turns out to be subject to contradiction when it is applied. A traditional right to collect firewood on the manor grounds is worrisome since the "villagers" now have central heating. The wad of purple in the weeds turns out to be a discarded candy wrapper rather than spring flowers. Regardless of her professional obligation to remain detached, Emma joins the walking party. Miss Vereker realizes that her nephew's willingness to do almost anything to serve her applies only "in theory." And Daphne is unable to decide whether she has protected her brother from the "grisly fate" of being pursued by the women in the community, or whether she has "stood in the way of his happiness" by preventing him from remarrying after his young wife died.

Daphne's resigned uncertainty at realizing her behavior is subject to equal and contradictory "bromides" serves as a clue to Pym's treatment of continuing traditions. Many of the novel's conventions are accompanied by contradictions of equal historical power. As a widower, for example, Tom is obligated to maintain a discreetly distant manner toward single women. Being carefully remote toward Emma is a problem, however, since she is the daughter of one of his old friends, and this second category requires him to be solicitous and welcoming. As rector, Tom is the "most important person" in a village where there is no "Lord of the Manor." On the other hand, he is also a "younger brother," which reduces his rank in the eyes of his sister. As a professional, as well as an old friend's daughter and a single woman, Emma's participation in the community takes a time-honored form. Her education compels Tom to wonder conventionally about her ability to type. At the same time, his personal interest in the seventeenth century forces him to recast the question by hoping she may be an expert on Elizabethan handwriting.

Other members of the community deal with contemporary situations by figuring out their historical equivalents, as well. Miss Grundy, for example, is suddenly confronted by a "modern young man" with "long hair" and a "brightly colored coat." The only way she can fit such a spectacle into her reality is to assume she has "seen something" out of the past. And Emma's mother, Beatrix, is able to devote herself to academic studies "with a clear conscience" only after her husband's death leaves her in the always respectable role of war widow.

Even when modern roles are not grafted onto the past, they are usually dealt with as if the weight of tradition were behind them. For example, Tom feels that it is "subtly wrong" for a woman to wear a hat with trousers, even though he is not sure what it is that makes him think so. Emma observes that one person dominates the other when two people live together and procedes to analyze examples. She decides which of two elderly unmarried women is dominant. Then she assumes that an older sister dominates a younger brother. The sometimes vague older doctor is probably dominated by his wife. She dutifully speculates about the possibility of an "equal partnership" in the case of two more modern couples, although she "suspects" the wife is dominant in at least one of these cases. The hierarchy of examples is traditional, but precedence within the pairs significantly is not.

Some modern roles are so irrelevant that they almost turn into satire. For example, Graham is the "perfect picture" of an "academic" writing "in rural surroundings," even though there is something "comic" about his self-consciousness in the role. Caught by the agent in an empty cottage on the manor grounds, Emma takes the role of a "bossy, caring woman" to escape accusations of trespassing. Insisting that all ladies can arrange flowers, Adam Prince explains that watching them do so was what he liked about being a clergyman. And the newest addition to the "newcomers" group turns out to be one of the oldest members of the community.

The villagers become so accustomed to such contradictions and irrelevancies that they are likely to react badly on the rare occasions when anyone seems to take some standard role at face value. For example, the florist, Terry Skate, tells the rector that he cannot do flowers for the mausoleum anymore since he took the job in the first place because he was a "church person" but has now "lost his faith." Tom is "stunned" and finally laughs at such an explanation. Similarly, the young doctor follows his medical school's recommendation of frankness and tells one of his geriatrics patients she is going to die. He is "indignant" when she responds by asking him if he believes in life after death. Emma decides she is not successful enough in her role as an "other woman," so she puts on a brighter and more fashionable dress. As a result, Adam Prince greets her with the "equivalent" of a "wolf-whistle," and Graham, for the first time, begins to "kiss and fondle" her. She decides the change was so successful as to be a mistake.

In addition to these unplanned reactions, traditional wisdom is sometimes deliberately rejected. Emma is sure that "the helplessness of men" is a "mistaken and old-fashioned concept." Observation of community rituals convinces her that Freud was wrong in thinking "every human activity was related to sex." Tom, also, draws contrasts between what he sees and what everyone believes. He irritably insists that having some "pious bromide at the ready" is an "outmoded" view of the clergy.

Scientific training as an observer sometimes raises doubts about both folk and scientific knowledge. The young doctor, for example, admits he does not really want to lengthen his mother-in-law's life, even though he takes the watchful care of her which his profession demands. His training builds on a normally conventional nature, however, and so he thinks in terms of modernized clichés, whenever possible. Where the old doctor responds to all female complaints by recommending a new hat, the young doctor knows hats have not been worn for years, and so he recommends a new hairstyle, instead. When Daphne confides that she wants to share living quarters with an old friend, he does not wonder if she might be justifiably bored by housekeeping and irritated by a brother who often forgets she is even human. Instead he speculates about lesbian relationships.

Confusion rather than enlightenment turns out to be the result of scientific training when the personality it is added to remains conventional. The young doctor is perfectly aware that a man like Adam Prince cannot be thought of as having a "bedtime," for example, but he goes on and tells Adam, a professional gourmet, to have a warm-milk drink at bedtime anyway. Confronted by Emma, who refuses to fit into his "prearranged categories," the doctor is "puzzled," rather than intrigued. Since his reactions silence him, Emma asks the questions, leaving him with feelings of inadequacy at the role reversal. She is the one who makes the usual suggestions--the rash on her hands might come from stress or from washing dishes without rubber gloves. The doctor has nothing to offer beyond mentioning Emma to his wife in hopes a sympathetic and womanly listener may provide the traditional cure.

Quandaries such as these show how limited scientific training is unless the mind receiving it is able to go beyond conventional views. Emma, for example, follows the common pattern when she is bored or feeling uncertain. She decides to watch other women so that she can take flowers to a funeral in the "approved fashion." She approaches a former lover's wife with traditionally mixed emotions. And even her professional behavior seems to follow conventional forms. Toying with the idea of doing a professional analysis of the village, she becomes excited about the possibility of studying "The Role of Women in a West Oxfordshire Community." But when she begins to assemble her observations, her list focuses on male roles, with women hidden behind associational designations such as sister and wife, or included repressively as "spinster" or "sad character."

Such a discrepancy between title and outline might suggest that Emma has fallen victim to a double load of cliches since her profession is as rule-bound as her society is. But this type of categorization turns out to result from observation rather than preference, in her case. When purely personal questions are involved, she responds so differently that her private value system is clearly separated from her social manners and her professional categories. She insists it is "humiliating" for people not to speculate about her relationships. When she has become interested in Tom, she is "disappointed" in him for speaking conventionally when they are not in the public eye. Since she is convinced that he is "essentially" rather than conventionally good, however, she persists in speaking to him "honestly" rather than falling back into social "murmurings."

Tom's politely empty responses turn out to be a bad habit based on his uneasiness about his role rather than being a genuine reflection of his personal value system. He notices a stranger in the empty church, for example, and automatically thinks, "Can I help you?" He does not say the conventional phrase, however, since it strikes him as being both "too trivial" and "too profound." His performance of a funeral is similarly dualistic. He speaks the traditional words so "beautifully" that Emma is moved by the ancient ritual. On the other hand, he refuses to include one of the hymns chosen by the family because its "wormlike submission" offends him as inappropriate. His behavior as an employer follows the same pattern. His organist is "not a believer." A musician, he works for the church because he appreciates a "fine instrument." Tom deals comfortably with this reality. He knows religious fervor will not induce the "splendid sound" he wants for the Christmas ceremony, and so he insures "grandeur" by the appropriately secular method of giving the organist a bottle of apricot brandy.

Because his profession is more traditional than Emma's, Tom's role is more heavily bound to the past. And since he is a "nice" man, he tries to avoid disappointing a society whose members seem to consider him as ancient as the church. The result is that he has more trouble than Emma does in speaking "honestly." He automatically begins a conventional explanation, for example, when she asks why he did not marry again. But his clichés make him sound "feeble," and he permits himself a more genuine agressiveness by suddenly accusing Emma of never marrying. The return attack allows them to laugh together and move beyond what is conventionally called correct.

Having discovered the genuine individuals behind each other's half-concealing politeness, Tom and Emma begin setting rules aside with increasing confidence. Emma decides fiction may leave more room than scientific articles do for a writer who wants to remain an individual, and Tom begins quoting Emma's social revisions along with his own. It is essential that they share this value since their personal pasts are active proof that neither of them will marry simply for the sake of the role.

Conflicting and irrelevant assumptions continue to surround Emma and Tom, while they work out their private agreements. Emma's mother dreads being a "conventional match-making mother," but she is nevertheless anxious about her daughter, who seems to be "in danger" of turning into an "old-fashioned spinster" without either poetry or painting to justify her "high-minded dowdiness." Tom's sister decides to continue meddling, too, since her move to Birmingham has not turned out well. The "helplessness" of men must be maintained in order to justify her plans to move back into Tom's house, and so she insists her brother's mind never moves beyond medieval fields and villages.

These conventional maneuverings seem inevitable and absorbing to the people engaged in them. However, their obviousness does not make them binding on people with something else in mind. While mother and sister invoke tradition, the subjects of their scheming inspect a display of "antique" medical and household items. But Emma and Tom are laughing together in a shared present rather than working their way imaginatively into the past.

Both the method and the fact of their separation from the past is symbolized by the private conversation they hold in front of the "antique" display, while the village watches. Tom suggests that Emma should give a professional lecture about the community, relating their present life to their history. But then he immediately rejects so traditional a topic by adding that she could "even speculate on the future."

The unpretentiousness of the suggestion is as important as is the escape it implies. Neither patient submission nor bitter defiance is required in a society where rules are chaotic enough to disconcert even the people who do live by them. Anyone wishing to be different will emerge undamaged from such ineffective norms. It is a social structure which leaves Tom and Emma free to explore their shared unusual values without sacrificing their amiability. At the same time, it offers the less independent community an equivalent freedom to remain absorbed in a traditional tangle of narrow and outmoded interpretations as they react to social change by feeling neither resentment nor control.

Diane Johnson's treatment of American social breakdown uses a very different literary format. The Shadow Knows is a book-length monologue by an introspective, hesitatingly independent woman who is driven out of conventional roles by her determination to be fair and accurate in social judgment and to be responsible and ethical in personal behavior. The combination turns out to be not normally available in late twentieth-century "North Sacramento," if it ever was, anywhere. By the time "N." completes her inspection of standard roles, Johnson has documented, not "society," but a conglomeration of contradictions involving statistical norms, pragmatic reality, individual emotional yearning, personality theories about normality, social class differences in value systems, and persisting traditional assumptions about what is theoretically "right."

    Johnson bases her commentary on the experiences of a woman who plunges into the conventions of a woman's role before she has gained enough maturity to consider whether or not they apply to her. Since she married in her teens, she did not immediately realize that being a wife and mother does not describe all of her capacities. By the time she notices that she is acting from a script, that the phrases of "wifely obedience" and "motherly concern" are "parroty," at least when she says them, she has four children and no marketable skills.

    Her first response is to look for a description which will provide a better fit rather than to reject categories altogether. Different types of mothers accumulate as she talks about her life. She originally assumed she was a "responsible mother," even though she knows other people consider her to be "careless and lazy" like a "welfare mother." She goes back to school, like other "restless mothers." And her dreams of being like the "beautiful mother in a diaper ad" do not prevent her from turning into a "neglectful" and "resentful mother." Finally, visualizing herself as a crime victim, she knows the newspaper phrase which will wrap up her life: "mother of four."

    Her understanding of herself as a wife undergoes a similar transformation. She discovers her husband to be an "antagonist" and begins analyzing their marriage in the language of criminal law and employment contracts. Insisting she will do what she wants to since her husband is not her "judge" and she is not his "employee," she begins to look for "female power" beyond that "legally" granted through marriage. "Adultery" is an immediate and obvious recourse, although it turns out to be no more than a way station toward other preestablished categories. Becoming a "divorced woman" severs her automatic social connections, and so she is transformed into a "woman alone." Estimating her future, she sits in the dark like an "old discouraged person" and foresees herself withering into an "anecdotal forlorn old crone."

N. does not turn away from categories altogether simply because wives have to pay their way with a "female brew" for which she does not have the "recipe." Instead, she resorts to the intensely personal role which is a standard alternative. Relieved to find she has the very different kind of "female power" which makes her lovers "pant and quiver," she becomes involved in a "serious love" with one of her husband's colleagues.

Working hard to separate the roles, N. "arms" herself against the "blinding, acquisitive dependence" which Andrew triggers in her by consciously defining wives and lovers. Andrew's wife is like all the other wives who fill "all the pretty houses," and so N. analyzes Cookie as a pattern. Cookie believes what people tell her, and though this means she is "a little stupid," it also gives her an advantage over N. Cookie knows the "reliable myths," and so she knows what to expect. When Andrew "looks within," it seems to N. that he falls in love with her because he has discovered his true nature. But Cookie has the "correct information" and knows "a little of this" is to be expected from men in their forties. Cookie loses weight, colors her hair, cries, and "tries." And since she is a "soap-opera" wife, she will get to spend the rest of her life sitting among the "beautiful objects" inherited from her own and Andrew's "mamas" in the midst of Andrew's riches.

N. knows that love is an equally "old story," and so she analyzes it in a parallel way. Her time with Andrew is like the Arabian Nights or a "dime novel." They know each other better than "husbands and wives" do. They "open their lonely hearts." Andrew discovers that he "can't live" without N., and N. confides to a dubious friend that Andrew is "perfect." She knows it is the "oldest and wryest" "secret female joke."

The source of the joke's humor is complex. It insists that lovers' privacy is so intense and personal that statisticians, marriage counselors, sociologists and "old wives" know nothing about it. It also assumes that N. really has found the "one real one" among all the "fake" men.

Part of the time, N. believes this, and yet doing so involves considerable editing of what she knows. She is convinced that the "true" Andrew is the one who comes to her "suffused with love." When her friend Bess insists that Andrew "never leaves" Cookie, N. admits there is also a "staid" Andrew who does return to the wife he "loathes." But Andrew says the "fact" is his love for N., and she is willing to explain his moving in and out as the result of his being "stuck down" by his promises and habits, and by other people's view of him.

Seeing only the lover half of Andrew makes N.'s view as much a joke as the convictions of the "statisticians" are since each involves suppressing half of Andrew's motivation. When his Christmas present to N. is a brief note cutting off the love affair, she convinces herself that Cookie "made" him write it, since he could not have done something which so betrayed his own nature and N.'s beliefs about love. But when he calls to apologize, two other truths become apparent. For one thing, he reveals that he, not Cookie, is to blame for the cruelty since he wrote the note himself and "meant it" when he wrote it. And by insisting that N. must surely "understand," he documents an intention to stop and start their love affair in the same way he alternately walks out and reconciles with Cookie.

Since such dual roles are traditional for men, choosing the "real" Andrew turns out to mean accepting him as normal for his type. While N. thinks he has left Cookie, rather than merely moving out on her as usual, she feels proud of him, as she would of a child who had done something "brave" and grown-up." The feeling shows that she has judged him, which is a contradiction of the "confidence" love implies to her. It also demonstrates her gradual belief that "grown-ups" must move beyond standard roles since conventions are, at best, no more than "tolerable substitutes" and "practice matches."

N.'s own transition into the "grown-up" stage is marked by her description of herself in a category which sets aside the various forms of the "woman's role" which have entangled her. Her absorption with Andrew makes her a "loony professor" of love, rather than a lover. Her belief in his individuality and difference involves her in a "disproved theory" which keeps her from being an "expert professor" of love. The images themselves are negative, but they underline N.'s determination to move outside the conventional options offered to women. She is determined to get a Ph.D., even though the divorce court insists that a "woman and a mother" is not entitled to a "turn" at self-development.

Johnson surrounds N. with different kinds of women in order to define the "woman's role." Osella is a huge black woman who does N.'s "work" while N. lives with Gavvy. That is, Osella cooks, cleans, babysits, entertains, flatters, takes Gavvy's side mindlessly, and even holds him on her lap. She is the "inspiring" and "terrifying" embodiment of a "superfemale." N. is convinced Osella is "mad," but N.'s opinion turns out to be irrelevant since Osella ends up as a stripper headed for a Las Vegas booking. Her fat and her passivity make her a "brilliant woman," and "little bitty" N. cannot bring herself to "sit down sisterly" with such a woman's image.

Ev, who lives with N. as her "dear friend" rather than her maid, embodies the extent to which N. loses her "powers" by divorcing. Ev is so scarred, battered, cut and burned that she seems like "Queequeg." When she finally dies, of a beating, or of pancreatitis stirred up by New Year's Eve, or of "love," her mother dismisses the confusion as her "nature," since Ev has always caused "problems."

That a mother could react in so cool and judging a way shocks N. Since she loves Ev very personally, and identifies with her as a fellow victim, it is disillusioning to find that Ev can be so easily diminished into a type. This difficulty is clearly with N. rather than with Ev's mother, as the behavior of N.'s other "dear friends" demonstrates. N.'s "dear friend" Bess denounces her as both selfish and lucky, and her "dear friend" Andrew fails to speak up for her when his partner handles the divorce for Gavvy. All these reactions reinforce the official courtroom opinion, which is that N. has chosen to stop being a wife and so she must accept the remaining alternatives of typist, telephone operator or nursery-school teacher.

N.'s sense of victimization coalesces around her conviction that what the police see as random nastiness is really a concerted plan to kill her. Conventionally, Gavvy is the person most likely to be her murderer, but it is her "dear friends" whom she really suspects of meaning to do her in. This dread is appropriate to their unselfconscious alignment with a society which deprives her of her personality. She does not have a personal name, since even her lover calls her "N.," and when she finds herself alone in a room, it seems to her the room is empty. She repeatedly thinks of herself as a table, a straight-backed chair, a stone, a rock, a picture with the face left blank.

However, society's depersonalizing view prevails only so long as the victim cooperates. N. decides to take a stronger position, as she meditates on Ev's death. Her own view is that Ev was a gentle and tolerant woman, even though Ev's doctor sees her as a rowdy drunk and the police see her as a career criminal. When Ev's death is officially described as being "natural," N. agrees in part, since she bitterly accepts that victimization of women like herself and Ev is common. Nevertheless, she begins to see the police inspector as a "force of darkness" who pretends to be a "force of reason." When this shock is added to her earlier discovery that fairness does not exist in family court, she concludes that "justice" is not a concept which can be trusted.

Justice and rationality are central issues for N. They are an organizing point of reference for her throughout her monologue. When she was trying to accommodate herself to the "ordinary misery" of mothers with small children, she read detective stories compulsively, because of their reassuring "morality" and "order." Once she notices that the "rules" help and protect men, but otherwise are full of "malice," she invents a "Famous Inspector" with whom she can carry on a running quarrel about society. As she refers various social situations to him and concocts his answer, she notices that he is "censorious," "sententious," and lacking a sympathy not because he is reasonable but because he is "a man." Because her goal was reasonableness and truth, rather than simply a man's view, she begins to reason for herself.

Since N.'s reaction is conventional, she gets into additional trouble. Deciding that the Famous Inspector is not fulfilling his duties, she takes over his role for herself. Forgetting that she prefers mercy to justice, she begins watching people "mercilessly." Her contact with the law has demonstrated that being "absolutely sure" is a routine substitute for being "absolutely right." Insisting on her own perceptions is congenial as a procedure, since she is constantly in search of "principles" which will apply.

Nevertheless, the result is unsatisfactory. N. has to recognize hate as the enduring link among people, if she is to embrace the "reform view" of "True Love" which Andrew's conventionality forces on her. And she has to believe that womanhood in the form of Osella, "sex goddess" and quintessential female, is her would-be murderer.

Both interpretations are too obviously partial to be maintained. Except for love and friendship, which she tries to keep as absolutes, N. has always done her thinking in broader terms. She is never sure whether or not the events of the novel have happened, regardless of whether they are physical facts, such as pregnancy, miscarriage, vasectomy, murder and rape, or whether they are emotional facts such as declarations of love or hate and offers of aid or explanations of betrayal.

If facts are so hard to establish, interpretations are obviously even more unsure. "You never know," N. says in the beginning, and she documents the difficulty throughout her monologue. You cannot tell by listening whether Osella is "shrieking" or singing. You cannot tell by looking whether God is "stupid" or "benign." You do not know whether a policeman will think Gavvy's being the district attorney makes him more or less likely to be a criminal. Equal evidence accumulates around both "passion" and "prudence" as the basis on which life is organized.

Rejecting standard views worries N., even after she knows they are too partial to be accurate. When she discovers that other mothers have handed on different "lore," she worries that she has given her children only her own opinion, which she knows society considers to be "deviance and eccentricity." She does not want mothers to be "various," even while she admits that they are. As she faces the fact that her "view of life" is "alluring and blandishing" because it is different, she feels like a "witch," luring victims. In other words, she clings to her preference for order at the same time that she recognizes her own contribution to the social chaos which is everywhere about.

Emphasizing this self-defeating aspect of limited views, Johnson includes modern as well as traditional forms. Bess, for example, governs her life on the basis of the psychiatric principle that everyone is estranged from their "inner mysteries." N. does not accept either the idea or the aggressive behavior which results, and so she converts the system into randomness by dismissing it with the hope that psychiatrists must be "right" sometimes. N.'s own fascination with linguistics is equally irrelevant to actual situations. It fills pages with arrows as she works on research papers, but it cannot teach Ev to speak standard English. N. is sympathetic to both the wish and the failure when Ev stops going to classes since she cannot learn the rules of English and feels they are not important since she is "speakin it, ain't I?"

The failure of all types of rational systems to describe or govern behavior causes N. to resort to her "inner eye." The less narrowing mystical vision which results allows her to see herself as a "monster of egotism" for demanding that her mind should understand the entire pattern of life. If she can treat her own craving for "principle" as no more complete a world vision than her study of linguistics is, she can avoid the despair which comes from roles.

Her problem is that she does not "approve of acquiescence." In a last outburst of the "elation" which false conviction brings, she decides she understands everything. She turns away from her earlier suspicion that biology and law are out to get her and converts her situation into a group of personal relationships instead of roles. Osella is her murderer, Andrew is her betrayer, Bess hates her, Ev has deserted her, Cookie has displaced her, Gavvy has replaced her. This new theory works so well in the abstract that it leaves her mind "blank" and her behavior "unwary." As a result, she is raped in her own garage.

Personality is the last of the partial patterns which N. must learn to set aside. Thinking everyone is nothing but an individual is as dangerous as insisting on seeing nothing but their role. The clear patterns which "satisfy your soul" always produce "badness" since they leave their believers unwarned against options. Wondering who raped her, N. runs down the list of possibilities again, this time adding meaninglessness in the form of "some madman neighbor." Finally able to conclude that it "doesn't matter," partly because it involves only her "bottom half," and partly because any interpretation is as senseless and as likely to be right as any other, she is at peace.

The only way to cope is to discount all social theories, as well as official and traditional roles. N. "feels better" once she realizes she can change her attitudes and views. Her old habits dying hard, she starts to downgrade herself as "spiritually sly" and then remembers and backs off from categories and describes her learning in more careful and neutral terms. She will "look around" instead of insisting on her own labels or believing blindly in the structures already supplied.

Since this new perception comes at the very end of the novel, The Shadow Knows does not go on to show a redesigned life. Such a structure is appropriate to the idea, since freedom from formal programs is the point. As the title suggests, inspecting the genuine and secret emotions lying behind events teaches individuals how false rules are and how delusive a hope for order is. Anyone able to tolerate the resulting chaos is left free.

The mental and social helplessness of individuals who cling to theoretical systems and prearranged categories is a continuous element in Diane Johnson's fiction. Other examples do not always achieve the muted hopefulness finally offered in The Shadow Knows. Burning, for example, ends with a similar suspension of social judgment, but the emotional result has more an air of confusion than of a strong-minded rejection of partial views. Unrelentingly hilarious, the novel documents the inapplicability of every social agency and intellectual system, from the fire department, which watches fires burn in order to discuss them on the TV news, to the psychiatrist who drugs his patients and then escapes to the safely emotionless plants in his greenhouse out back. Even though the novel does not finally offer alternative guidelines, it constitutes a recommendation overall in that conventional categories are too ridiculously irrelevant to hurt. The characters fling themselves into the resulting chaos with such bewildered gallantry that their lives are intense and personal, regardless of their situations.

Social breakdown is not always the basis on which individuals escape from roles. Elizabeth Gundy's Cat on a Leash shows a rather conventional wife choosing to desert her role, even though her husband is not abusive and she has no clear alternative in mind. He tries to lure her back from the subsistance living which is all she can provide for herself, and he tempts her with the "wonderful" children whom she has deserted. Being wonderful does not make the children "anything special," in her mind, however, and so they do not constitute a sufficient justification for a role she has no wish to accept.

Unspectacular resistence to convention also underlies Elizabeth Wilson's Love and Salt Water. This low-keyed novel depicts the mutual toleration and the social adjustments which make it possible for individuals in various love, friendship and blood relationships to choose lives which suit them. Since Wilson presents the procedure as an ongoing series of decisions rather than as a single act of commitment, choices sometimes fall into step with the norm and sometimes they deviate. Such flexibility is easier because neither personal contacts nor society in general tries to tell individuals how they "ought" to live.

Freedom inside a social structure is sometimes paid for, rather than granted. Elizabeth Hailey's A Woman of Independent Means follows its heroine from puberty to death in order to document the basis of her independence. Financially independent and strong-minded, she becomes committedly self-reliant when death deprives her of her natural advisors--her mother and her first husband. Accepting the price along with the independence, she admits that she makes mistakes, is often misjudged, and sometimes alienates conventional people whom she would rather not have offended. She discovers that society changes its opinion, with the passage of time, and that the rules are not the same, at different stages of a woman's life. Because she wants to get things right, she take responsibility for planning everything, from warding off her husband's bankruptcy to writing her own obituary notice. It never occurs to her to question the price, since the rewards of independence are full self-development within a social milieu.

The discovery that social norms are advisory rather than required is an international route to independence, in the twentieth century. English examples include Nina Bawden's The Afternoon of a Good Woman, in which a dissatisfied wife undertakes the conventional escape of running away with a lover. At the last moment she decides on the less conventional step of simply running away without depending on a man. This choice allows her to see that her lover was meeting her out of duty to his role, and she is rewarded by the realization that her independence has freed them both.

Elizabeth Jane Howard's Odd Girl Out depicts independence as somewhat more disruptive. Since the young heroine is independent of sex as well as social roles, she makes love to both the husband and the wife of the married couple who take her in during a stressful period of her life. What she is doing, in her own opinion, is trying to get them both to love her. In explaining lesbian arrangements to the wife, she points out that she can do everything for her except present her with a baby. However, since she has become pregnant by the husband, she turns out to be able to offer a family baby, as well. Her freedom from rules causes the husband and wife to become more conscious of what they are doing and what they think their marriage means.

American versions of these ideas tend to be more categorical, although the result is similar. Firth Haring's A Perfect Stranger, for example, focuses on the struggles of a traditional wife and mother to find some reason for her existence, after her children are in school. She tries bricking herself up in a walled garden, and then takes a lover. Only when more routine recourses fail does she think of depending on herself and developing her own talents.

Similarly, Zane Kotker's Bodies in Motion places the story of a young marriage against a background summary of all the standard reasons for conventional responses, from urban overcrowding and suburban isolation to primate behavior and patriarchal religion. Tactfully, every explanation does apply. But since there are so many programs for development, no one pattern takes overwhelming precedence, and so the characters are left reassuringly free.

Some writers who see multitudes of categories may consider them as binding, when they apply at all. However, the importance of any one role may be weakened if it is dealt with as a developmental stage, rather than as an absolute. In her All Passion Spent, for example, Victoria Mary Sackville-West allows her elderly heroine to escape from social confinement now that she has patiently fulfilled all her roles. And Doris Lessing, in her Summer Before the Dark, insists that, although the woman's role is crushingly confining, its prison-like narrowness is required only of the young. Older women, if they want to, can move on out of the caretaker role.

Underneath an enormous surface variety, all these novels emphasize the essential freedom of twentieth-century individuals to go their own way. If they are conventional, they will find that traditions have carried over from earlier times. If they want change, they can fit themselves into new beliefs. If only variety seems to leave them in touch with themselves, they are entirely welcome to refuse both old and new beliefs. In this kind of fiction, they are not even asked to come up with alternatives. They are simply free.

Note

1 *Australia Felix* (London: Heinemann, 1917); *The Way Home* (London: Heinemann, 1925); *Ultima Thule* (London: Heinemann, 1929).

8. THE SUM GREATER THAN THE PARTS

Dame Rose Macaulay, The World My Wilderness
Doris Lessing, The Golden Notebook
Dorothy L. Sayers, Gaudy Night
Margaret Drabble, The Realms of Gold

others:
Doris Lessing, "Our Friend Judith"
Nina Bawden, A Woman of My Age
Nina Bawden, A Grain of Truth
Barbara Pym, A Glass of Blessings
Margaret Drabble, The Ice Age

  Writers who see twentieth-century upheavals as a social opportunity sometimes take an aggressive approach. When a society has lost confidence in its own values and in its ability to enforce its views, optimistic individuals may think of it as being less restricted, rather than as breaking down. This attitude is particularly available to English novelists, perhaps because England's longer history has included several episodes of extensive social change.

  Fiction based upon this principle begins by emphasizing diversity. Differences may be presented as new forms of old alternatives, as in Dame Rose Macaulay's concern with splintering religious views. Or new freedoms, such as the educational opportunities for women which intrigued Dorothy L. Sayers, may seem to demand a revising look at how people expect to live. But regardless of whether change is supposed to have come from war or disillusionment or a rebellious underclass, it leads to a new way of thinking about society. Writers working on this topic do not suggest a replacement value system. Instead, they redefine old terms and propose new unities in order to provide a more inclusive view which leaves variety intact.

  The violence of twentieth-century politics is so frequent a contemporary topic that the aftermath of war is an obvious entry point for writers who wish to deal with social reorganization and change. Dame Rose Macaulay's The World My Wilderness, for example, gives every sign of being a war novel. The ruins left by bombing raids are a constant presence in every part of the London scene. The natural setting includes them as the narrative lists the flowers and vines which have begun to turn them into natural gardens. The financial world is represented by the businesses which have moved elsewhere and by the thieves and fences who have replaced them. The prewar social function continues in the form of picnics which substitute for restaurants and rough offers which perform the prewar function of affectionate courtship. The spiritual world remains in the litany of bombed churches, in the celebrations of hell which the street children perform, and in the terrors of a clergyman gone mad from fire.

Because France was occupied instead of being bombed, the results are different there. The cities and the countryside remain beautiful, but the people have become less so. Orderly behavior is considered to be "collaboration" and is therefore punishable by unofficial death. Only furtive lawlessness is respectable, while dirt and violence have become replacement virtues.

In addition to these different kinds of evidence, Macaulay places several of her characters in a position to speculate about the results of war. The children who grew up under the occupation regard the "maquis" as a kind of club. An observing psychiatrist remarks that they continue their criminal behavior out of a habit which turns them into "unfortunate automata." "All" young people have turned to stealing, according to a returning English soldier, and one member of the British privileged classes moves beyond contemporary observation to wonder to what lower-level moral standards will descend after yet another war.

At first, such drastic views seem justified. Postwar rationing curtails English life and the black market beggars the French. Scholarship and the humanities have been "trampled" in England, while family life has been disrupted by the slaughter in France. But behind the glib and constant current explanations, older patterns from a less simplistic frame of social reference are also applied. Both patterns are consistent in themselves, and so, even in the war generation, they vie with each other as fashionable or old-fashioned ways of accommodating to situations which have always been present and have always been officially deplored.

Barbary embodies the civilian aspect of the war, since it is her constant frame of reference about herself. At seventeen, she is sullen, dirty, almost illiterate and has become a liar and a thief. Her widowed mother has cooled toward her because she is a member of the group of resistance workers who killed her stepfather on the grounds that he collaborated during the war. In Barbary's mind, such behavior is justified by the fact that her social life is the maquis and the ruins are her "spiritual home." She has been raped and "questioned" by the occupying army, and though she later lures her rapist into a trap to be killed by resistance workers, this single, personal revenge is not enough to quench the universalized hate and fear with which she confronts authority.

Barbary has identified herself so totally with the maquis that her mother feels justified in sending her away "for her good." Helen's grief and anger over the murder of her husband make it difficult for her to offer any emotion to Barbary. Several less personal reasons also point toward the same solution. For one thing, Barbary's father, Gulliver, was appointed as his children's guardian when the parents divorced. Also, he is a lawyer and therefore accustomed to dealing with criminals such as Barbary. In addition, he is a "very civilized man" who might hope to exert a wholesome influence on a teenager around whom images only of savages and jungle creatures collect.

From Barbary's point of view, the move has almost nothing to do with the explanations which surround it. In London, she joins what she thinks of as the "resistance." But since Londoners do not have the excuse of hating a foreign ruling group whose authority is based on victory in war, the individuals who repopulate Barbary's personal maquis are perfectly standard members of the perpetual London underclass. She continues as usual as long as she is content to steal from her father and from people on the street. But when she wants to be more English, and steal from shops, she is warned that she will have to wash and curl her hair and dress neatly, since store thieves must look "respectable."

This conflicting net of categories continues when the family goes on holiday to Scotland. Barbary steals from her aunt in her usual way, but the aunt blames the new maid, as English traditionally have done. When Barbary steals from a neighbor, her uncle asks her to talk to him in private about her situation. Talking is against the rules, to

Barbary, who remembers being interrogated by enemy soldiers. As a psychiatrist, her uncle notices how out of touch she seems, but he does not blame the war. To him, all women and girls are "a little mad." Although they cannot hope to be "cured," they can sometimes improve enough to "pass muster," if compared only to other women and girls. He would like to help Barbary reach this stage, even though she has two strikes against her, coming from a "dissolute mother" as well as growing up outside the reach of English respectability.

There is some justification for blaming Barbary's genes as well as her hormones. Coxy, the London maid, warns Barbary against "trusting" the street people she meets and insists she cannot be "too careful." Hearing herself, Coxy then silently revises the phrase, recalling that Barbary's mother was never willing to be "careful enough."

Since Helen provides part of the environment as well as the inheritance, she constitutes another conventional explanation of Barbary's uncontrolled behavior. The possibility that divorce produces sociopathic children is an idea of long-standing fascination. When Gulliver sees his daughter Barbary for the first time in seven years, he reminds himself that she has come from "the enemy camp." He would like them to become friendly, but he suspects she prefers her mother too strongly to be interested in him.

Since Gulliver is the image of "law and order, honesty and reputability," it is appropriate that he should provoke Barbary's most conventional set of responses. Admiring him makes Barbary "uneasy." But there is one aspect of his life which she easily understands. He has remarried, but Catholic France considers Helen to be his wife still, regardless of divorce. Barbary is not a Catholic, but she nevertheless pleads for her father's "woman" to be sent away and her mother to be summoned back to her place. Since Pamela is just as quick to call Barbary a thief as Barbary is to dismiss Pamela as her father's "chère amie," Gulliver's war imagery turns out to be entirely appropriate on the conventional, domestic front.

By the time Barbary's situation has been established, Macaulay has included a variety of explanations for her behavior which are accepted as sufficient by the characters who believe them. Madness, femaleness, parental immorality, bad company and divorce all are perfectly reasonable contexts for such a child. War is simply one more proposed rationale for behavior which is by no means new.

Macaulay further limits the usefulness of war as a social explanation through her characterization of Richie, Barbary's older brother. If anything, Richie's situation should be worse, since he received a soldier's training in "dreadful deeds." But he takes after his father in being civilized, and so his reaction to "messy, noisy and barbaric war" is to recoil more strongly into "exquisite niceties."

Regardless of his orderly instincts, Richie does cheat the customs, as all his friends seem to do. And like Barbary, he assumes smuggling is his generation's reaction to war. However, the topic comes up because he has discovered that his mother is entertaining herself by forging twelfth-century Provençal poems. Describing himself as a "gentle, civilized, swindling crook" lets him excuse his mother, even though he disapproves of her lack of a "scholar's conscience." He is more interested in being tolerant than in being judgmental, and so he is satisfied with finding her unruliness "a little odd" since she is "middle aged." Helen reminds him that scholars have always forged and cheated and destroyed evidence, so her behavior is nothing new. She qualifies his view of his own generation by adding that his English stepmother would never cheat, even though she is "a long way under forty."

Their effort to fit their own and each other's behavior into current conventions about war ends when they charmingly wander onto other topics. Since both of them are interested in conversation more than they are in making any particular argument prevail, noticing holes in the theory is enough. Richie is too civilized to make himself unpleasant about re-creations which accurately reflect his mother's character and talents, and Helen is too tolerant to be exasperated by qualities her son shares with his father. The result is an exchange of affection not available to people who insist upon the rightness of a single view.

So many theories about behavior are proposed that the beliefs of characters seem almost as individual as their experiences are. Because of this diversity, their efforts to live according to their beliefs produce often unexpected results. When the psychiatrist complains that Barbary has run away rather than talk about her problems, Barbary's father agrees with Barbary that people are better off not "chattering" about their affairs. Coxy begins worrying about Barbary and asks her policeman nephew to watch out for her. The result of her kindly intentions is that Barbary is caught stealing and almost kills herself by falling as she runs away. When she was Gulliver's wife, Helen routinely left the house when "bores" were invited to dinner and at other times filled the house with gambling men, though Gulliver did not participate. Gulliver accuses her of rejecting "decency and integrity" along with him, when she leaves him. Even though they both remarry and have new families more suitable to their own habits and views, Helen's glamorous independence makes it impossible for Gulliver to stop loving her, in spite of all his disapproval and outrage.

Such problems are the result when individuals of clear views regarding what is "for the best" try to enforce their opinion outside their own mind. To Barbary, Coxy is an "informer." To Pamela, Helen is an "intellectual courtesan." To Gulliver, Barbary is at best "bohemian." And despite their efforts to classify and explain what right behavior is, they have no effect beyond hurting each other's feelings and seeming rigid and in the wrong.

Even when they seem to have a topic in common, these judgmental people flounder since their definitions are at cross purposes. Most of the characters in the novel include "hell" in their system. Yet sharing so traditional and so fully defined an idea does not really give them common ground. To the mad priest, hell is London's bombed churches. To Barbary, hell is her mother's absence. To Pamela, hell is the presence in her house of her husband's first wife.

Macaulay uses these scattered views as one approach to her theme. Each modern version of "hell" is a recasting of one single aspect of a concept which has a complex form. Characters who insist upon a narrow vision inevitably disagree, since partial views leave out too much that is also relevant and equally true.

The opposite approach to common ground is more likely to achieve its ends. As Helen sits in her French home, talking with her son, Richie, her lover, Lucien, and the abbe, her friend, the group seems to be hopelessly at odds in what they stand for and in how they live. Yet their readiness to admit their different standards is itself a basis for enjoying each other's company. All of them are willing to be "courteously oblivious" to aspects of their individual relationships which might cause them to reject each other. And, they look for attitudes they can share, rather than assuming they are alike in any way. Amusingly, they find they can all call themselves "reactionary" if they accept enough different definitions of the concept. Thus, they share a pleasant evening, during which no one is either shocked or hurt.

The social usefulenss of tolerance and diversity is expounded directly by Helen, as she talks to her son about her life. In addition to the men by whom she is surrounded in the course of the novel, she explains that she has always had women friends, and they have never bored her. She likes people who are clever, curious and funny. So long as they are "first hand," she does not care whether or not they are cultured, Philistine or bawdy. Only a lack of genuineness causes her to draw the line. She explains that she has found such women everywhere--Paris, London, the universities, and "even" Ireland. Richie listens thoughtfully and moves to the opposite extreme. Like his father, he prefers his women "ladylike." But he has his mother's tolerance, as well as his father's "civilization," and so he enjoys his mother's charm while he quietly discounts her ideas as they might invade his own life.

The value of accommodation as a social response includes more than amiable conversations, as the final conflict between Gulliver and Helen proves. When Barbary almost dies in London, Helen admits to herself that she has sent the child away out of grief for the husband Barbary's group has killed. Barbary's accident reminds Helen that losing her daughter will not bring her husband back. Without abandoning her mourning for a man she admired as well as loved, she accepts the reality of the past and plans to take Barbary back to France. Gulliver refuses to release his daughter, insisting that Barbary must be civilized. However, he admits that he may simply want to keep a connection with Helen, whom he cannot quit loving. When persuasion is useless, Helen attempts accommodation, pointing out that they have no real reason to pretend they do not care for each other. She suggests they meet occasionally in France. Gulliver's "honor" makes such a solution seem "ignoble." His rigidness and righteousness leave Helen with no basis for negotiation, and so she has to give up on love and resort to hate, instead. She explains that Gulliver is not Barbary's father and therefore has no real claim.

Gulliver's reaction is painfully "civilized," in one way--he asks what phrase he should use in reply to Helen's belated news about her daughter's parentage. But emotions are not "upright" and "incorruptible," regardless of Gulliver's preferences about behavior, and so he descends to the same distresses any man would feel. He bitterly wonders whether she betrayed him emotionally as well as physically, and in an unexpected way, the answer he provokes betrays him more painfully than the long-ago and unsuspected infidelity did. Remembering, Helen explains that she may not have cared at all for Barbary's father. But she certainly did not love him as she loved Gulliver before he began to find her so annoying. Helen's calm statement that Gulliver's rigidity drove her away is a more painful rejection of his personality than any physical betrayal could ever be.

Because her values are so strongly oriented toward indulgence, compassion, adaptability and affection, Helen wants to feel that she has not been cruel, even as a last resort. She does not ask to be "forgiven." Instead, she speculates that her revelations will have "killed a tiresome love," so Gulliver may be glad to know details which are painful in themselves. But emotional flexibility is not one of Gulliver's qualities, and so Helen's attempt to review his situation in terms of her own values merely describes herself and leaves him still uncomforted.

The direct confrontation between these two approaches to judging underlines the importance of accommodation. When Richie says that Barbary and Pamela should be able to live "side by side" even if they cannot be "matey," he is describing his own cool version of Helen's more passionate intensity. In fact, Barbary and Pamela cannot get along "without fighting," since both are rigid, self-righteous and quick to feel betrayed, although they are entirely different from each other in every other way. On the other hand, Richie is able to get along with either of them. He appeals to Barbary to feel less tragic, even though their father "takes living up to." And he reminds Pamela that divorced people do meet, so Helen's presence need not be hell.

In each of these relationships, the worst of the suffering comes from a "high-minded" refusal to deal with things as they are. Unfortunately, people who insist upon their own version of "honor" bring grief to others as well as themselves. The maquis felt justified in killing Helen's husband, and "incorruptible" Gulliver agrees that their violent act was justified by Maurice's collaboration.

For Helen, Maurice was "the best" of life. Since he is dead before the novel starts, it is her list of his virtues which is important to the book. He never betrayed anyone. He made the best of things. He was "on terms" with everyone including victorious invaders. He was "genial" and "accepting." His "only fault" was amiability.

Because he was the only person who shared her view of life, Helen is temporarily shaken from her own form of "collaboration" by his death. She allows herself to retaliate. However, she eventually realizes that she has betrayed herself by accepting even provoked anger. Determined not to lose her values, as well as losing a man she loves, she says she does not mean Barbary's betrayal of her and Maurice to matter anymore. She has made up her mind to accept Maurice's death, as Maurice accepted his country's defeat in war. And she will take Barbary back to France with her, in the same way Maurice adjusted himself to German "occupiers."

When Helen informs Barbary that it is possible to love people without trusting them, and in fact, makes sense to do so, she has survived Macaulay's central test for coping in a diversified society. Emotion which fails to take the loved one's nature and personality into account is really an attack, regardless of the way it may be described by the person feeling it. Similarly, withholding love from people who live according to a different personal code is an act of enforcement, as surely as murder and betrayal are. Therefore, Helen finally sees that she will have to accept Gulliver's need to deal in hate, and Barbary's addiction to sneaking and conspiring to betray, if she is to return her own value system to the center of her life.

Unjudging love is so exceptionally unusual a social value that its results to Helen are unexpected and awkward in some ways. Her ability to accept and make allowances for other people's "maxims" turns her into the focal point of a remarkably varied social group. Since she understands people rather than "forgiving" them, she becomes an "enchantress" from whom no one is ever "quite free."

Macaulay uses Helen's entrapping charm to represent accommodation and inclusiveness, just as she uses war to symbolize an enforced cancellation of diversity. When the two value systems come into direct conflict, there will be destruction and deaths. Nevertheless, in the long run, war succeeds only in driving variety underground, since nothing can abolish it.

In their wide-ranging, cultivated conversations and in their eclectic backgrounds, the characters in this novel document the long history behind what otherwise might be mistaken as a temporary aftermath of a specific political breakdown. Modern psychology insists that repression leads to disease. "Western civilization" segregates the forgiven from the damned. And even pagan gods, who were not at all absorbed in "justice," would refuse "help" when they were offended.

To make her twentieth-century Helen as compelling as the original Helen was, Macaulay creates a woman who is inflamingly capable of love. Then she defines the term in its largest sense. Love is the ability to accept everyone along with their own values and formulas. Equally important is the fact that it is the result to herself which Helen seeks. She is determined that she can know other people's reality without judging them for it, and she can admit their shortcomings without accepting defects as helpful or good.

By remaining "carelessly attached" and "fundamentally detached" in this way, Helen is able to take what pleasure there is, while remaining uninterfering, unthreatened, comfortable, interested, and, sometimes, amused. She demonstrates the value of unforced eclecticism to herself and to the diverse people around her who have in common nothing beyond their willing acceptance of her kind of love.

Bombed London and occupied France seem almost peaceful in comparison to the multifaceted disasters dealt with in Doris Lessing's The Golden Notebook. Considering the impact of public disorder on personality, Lessing includes war as only one element in a spectrum of activities representing the current social environment. In each case, the goal is to establish order so that life can continue. But the separate topics defeat themselves by fastening on limited aspects of a social disturbance which is universal.

In order to suggest that every intellectual system is too narrow to organize the actual world, Lessing divides her material into several "notebooks," each of which is dedicated to a particular pattern. The organization dealt with in the separate notebooks is necessarily limited, and within the area covered, basic principles are broken down into paired ideas, each half of which again divides and subdivides until all hope of inclusiveness is lost. Finally, only splintering and fragmentation are generalized. After she has demonstrated how inevitable it is that standard methods will fail, Lessing reconstructs her material into an alternative approach to "form" which is inclusive enough to heal her characters' psychic wounds.

Politics is one of the major elements in The Golden Notebook. In her workmanlike way, Lessing divides the idea into a theoretical and an applied form. Each of these halves includes its own version of the same division. And all the divisions which result are further modified as they work themselves out in individual lives.

The theoretical aspect of politics is represented by the Communist Party. The heroine, Anna, joins the Party because of her impulse toward belonging to an "anonymous whole." Inevitably, according to Lessing's pattern of analysis, Anna has two kinds of experience as a Party member. In Africa, membership gathers up people who have "nothing in common." Still, they accomplish a kind of involvement since they have been "thrown together" by a local war. In England, on the other hand, there is a great sense of mental unity which is fostered by nonparty members who insist on believing that "a communist" is only one thing. Despite this common front against outsiders, however, Anna discovers that her work assignment for the British Communist Party is divisive. Because she is a writer, she is expected to bring Art into line with Party goals.

Anna's writing about her political experience highlights the inner defects of the Party in both its African and its British form. War is the practical outcome of the African experience. But Anna rejects her successful novel, Frontiers of War, because its "nostalgia" lends a false glamor to battle. War implies that conflict is a matter of frontiers and soldiers. In fact, Anna knows that shooting is only one way people work out definitions of abstract issues. It is not even the best way to discuss international imbalance, internal analysis and debate, and personal impulses toward cynicism and cruelty.

Even more important is the fact that war is a delusion

in itself since it creates a state of crisis which encourages a false impression that unrest is localized and temporary. Only the willfully blind believe that a simple win on a battlefield will end political debate. After the shooting stops, there still remain real conflicts between classes, colors, generations, economic levels, political parties, marital statuses, social conventions, intellectual levels, and sexual identities, including masculinity, femininity, heterosexuality, homosexuality, virginity, celibacy, and promiscuity.

When Anna writes about the British Communist Party, it demoralizes her in a parallel way. Her duty is to apply the politics of "the masses" to art by arguing against individual talent. Anna is able to maintain her integrity and still embrace a "Twentieth Century Anon," in theory, since medieval art produced undeniable, unsigned glories. However, when she takes this idea off the lecture circuit and out of the Middle Ages, efforts to apply it in a current way embroil her in the same conflict with diversity which defeats her treatment of war. The officially "healthy" novels which are submitted to her for editing are pathetic banalities. The politically "unhealthy" personal letters of transmittal are alive with literary power. Anna would like to collect and publish these letters because of their intense and personal vitality, but doing so is a dangerously "anti-party act."

Whether politics produces soldiers or authors, it accounts for only a small part of the activities of both nations and individuals. Political ideas which lead to war can force a temporary uniformity, since less basic questions are set aside in the face of a struggle merely to survive, but in the long run, war is too simplistic to be anything other than distracting. Doctrines which rely upon tools which are themselves destructive bring about their own defeat. Even outside war, politics aggressively intends to deny personality and individuality. Cutting people to a common pattern is no better than killing as a way to organize them into groups, and so politics in The Golden Notebook proves its social uselessness.

Lessing turns to love to represent the opposite extreme. As she did with politics, she establishes chains of categories which divide and classify this most private basis for connection between people. Some relationships are worked out individually, without the help of rules. Inevitably, the freedom of such intensely individual extremes offers little in the way of models which can help other people find patterns which will work for them. On the other hand, many relationships do fall into age-old patterns. When this happens, what seems like personal feeling turns out to be a ritualized performance of family and sex roles. Privacy is lost under such unintended predictability.

Countering this defect by suggesting that love is unstructured in its nature, Lessing presents a range of love connections which are recognized but not approved. Those interested in sexuality may turn to incestuous or homosexual love. Nonsexual friendship between women is seen as "twin old-maidhood." All such relationships take place outside the standard rules. For this reason, they offer little to an official understanding of society. However, the fact that they are admitted even while they are disapproved helps to establish the limits society places on its view of love.

One form of essentially emotional love can be included inside a social pattern, since it is considered to be a standard option. Anna is involved in a love affair with a married man. She thinks of her situation as an absolutely private matter. In fact, however, the role of the other woman is so routine that its terms and outcomes have been fully charted. The role begins with an intensity which makes it overwhelming. This feeling produces an involvement which leads to a longing for permanence. But permanence, by definition, is not part of the plan. Wanting the love affair to last may lead to divorce and remarriage, after which the traditions of marriage apply. Or else, a break up may resolve the bitterness of loving without having control over the loved one. These alternative endings feel very different to the participants. Nevertheless, the outcome is similar, in terms of love, since both mark the end of the affair.

If love is to have meaning outside the feelings of the two people who are directly involved, some kind of social framework is required. Marriage is supposed to perform this task by organizing love and making it reliable. Its orderly nature should put an end to the painful ups and downs which less official love involves. As it works out in fact, however, marriage merely removes the high points of feeling without relieving the lows. In her appallingly vivid analysis of a marriage for love, Lessing shows that the husband is "trapped" and has put his wife in a "cage." The problem is that marriage is a social institution which incorporates a concept of "family." The married pair have privacy only in bed because they are shut up with their parents and their children. Love makes their situation worse because their refusal to separate means they are "trapped without hope of release." A loveless marriage works out better, since the husband is free to leave, and the wife is "perfectly happy" with the isolation which results.

The family as an institution afflicts children, also. When marriages break down, overcrowding is relieved but children do not escape. If anything, divorce makes childhood more claustrophobic. Remarriages add stepparents to multiplying ranks of unwanted dictators. Also, divorce automatically makes parents cling to their children more. And a clinging parent, whether custodial or absent, is a burden.

The other side of this nightmare is that parents are more likely to become dictators when divorce removes the resident critic who could be counted on to deflate their will to power, as long as marriage applied. Living without adult companionship, single parents are able to deceive themselves that they are always right. And remarriage does nothing to change this sense of absolute authority since the new spouse cannot claim a parent's rights.

What starts as a lack of conflict turns into a lack of balance which can make parents seem overwhelming. In order to resist, children may turn to impersonal forms, as Janet does so successfully that her mother laments her as a "processed pea." Or, at the opposite extreme, children can resort to self-mutilation to fend off the growth and glory which their parents care too much about. Tommy, for example, frees himself from his parents' hopes and plans by shooting himself in the head. The gesture of defiance leaves him blind rather than dead. Released by his handicap, he becomes confident and even aggressive. He has destroyed parts of himself from which conflict can spring, and so he is finally "all in one piece."

By the time Lessing has finished with them, both structured and unsanctioned forms of love have defeated themselves. The family umbrella which includes all kinds of institutionalized love is limiting enough to be crippling, whether traditional repressions or modern laws are used. And the "freedom" to which love is otherwise exposed is so bewilderingly lacking in rules that connection with anyone outside the self becomes a doubtful task. To illustrate her point, Lessing fills her book with marriages which puzzle, frustrate and entrap. She adds a clutter of personal options which also divide into a complexity which bewilders and betrays. Adults may be celibate with or without love. If they prefer, they may be sexual with or without love, with or without satisfaction. They may have children with or without fathers. Children may or may not have biological mothers. Whatever an individual decides to do in the face of such chaos--whether to make a choice which leads to self-limitation, or to break down and refuse to choose--the outcome is a narrower life.

The end of one of the novel's love affairs shows how the lapse of traditional structure leads to isolation rather than to freedom. The man picks a fight with his lover because he has heard that a woman no longer needs a man in order to have a baby. She can "apply" ice to her ovaries "instead of a man." The woman answers that no one "in her senses" would prefer ice to a man, but of course, she is missing the point. The quarrel is a sad proof of the real basis of the love affair. Lovers normally seek to avoid pregnancy. Still, the ability to impregnate implies a sense of power which this man refuses to yield. At least for him, the heart of the matter even for unstructured love is not an exchange of feeling.

In The Golden Notebook, love comes to the same thing in the end, whether it leads to the trap of married roles or to the isolation of rejecting lovers. Both structured and unstructured forms of love add up to sexual politics. Politics of any kind are limiting. Therefore, governments, parties, marriage, and love all break down as social explanations.

Anna's attempt to write about her personal life parallels her writing about war. She starts by keeping a diary. When she get nowhere in private efforts to understand her experience, she turns to psychotherapy. Analysis is a useful symbol, since it is a method of thinking about the individual personality against a background of theoretical categories. Still, psychoanalysts think in terms of cures, whereas a serious writer must search for some way to accept experience as it is and make it coherent as it is portrayed. So serious a conflict in goals leads Anna to a gradual deepening of her writer's block.

When diaries and dream journals fail her, Anna turns to journalism in search of some connection with other people. No longer able to write for herself, Anna begins clipping the newspapers. Her notebooks become scrapbooks which fill and overflow as she tries to organize her clipped reality. She resorts to covering her walls with clippings and is finally overwhelmed. The separate nuances of actual events suggest so much diversity that categories scarcely apply.

Anna also attempts a work of fiction which is to do for domestic life what her early novel, <u>Frontiers of War</u>, did for politics. She tries to turn her diary into fiction, and as long as only isolated episodes are involved, she succeeds brilliantly. The most emotionally effective passages in <u>The Golden Notebook</u> come from Anna's fiction about herself. But this power is itself the source of her writer's block since it comes from a literary tradition which she finally rejects. She cannot work in established literary forms which are as narrowing about personal life as they are about war.

As long as Anna continues to use traditional systems to think with, she succeeds only in proving to herself that order leads to limitation and therefore mutilation, and at the same time its force causes fragmentation and therefore chaos. Tradition is nostalgic about the past, and this is a false response, as her two books prove. Equally damaging, it leaves the present disorganized. At home, she is buried under newspaper clippings. In the community, she finds "somebody there in pieces" every time she opens a door. Also, these systems project a hopeless future. She has to face the fact that her own and her friends' children are self-destroyed.

Art is the one idea which can rescue her. It is the only system which can fit "conflicting things" into a "whole." She dreams of a "casket" holding fragments "from everywhere." These fragments turn into a crocodile, when fitted together. Anna's interpretation of this dream is that art can transform dead and scattered fragments into a living whole which will be beautiful because it is inclusive and alive, even if it is "sardonic," in itself.

The applied form of Anna's dream theory produces the sequence which gives the novel its title. Anna plans a new writing project which will include "all" of herself in one book. She buys a "golden" notebook for the purpose, but she loses full control when a friend demands the beautiful new notebook as a gift. Anna writes the first sentence of "his" novel in it for him. The sentence she gives him comes from a dream in which she is a variety of people not at all like herself, including men and soldiers. In exchange, he starts her novel for her. The sentence he sets for her is the opening sentence of <u>The Golden Notebook</u>, slightly edited. By the time the artistic exchange is completed, Lessing has linked these two people in a mesh of identifications which erase the division between male and female, waking and dreaming, writing and being blocked. Also blurred are distinctions between nationalities, between emotional functions such as friends and lovers, and between the behavior of critics and writers.

In order to be thorough, Lessing also offers Anna's doctrine of inclusiveness in a nonwriting mode. "Marvellous, mature, wise people" are those who can stand on the top of a mountian and meditate about the "nature of space." There are two ways to reach this situation. One route is that of the Sisyphus-like worker who pushes a boulder up the mountain of human stupidity. The other possibility is to be a "raving cannibal," rising on the "sad bleeding corpses" of the ignorant victims who litter the road of "great men."

The major test of Anna's theory comes in the temptation to choose between the methods. But by this point in the novel, Lessing has proved that any choice means chaos since it implies division. Newly able to synthesize, Anna passes her theory's test by electing all three options. When her friend asks if she is a cannibal, she answers, "Yes." And then she goes on to add that she has "dished out aid and comfort" and so she is a boulder-pusher, too. In addition, her cooperation with him makes her a willing "corpse" in his road. In other words, Anna demonstrates that in life as well as literature, the "correct" choice is not one of a set of options. The only possibility for order is to choose it all.

Lessing then takes up this theoretical insight in an applied form by allowing it to govern the plot. The reference to "two women" with which The Golden Notebook opens turns out to be a cut-off form of the actual idea. The "two women you are" is the sentence her friend wrote for Anna. As "Molly," one of the two turns into a willing victim by marrying without emotion and moving to Hamstead where she will live a perfectly "normal" life. Under her own name, the second woman will lead two lives. In one aspect, she will live like a "boulder-pusher" by counselling other people about their marriages and teaching other people's children. And in her "great man" aspect, she is an obviously no longer blocked writer--she turns her friend's brief sentence into The Golden Notebook's quarter of a million words.

Since this novel has been surprisingly easy to misread through overemphasizing either its politics or its sexual politics, Lessing has been moved to point out that the meaning lies in the "form."[1] When Lessing's advice is taken, the book's careful structure can be seen as gathering coherence from an initially daunting array of extremes which are too narrow to be correct in themselves and too contradictory to function as a central idea. Politics are too depersonalizing, while literature is too private. Love is "too difficult," but sex is "too cold." The masses are repulsive, and yet isolation is "insane." The past is a lying nostalgia, whereas the future is "blind." Efficiency dehumanizes and tenderness betrays. "Brooding" is inclusive but immobilizing, while "fighting" gets results at the cost of mutilation. Only some larger vision could hope to rise above so bleak a gathering of self-defeating partial views.

Art is Lessing's nomination for an inclusive ideal. The Golden Notebook begins with a "formal" novel, whose literary conventions are restricting enough to make it both short and limited. However, it turns into an envelope for the "notebooks" which sprawl off in every direction in order to introduce a variety of writing forms, personal situations, public roles, and systematic theories about humanity. By the time the formal novel reappears and brings The Golden Notebook to an end, patterns of analysis which led to breakdown have been reversed. It turns out that ideas in pairs can flow together as coherently as categories divide. This process means that synthesis is possible, provided the need for it is recognized.

For Lessing, art is the one coherency which depends upon including all the other forms for feeling, thought and action. Therefore, even when it is joyless, it makes beauty out of fragments. In this way, it achieves its goal.

Some celebrations of inclusiveness use twentieth-century topics to organize their twentieth-century forms of chaos. Dorothy L. Sayers believed that granting academic degrees to women was a turning point which would change every aspect of life. Her vigorous essay, "Are Women Human?"[2] grows out of her belief that equality in education should have a domino effect, resulting in a quiet revolution in social attitudes and behavior toward women in every context. However, her experience in the literary marketplace kept her intensely aware of how relatively little impact an essay is likely to have, when it speaks directly about a topic on which everyone already knows what to think. Equality for women had been prejudged for centuries. Therefore, she tried a second, indirect approach by embedding her argument in a type of fiction where it could carry with it its own kind of proof.

Gaudy Night is an academic novel. It is also a detective novel. And it is a novel about women. Since all three patterns are coherent within themselves, the book is often appreciated in no more than a single area, in the same way that Lessing's The Golden Notebook is sometimes misunderstood because a partial view can be almost too intriguing.

Sayers' reputation means that Gaudy Night is most likely to be encountered as a novel of crime and detection. Recent interest in the study of women in groups also focuses attention on the community of female scholars in the midst of which Gaudy Night's crime takes place. Both approaches are important to the novel's organization, although either may mask the presence of the other since their procedures are so similar.

Both academic research and detective investigation depend upon gathering data and organizing it rationally in order to arrive at the facts of the case. Only the target of the inquiry is different. Detectives work in the physical world, examining crime scenes and listening to witnesses. Scholars operate in the realm of the mind, inspecting original documents and weighing the conclusions of other scholars.

It is this combination of similarity and difference which allows Sayers to expand her treatment beyond the limits which ordinarily apply. Academic research is absorbed in the past, and so it is appropriate that the long tradition about the role of women should crop up constantly. But focusing on the past means that women will be considered more as a topic than as an active agent, since in history, only exceptional women escaped the conventional rules. Women who are scholars themselves, rather than subjects for scholarship, are so new an option as to require contemporary investigation, if they are to be studied. This means that analyzing how women actually live in the modern world is work for detectives rather than for academics.

Detectives qualify for the task in several ways. Not only do they observe the people around them, but they deal with behavior which is, by definition, outside the rules. In order to reconstruct criminal sequences, they must be willing to accept the idea that some minds operate on a completely different value system. A detective who can observe crime and admit that it comes from a rational process of its own may be able to face the possibility that actual women are not what ancient convention describes. To detect what women really are requires the analytical skills of investigators trained to set aside their own feelings and beliefs in order to focus on what in fact is going on.

Bringing these attributes together in an orderly way, Sayers establishes a central character who has placed herself outside conventional behavior in the full range of ways. Harriet has been tried for murder, and she is also a scholar, a crime writer, and a practicing detective.

The context of the novel echoes this inclusiveness. A women's college might seem to stand for retreat and selectivity. But by the novel's end, Shrewsbury College has revealed itself as a gathering point for every imaginable accommodation to life, including the primitive as well as the "overbred," and for men as well as women.

Academic in both topic and method, the novel begins when the central character returns to Oxford for the "gaudy" which also attracts other "senior members." As Harriet identifies people she used to know and hears the life stories of other former students who have not returned, she assembles and classifies a list of female career possibilities. She adds a second tier of variation by thinking about the results of their choices. Among them, they have married everything from a missionary to a farmer, and, in a separate spectrum which cuts across the marriage question, they work at a full range of activities from academic research to breeding dogs.

This gathering of women can be analyzed on a more internalized basis, as well. Some of them return naturally to an academic environment. One former student is clearly an "oddity" in her social behavior, but she is respected for being "extremely sound" on the "life-history of the liver-fluke." Harriet herself has been a public scandal--for living with her lover, for being charged with his murder, and for subduing her writing talent to the type of publication which leads to fame and wealth. Nevertheless, at Shrewsbury, she is respected for maintaining a "scholarly" standard of English in detective fiction.

Not everyone who returns seems right to have done so. One of Harriet's old friends is too ill to make use of the contacts which are offered. One "brilliant" woman who married a farmer is so demoralized by the utterly physical life which accompanies such a choice of husbands that she can respond to nothing academic except the cultivated voices. And others who seemed to show brilliance as students turn out to have been no more than precocious, as their present boring wordiness proves.

The point of such diversity is established from the beginning. One of the weekend speakers focuses his remarks on an appreciation for the "diversity of gifts" which share the "same spirit." This concept of "equal citizenship" regardless of unequal talents and life details organizes the responses of everyone who wishes to participate. It makes Oxford a "paradise" of "spiritual peace" where even the prayers are "undenominational" and people do their work simply for the "love of the job," regardless of what the "job" might be.

Definitions of "the job" do differ, as Harriet notices, and ongoing discussions of this idea become one of the important ways in which the book is organized. There are two basic elements to the concept. In addition to the job itself, there is the question of whether or not it is "your job." However "grand" the job may be abstractly, it will not turn out well in an individual life if it is not the job toward which each person's talents and energies naturally incline. One of the current students illustrates this difficulty. She is at Oxford only because her parents insist upon it. She wants to be a cook, and there is no school of cookery at Oxford. As a result, she spends her time drinking to excess and getting into trouble.

Women have the additional problem that they are likely to marry into someone else's job. The woman who mentions this difficulty has ruined her life with a marriage which seems to have hitched a "Derby winner" to a "coal-cart," which makes her an illustration as well as a mouthpiece for the idea. People who believe that marrying is the only job for women are likely to think only as far as the marriage and push aside secondary questions about the individual man whose way of life defines the job of marriage for the woman.

Carefully maintaining options in illustrations as well as definitions, Sayers balances this "Derby winner's" tragedy against the experience of a historian who married an anthropologist. Because their jobs can be pursued together, they are able to achieve mutual happiness. They go around the world together digging up "bones and stone and pottery." They also fulfill the more usual expectations of marriage by producing successful children whom they casually "dump" on "delighted grandparents" until the children are old enough to begin digging along with their parents. So energetically joyous and successful an outcome proves that marriage need not necessarily cut women off from their own identity. If the life after marriage will make use of the woman's genuine tastes and talents, as this mating between history and anthropology does, then marriage becomes a mutual blessing. On the same basis, even a very traditional marriage may be satisfactory, provided that the woman really does want to be a cook and nurse, as one current student does.

The danger is that women who are well-suited by traditional marriages may feel rebelliously self-righteous, knowing that their opinion is backed by centuries of approval for self-cancelled wives. Women in such circumstances are likely to be sure that all women are obligated to live as they do and that any other option is unwomanly and destructive. The genuine diversity which is at the heart of academic process includes this option along with all the others, even though its own point is that women have only a single possible function which leaves no room for tolerance in return.

Sayers suggests the importance of the traditional view by showing how academics work around it and by including displays of the hostility and disbelief which academic accommodation provokes. The men's colleges stand behind Shrewsbury without any hesitation, once they make the decision to admit women into the Oxford community. Lord Peter, a senior member of Balliol, refuses to believe that the education of women is "still a question," and his insistence that he has no right to an opinion in the matter illustrates Oxford's belief that the admission of women into the community of equals automatically denies both men and women the right to rejudge the matter since they are now on a par.

On the other hand, some of the people who live and work inside Oxford's "serenity" are not members of the university. The Shrewsbury College porter, for example, turns out to be part of Lord Peter's world on an entirely different basis. The two men were soldiers together during the war, but Padgett's admiration for Lord Peter, and Lord Peter's friendly response in that strictly man's context, does not mean they hold any views in common. Padgett is a careful and generous-spirited porter, but his helpfulness toward women turns out to result from amusingly traditional views rather than from acceptance or liberality. He used to work in the camel house and came to Shrewsbury only because he had to quit his interesting job at the zoo. He was bitten by a camel, and his idea of universal order is revealed when he points out that the misbehaving animal was a female. Still, the rules of chivalry do apply, and so his treatment of the Shrewsbury women is resourceful, reliable, generous, protective and kind.

Enforcing the repressive tradition against women is left to women, since the male response to it is protective, as Padgett shows. Gaudy Night's villain reveals how this idea works. The criminal is a woman so dedicated to the tradition of a single choice that she vigorously insists to her daughters they must be wives and mothers. When one of the little girls protests that she wants a motorcycle instead of a husband, Annie is resentful and annoyed. Such a reaction is a slightly more manageable version of her feelings toward dons and scholars. When the members of Shrewsbury College show how committed they are to the "impersonal job," as distinct from a husband, Annie is driven to assaults against them which begin with poison-pen vulgarity, move on to increasingly invasive property destruction, and finally culminate in a murder attempt.

Annie's experience is symbolic as well as painfully personal. She used to be a don's wife, which is the academic relationship she considers appropriate for a man When her husband died, she returned to a college connection in the only other traditionally acceptable role. As a scout, she is now a servant to resident scholars, this being the position for which she qualifies by her own talents.

Annie's association with female scholars is particularly painful because it was a woman who caught her scholar-husband in the unforgiveable act of suppressing evidence which contradicted his research. The unmasking was a perfectly automatic and impersonal dedication to "the job," in the mind of the woman scholar who made the discovery. But placing "honesty" at the top of the value scale seems like a wanton betrayal, to Annie. She insists a decent woman would not take a job which might lead her to expose the defects of a man. Annie is passionately sure that the only possible function for women is to stand behind men, regardless of anything.

With the confidence of centuries, Annie attacks the don who discovered her husband's crime against scholarship. Her indignation expands when Oxford does not even consider casting Shrewsbury College out of the university, despite the antiacademic disorder she is creating. And her attack enlarges to include the whole school when the dons and students of Shrewsbury College survive as a community by accepting a criminal presence among themselves without gossiping, without losing their sense of themselves as scholars, and without faltering in their loyalty to their work.

In <u>Gaudy Night</u>, Sayers assigns all the basic detective-fiction roles to women. Women are the victims, the criminal, the witnesses, and the investigator. At first glance, such a cast of characters suggests that Sayers has set up a separate world, where women can escape from male violence and power. Certainly this is Harriet's first hopeful vision. She notices that one of the dons who specializes in literature knows "all the sins of the world by name" but cannot recognize sins in their real life versions. The distinction is important to Harriet because she is eager to feel that Oxford is "her own place," even though she has "broken half the commandments." She dreams that Oxford is the "heart of rest," where Lord Peter, who "stands for London" and an "upsetting world of strain," has "no niche."

Harriet's vision is defeated by the fact that women themselves bring crime and disruption into the "still center." "London" cannot be shut out. "Rome" and "Warsaw" intrude as well, since the foreign office calls Lord Peter away just when Harriet wants help from him. Calling Lord Peter into the mess is distressing to Harriet in several ways. She is shocked at herself for needing the help of an "alien" to work on a woman's crime. But Lord Peter avoids the traditional and simplistic label by dividing people according to their work instead of their biology. He insists that "feeling like Judas" is part of a detective's job and does not come from being a man. The wistful simplicity of Harriet's labeling is further challenged when she sees Peter in his academic robes. She reluctantly admits that he is a more comfortable senior member than she is. Women are a very recent presence in Oxford, but men like Lord Peter have "grown there from the beginning."

The pure form of what Lord Peter represents is embodied in his nephew, Saint-George. "Six centuries" of privilege have given men like these a "cheerful readiness to take and have." Saint-George masks his making use of everyone around him under the "grace of gratitude." His breeding makes him charming, but it does not improve the balance of his nature.

Like his more delightfully attractive nephew, Lord Peter also has "everything he could possibly want." But in Lord Peter's case, the centuries of possessiveness included in the family background are balanced by his personal life-long cultivation of "over-sensitized intellect." The result is an attractive "diffidence" of manner which is in crucial contrast to his nephew's "impudence."

This distinction is important since Lord Peter functions in the novel as an image of balance. Harriet calls him an "Augustan," and he admits that his most important companion-of-the-mind is John Donne, whose spiritual writing emerged in physical imagery and whose human enjoyment was expressed in spiritual terms.

In addition to being balanced within himself, Lord Peter behaves in such a way as to show how a shared balance including other individuals can be achieved. Sensitively adaptive, he constantly redistributes his own weight in order to adjust to his situation. In physical terms, he teaches Harriet how to resist being strangled by using an assailant's own weight to overbalance him. Then, when she practices his method on him, he manages to compensate quickly enough to keep his feet. He demonstrates the same principle intellectually by accepting Harriet's organization of evidence in the Shrewsbury case. He does finally add his own interpretation, but only after it is clear that her guilt and involvement prevent her from being dispassionate enough to do the work herself. If he had wanted to strut as savior, intellect, or man of privilege, he could have assembled the information as well as interpreting it. Instead, he insists that a solution is his only goal. His seriousness about this humble response is proved by his refusal to be thanked when the crime is solved.

Emotional balance is harder for Lord Peter to maintain. During the five years since her trial, Harriet's one goal has been to withdraw. In order to counterbalance this single-minded isolation in a woman he wants to share his life with, Lord Peter has patiently repeated an offer of marriage. Harriet tries to shut him up by proposing to live with him. He responds by refusing to let her pretend that his interest is merely physical. She debases herself in a prickly gratitude for his having saved her life by proving she did not kill her lover. Lord Peter counters by insisting that he hires tactful dependents when he wants them, and he will not accept such a relationship from a person who "ought to be" an equal. She tries to retreat into the life of the mind, and he remarks that some people have both hearts and minds.

When Oxford turns out to be as open to crime, sin, passion, and disorder as London is, Harriet finally begins to see more than one side of the question. In her uncertainty, she wishes to be "ridden over rough-shod," but she recognizes that Peter will never offer so traditional a relationship. He is as "protective as a can-opener" on all levels. He assumes she will not retreat from danger. He suggests that she set aside her usual self-protective "jigsaw" approach and write a novel about "human beings," even if the process stirs up her own feelings in a painful way. He counts on the absolute priority of "honesty" in her value system by carrying on with an investigation which he knows will lead to an exposé of the madness which "love" may sometimes provoke.

Lord Peter's anxiety about Harriet's ability to deal with Annie's mad form of love is well-founded. Harriet's response to Oxford shows that she does tend to think in absolute terms. She is very ready to see Annie's perverse and angry love as proof that the horror of her own past is normal, not unique. If she defends herself from her violent memories by deciding that love is destructive in its nature, even Lord Peter will not be able to counterbalance her belief.

The resolution of their relationship comes through the artistic expression which is central to each of them. To Harriet, words are everything, and so the stages of her understanding are marked by examples of different literary forms. Belatedly realizing that Lord Peter is a vulnerable man, as well as her savior, she writes him a kind and human letter about his nephew. And then, for the first time, she adds some personal interest in Lord Peter, himself. Lord Peter is astonished by the change. When he next sees Harriet, he responds by exposing "all his weaknesses," to counterbalance her sudden discovery of her own strength.

Complex personalities cannot be brought into balance with a single adjustment, however. Lord Peter withdraws again when he comes across a poem she has been working on in the midst of her notebook about the Shrewsbury crime. The "singing voice" has returned to her, after five years of silence, but it has produced only the octave of a sonnet.

Her fragment shows that she is groping toward a balance which still escapes her. She has written about the "still center" without following up on the full implications of using a spinning top as an image for the world.

Counterbalancing as always, Lord Peter writes a sestet which is "better" than the octave, as it must be, since it is shorter. His lines respond with the image of a top as stable through tension, not through rest. The balancing "turn" shows Harriet that Peter wants a "central stability" which he can achieve only when stimulated to a "precarious balance" by "opposing forces." Since she is able to respond to poetry with the "detached intellect," she is able to use their collaboration as a way to understand what balance means to Lord Peter and how he accomplishes it with her, as well as within himself.

Harriet begins to understand the usefulness of balance as a goal when she realizes it enables Lord Peter to accept everything life offers. In contrast, her instinctive reaction--withdrawal--has not protected her from violence or grief, and it has cut her off from the compensating benefits of love and trust. Her recognition reveals its last stage when she begins revising the novel she is working on, in terms of Lord Peter's editorial comments. With the habit of years, she still hesitates at the thought of a life commitment. Still, her growing personal balance makes their relationship manageable, so that Lord Peter can find "the word" which helps Harriet accept her own version of the balance they both seek.

It is part of Sayers' point that Lord Peter should already have the balance which Harriet must learn to value. Privilege makes many forms of "grace" possible. But privilege for one group implies disadvantage for another. If women are released from the repression of history, the concept of privilege will have to be separated from sex roles. On the other hand, thinking of privilege as male is so ingrained a social habit that women continue to react with anger, and men continue to be "impertinent," even after the inequality which justifies such attitudes is gone.

Lord Peter is a musician rather than a writer, and so he expresses this idea most comfortably in musical terms. He waits respectfully while a soloist performs, but his real interest in in Bach, who is not a matter of "autocratic virtuoso" and "meek accompanist." When he asks Harriet if she wants to be either, he is documenting his acceptance of women as "fellow-creatures." Significantly, he does not assume that the "accompaniment" is automatically provided by the "girl." His musical terms for equality go even farther. He willingly leaves "harmony" to other people, provided he and Harriet can have the "counterpoint."

The balancing idea is equally true. If women are to move beyond the traditional trap, they must develop a more balanced view of themselves. They must set aside their own "distorting-glass" and accept the fact that a woman who is a "kindly, intelligent human being" may run a college as "normally" as she would preside over a "household." Only when women accept this idea of themselves will they be able to take an equal place beside men who have restructured their own balance in order to make a place for them.

Being treated with the respect of an equal means that the patronizing protectiveness of traditional males must be sacrificed. At first, the loss may seem "brutal," even to women like Harriet, who insist upon it. Tradition made life simpler by offering a single role. Under the old, unbalanced system, when options were possible at all, they involved a clear, lopsided choice between marriage or career.

In the past, male protectiveness was appropriate since it counterbalanced female self-limitation. It will remain an option as long as individuals of either sex continue to choose traditional roles. Still, educational equality confronts twentieth-century women with the same spectrum of possibilities which men confront. Individuals of either sex can be anything that feels right to them, from traditional to mad. Or, they can be balanced, if the trouble seems worth the goal. It is a new freedom from deliberate repression which makes "very great happiness" possible to those who place more value on facts than on conventions and use dispassionate honesty to interpret what they see.

The importance of a balanced view is established in Margaret Drabble's Realms of Gold by the presence of a narrator. As if distrusting the ability of any character to be suggestive beyond the limitations of a single role, Drabble allows a disembodied voice to break into her story from time to time in order to comment or speculate on action, motive, fictional technique, or probability.

This narrator is not necessarily in control of the

story. Sometimes it is unsure of what characters are thinking about. It apologizes for plot changes and offers to negotiate with the reader about endings, about beginnigs, and about boredom. It finds extremely complex motivations bewildering, and so it sometimes has trouble foreseeing how things will turn out. It worries about being criticized for coincidences in the plot and defends itself by referring to both life and literature. It laments the suffering it describes. And sometimes it interrupts itself and tries to explain what its phrases mean.

The overall effect is one of meditation. The reader watches as a story is pulled out of a welter of characters, events and kinds of life which finally ranges from happy innocents and survivors to sadists and victims, from disasters and scandals to emergencies, triumphs and pleasures, and from coping energy to luck, Fate and personal entrapment. Since events and characters are so tumbled together, and since the assumed meanings depend so much on the mind of the observer and the proportion of the situation which is perceived, attention is increasingly focused on the calmly pondering narrator, striking a balance between the inclusiveness which makes explanations possible and the ruthlessness which rationalized order requires.

Having a point of identification outside the central character is especially helpful in The Realms of Gold because Frances Wingate is an individual of such energy and charm that the urge to identify with her single perspective is irresistible. Frances frequently calls herself greedy, and the term is at first easy enough to take literally since she is introduced in the context of her appetites. She drinks too much while entertaining herself with the possibility of becoming an alcoholic like her brother, who gets "good results" even though he suffers from "side effects." She enjoys a banquet made up of many small dishes and remains undaunted even while speculating that she might have been expected to choose among the first variety in order to save her appetite for a conventionally large main course. And, while being entertained as a visiting dignitary, she assesses the personal availability of her various hosts, a process she excels at since she has sometimes been unable to "stop herself sleeping with people" when traveling.

But greed, for Frances, is far more inclusive than such details imply. She is just as ready to absorb herself in physical distresses as she is to indulge her appetites.

Getting sick on a desert journey, she assumes she must have typhoid. Suffering with toothache, she hits herself on the other cheekbone so both sides of her face will ache. She takes pride in the fact that her skin is weathered and scarred by her work as an archeologist, and she inspects her wrinkles acceptingly, confident that her lover enjoys them.

Since Frances gets full value from every feeling, her kind of greed applies to emotions, as well. Depressed, Frances plunges into the experience wholeheartedly. Tears dripping off her face, sobs choking her, she paces and drinks and times herself to see if this depression is following her usual pattern. Waiting through a praising lecture introduction which lists her professional accomplishments, she is impressed with what she has done and pleased to think of herself as a "vain, self-satisfied woman." Drinking with a young man who says he admires her, she is intrigued, despite his "insolent" look. And she likes it even better when he irritably accuses her of being a "golden girl," since "malice" is a more "real acknowledgement" than flattery. In love, she works assignations into her schedule without diminishing her attention to her profession or hampering her devotion to her children. In hate, she flings all the coffee cups at her husband's head, one at a time, before ordering him out of the house.

Despite her self-satisfied claim, Frances does not finally fit into any usual definition of greed. What she craves is variety, since almost any change will relieve boredom. Her unusual energy turns out to be a determination to "keep moving" in order to escape depression, and the money and fame which result are only side effects. Further, the things she "has" are not the dreams of an acquisitive nature. She "imagines" a buried city, an ancient trade route, a career, and these things exist. But she is not bothered by the sight of her normally privileged guests eating off plates randomly decorated with pictures of Babar, and so she never gets around to buying a set of plates for the dinner table. Satisfied that her reputation and conversation are enough to make her socially effective, she does not bother to provide herself with even minimally attractive clothing.

In view of such priorities, intensity, more than "greed," emerges as the key to Frances' behavior. She appears to be totally committed to whatever she is doing at the moment, even though she has her eye on the clock for each activity, not just for her depressions. For example, she wholeheartedly enjoys her four children. Nevertheless, she decides her "programming" for motherhood is wearing off, as soon as her children are old enough to be somewhat self-sufficient. And even when they are small, she does not hesitate to leave them with an au pair girl or with their father and stepmother, when conflicting activities catch her fancy.

Her approach to other conventional situations is similarly intense and contradictory. While married, she buries herself in all the social and private rituals, giving elaborate dinner parties, battling over whether she is entitled to continue her education, and taking long vacations by car which lock the family together in bitterness and shouting. But once she divorces, she just as passionately rejects the very idea of the "nuclear family." If both parents are present in a family, she insists one must be a "drag" on the group. During this stage, she is convinced that women can "manage" a man or children, but not both at the same time. No more loyal to this than to any other opinion, however, she and her lover both bring their children with them when they finally marry. The combined household includes seven children in addition to the two parents Frances at one time rejected. Embracing her new situation with her usual enthusiasm, she decides compounding families is good for her since it taxes her energies.

Frances approaches her professional life with an equivalent disbelief in permanence. When she tries to phone her former professor and is told no one of that name is there, she does not think she has a wrong number, she concludes her entire career has been an "elaborate mistake." Wholehearted as always, she laments the "lengthy delusion" of her recollections of student days at Oxford and what seemed like memories of her archeological expeditions.

It is this ability to become totally involved with the experience of the moment which constitutes her charm. Her lover delights in her utter responsiveness when her face turns gray with shock as they are reunited, and she is as impressively ready to enter into the lives of other people as she is to intensify her own experiences. At a professional conference, she lends a bathing suit to another woman and then engages in a poolside competition, which she wins, despite her additional ten years, ten pounds, bad teeth, and lack of genuine interest in any of the men. Meeting her timid cousin, Janet, she lies about her domestic pleasures in order to fit obligingly into the negative stereotype

Janet holds of her. And when her cousin's strutting and abusive husband comes home, she enters into Janet's claustrophobic cringing as if he were her own tyrant. When her lover's wife decides to be a lesbian, Frances attends familiarization meetings. When her reclusive aunt dies, Frances sits in the aunt's neglected cabin, experiencing the life of a recluse--for a few hours.

It is not only women who provoke her empathy. Her childhood involvement with her brother progresses to tolerant understanding when he becomes a "drunken grandfather." When her brother's son kills himself and his baby, Frances accepts the young man's belief that he has had a "revelation" which shows that life is sordid enough to make death the only option which leaves personal dignity intact.

Her ability to identify with the lives of others is not limited to the people around her. In her professional role, Frances enters into the lives of the ancient Phoenicians, suppressing some of what is known about them in order to defend her conviction that they cannot have been as bad as they are accused of being. Equally busy with family history, she visualizes the lives of the generations of farm laborers who eventually produced her father. And her dead aunt's letters involve her in a long-ago heartbreak which leaves her weeping and wishing for a picture of the charismatic, long-dead lover.

Nor is it always humans who stir her powers. She throws herself into the implied lives of country cottages. She reconsiders her relationship to biological function as she watches an octopus who lives in a plastic box, and she "loves" the sight of a drainage pipe so crammed with frogs that a "law of nature" seems to have "gone wrong."

Frances' ability to empathize has an enormous range, but it is not all-inclusive. Rocks are outside her reach, as she discovers while getting acquainted with David Ollerenshaw, a geologist who turns out to be her cousin. Her contact with David shows her that her enthusiasm is limited to life. To be sure, life is a larger term to Frances than it is to most people. She expands the concept to include death, in both its archeological and its family aspects. Still, her lack of response to rocks contrasts with the eagerness of her involvement with everything else and turns her into a warning of the limitations inevitable to any individual "approach."

The structure of the narrative underlines this idea. The Realms of Gold begins inside a depression which is engulfing Frances. However, depression is a small part of this character's overall personality, just as Frances is only a small part of the novel's world. Counteracting Frances' tendency to overpower her environment, the narrative voice gradually shifts reader identification toward a more inclusive viewpoint, until finally the narrator and the reader are bargaining directly. At the story's end, the narrator gives the reader permission to "resent" Frances, since Frances is "not listening" and "will not care."

The narrator's offer is a surprise, at first, since it seems impossible to do anything other than agree with the young man who offers "immense" admiration to a woman who struggles to absorb everything she encounters, and fails only when she encounters rocks. But when her behavior is compared to her lover's procedures, some additional limits emerge. Frances fears boredom, rejection, and being "underemployed." Only change lets her escape these things. As a result, even things she values must not last too long.

The most crucial illustration of this principle is her breaking off a perfectly satisfying love affair which fits into the rest of her life in an ideal way. Frances begins parroting standard phrases which "come from nowhere," insisting that she is "ruining her career" over a man who will not marry her. She knows her career in fact is flourishing, she admits she does not particularly want to marry, and normally she is "amused" rather than convinced by folk wisdom and clichés. Nevertheless, the phrases offer her an excuse to recoil from a perfection which includes the continuance she dreads. Any activity loses its "charm" for her, as soon as she is "good at" it.

Her lover, Karel, believes in an entirely different approach. He insists he will not "make distinctions." He limits himself to human beings, but within this category he refuses to attempt to "redress the appalling imbalance" of life. Rejecting the arrogance of trying to create a "justice" which does not exist, he longs instead to love everyone indiscriminately, as if they all deserved it. A college teacher, he is as unfailingly responsive to his students as he is to his masochistic wife. He beats his wife because she wants him to be offensive enough to justify her distaste for heterosexual arrangements, and he spends a "lifetime" listening to the boring, malicious, manipulative student failures who cynically exploit his desire to achieve an "unforced, real, shining love" which will "transform" them.

So ambitious a view of love fails when Frances leaves him. If he cannot have the love of the one person he chooses, he refuses to love anyone. He begins to approach everyone with "rancor," "blaming" and "criticizing" them and dwelling on their worst features. Although this attitude maintains his commitment to equality, it also exposes the defects of such a value system. Being an "egalitarian of love" really includes a double goal, and under pressure, he discovers that he cannot maintain both parts equally. He will have to restrict his attention to a "chosen few," if he wishes to remain compassionate. Or, if he insists on equal treatment, he will have to "hate" everyone.

When it is applied to actual life, Karel's equality turns out to be as limited as is Frances' greed. He can offer to love everyone only as long as Frances loves him, and he can hate everyone only as long as she deserts him. These problems curtail Karel's highly theoretical approach, just as the need to "keep moving" limits Frances' more physical approach. Between them, these characters demonstrate that neither desire nor energy can help individuals escape from the confines of their single vision. Their limitations return attention to the narrative which expands beyond both the theoretical and the worldly attempt.

A more balanced and more expansive view of life is represented by David Ollerenshaw. He enjoys being with people "intermittently," and he is good company. But, unlike Frances and Karel, he also likes complete isolation and deliberately provides for time alone, so that he can think about "inhuman things." Listening to a married colleague describe a love affair with a married woman, he feels relieved that such things do not happen to him and entertains himself with how "unexpected" people are. Attending a funeral, he contemplates death as a function and thinks how much more pleasant "inorganic" process is.

A geologist, David takes a longer view of history than Frances and Karel do, since their work ties them to human history, which seems brief and insignificant to David. His fascination with volcanos and prehuman rock formations allows him to watch human upheavals with amused detachment. The narrator balances David's absorption in the farthest past by suggesting that his "significance" will become clear in the future.

This emphasis on David's balance lends an importance to his method which might not emerge simply in terms of the proportion of the novel's action which focuses on him. Neither flamboyant nor aspiring, David enjoys a composure which is almost unique in the novel. His success in this regard comes partly from the fact that people who live alone are able to be themselves, as his great aunt is. But unlike his bitterly reclusive aunt, David is able to be "himself" even in company, because the enormous range of his vision makes any particular social rule amusing rather than confining or exasperating. His freedom is a comment on more social and therefore more restricted lives. Both Frances' archeology and Karel's history document the fact that society changes its demands, over time. But this idea alone is not enough, since every human study shows that rules of some sort do apply. David, on the other hand, sees humanity itself as insignificant and temporary. It is an attitude which makes all human rules seem brief and trivial to him.

David's personal freedom exists in the midst of a family where adherence to a particular and temporary code ruins individual lives. His cousin Janet, for example, limits herself deliberately to a voluntary misery, since the only way she can think of herself as the center of a moral vision is to believe she is a martyr. His Aunt Con turns herself into a "mad" recluse, since she can think of no other role which will include her consummated and thwarted love for a married man.

This idea emerges in its opposite, as well. According to current attitudes, Stephen murdered his baby when he tenderly poisoned her along with himself. But history supplies a wider view. The past includes many societies where sacrificing infants, particularly females, was perfectly routine. Since the label for even such a clear-cut act depends on when and where it happened, less definite choices obviously must benefit from the changes which the passage of time automatically brings.

Even without death or cultural relativity, "escape" is possible. Some of the Ollerenshaws of the past managed to climb out of the "slough" of peasant poverty. And modern life offers such diversity within itself that only the deliberately self-restricted need to accept their misery.

The Realms of Gold documents the process of freedom in copious detail. A battered wife can become a happy lesbian. A picture-perfect wife can join an encounter group for the families of alcoholics. Sexually eager couples can choose to remain childless. Energetic women can become famous in their own right. Solitary children can treat themselves to professions which commit them to deserts. Compassionate teachers can reduce their office hours.

The narrator concludes its story by summing up all the characters it has described and distributing outcomes which are individually appropriate to widely different lives. It insists on "happy endings." But what makes an ending happy depends on the personality of each character, their beliefs, blind spots and accommodations, their friends, their work, their neighbors, as well as an assumed reader's views. In the midst of such an array, "justice" can be discounted except by people who actually want its limitations, since all human value systems are inevitably temporary, compared to geologic time.

In terms of novelistic structure, the narrator's process is reminiscent of the nineteenth-century "afterword," and on the surface, the happy ending into which Frances and Karel disappear seems highly appropriate to such a form. Still, their happiness rises out of as much "confusion" as that which produced tragedy, in Aunt Con's past. This parallel allows the narrator to update the response as well as the literary form. Consenting divorce, happy remarriage, and quasi-incestuous satisfactory marriage between teenage members of stepfamilies all seem like social options which belong to the late twentieth-century rather than to earlier times. But Drabble has remarked that happiness for Frances will offend those of her readers who object in principle to the idea that a heroine might be happy with a man.[3] Drabble's comment calls attention to the importance the novel places on both permanence and change in value systems. Like the nineteenth century, the twentieth century still finds grounds on which to believe that Frances should be "punished" for going her own way. At the same time, present-day diversity also makes room for people who accept happiness as a suitable reward for individuals who live up to their own values, so long as there is "no harm done to anyone."

The narrator emphasizes the full range of these attitudes by negotiating behind Frances' back with readers who do not want Frances to be happy, or who wish she would believe in a different basis for happiness. By making such a gesture, the narrator expands the novel to encompass even greater diversity. Not only do the characters receive endings which are personally suitable, but the readers, also, get to please themselves. This innovative form also incorporates the possibility of denying that patterns exist, in any rational way. Invoking the past and suggesting the future, events are variously described as resulting from chance, Fate, luck, talent, pity, despair, energy, inspiration, pagan ritual or answered prayer. Each person and theory is correct enough, because none is right exclusively.

Since the narrator helps the novel escape from any single time, place, or point of view, the book overall succeeds at establishing "unnecessary" variety as the actual context for everyone's life. This background provides for entirely individual results since it accepts the "teeming world" as "nasty" and "horrible" for those who recoil from confusion. But for individuals who are energetic and therefore free, both the causes and the results of "creation" are "delight," "excitement," "joy" and "fun. "

In a context where social variables are almost infinite, even though individual attitudes are far from free, people like Frances Wingate do not have to discount themselves as "freaks" and look for new worlds or optional groups in order to survive intact. They can see every human possibility as normal and celebrate greed by trying to experience all lives in the short stages which keep roles from turning into traps. The present world makes room for unself-conscious individuals who simply reach out their hands for what they want and assume that everyone else is equally at liberty.

One result of currently flexible social regulation is that remarkable individuals may not be forced to define their goals so clearly as eccentrics in the past have had to do in order to know what they need to survive. When individuals themselves are not forced to be so self-aware, the normal people around them may not identify them any more clearly than they do themselves. The result is a type of recent fiction in which the conventional world is in the forefront of the novel. The unusual person is allowed to move unconcernedly through the story, spreading a "confusion" which triggers at least tolerance and sometimes admiration and love.

An unusually vivid example of this process is Doris Lessing's story, "Our Friend Judith. " Strangers meeting Judith for the first time place her in a social category without the slightest hesitation. But the women closest to her are entirely baffled by her. She seems to be dowdy, though she is seductive when she dresses to show off her figure. She appears to be an intellectualized old maid, and yet she has fascinated men enough to be a mistress for years. She does not conceal her way of acting and judging, but she does not offer to explain herself, either, and so her friends are constantly startled by the details of her life. When they compare what she has done with what they expect her to do, she has a standard response. She finds them "extraordinary." The label sums up her case since it satisfies Judith, and the rest of them are too fascinated to cast her off and too baffled to contradict.

Nina Bawden uses the traditions of the love triangle as a less explicit way of presenting this pattern. A Woman of My Age focuses on the emotions of a conventional middle-aged wife who discovers that her husband has betrayed her. The wife's problems are intensified by the fact that her husband has not fallen in love with a younger woman, whose appeal would be both conventional and temporary. Instead, he has been unable to resist the attractiveness of another middle-aged woman whose seductiveness consists of being energetic and charmingly free from standard social roles and empty formalities.

Bawden's A Grain of Truth also examines standard behavior by contrasting it with a more individualized life. In this novel, a highly manipulative conventional wife brings grief and guilt to the men she flirts with in a fantasizingly empty and self-flattering way. Since her behavior is traditional, her destructive outcome offers a comment on conventions about the woman's role, particularly since it contrasts so sharply with the social impact of a neighbor and friend. The neighbor is interested in actuality, and so she frankly offers friendly affairs, when she is attracted. On the other hand, when sexuality does not interest her, she omits it altogether. The honesty of this behavior produces good relations with almost everyone, including her husband. Nevertheless, it is a demoralizing shock to the traditionally furtive and fantasizing main character.

Barbara Pym's A Glass of Blessings also represents the surprises which may result when men are surrounded by a variety of conventional and unconventional women from which to choose. Like Drabble, Pym presents a pattern of multiple variables as the most successful way to deal with freedom of choice. Traditional women need conventional men. Both will be better-suited if they choose each other.

Normal men may be temporarily dazzled by exceptional women, but neither will thrive if they try to share their lives. In order for remarkable women to have a happy life, they must live alone, surrounded by their friends. Or, they may marry happily, provided that they find a man eccentric enough to appreciate their charm.

In all these cases, no matter what life the individuals choose, the reasons and the outcomes remain much the same. Everyone pursues the way of living they like best. They are startled and amazed by other people's values. But they are nevertheless dependably tolerant of the way other people choose to live.

In The Ice Age Margaret Drabble confronts the problem more directly than most authors do. Turning to a population which lacks both the energy and the will to inclusiveness which makes The Realms of Gold so triumphantly free, Drabble reexamines current patterns from the point of view of people who are at least tentatively willing to live the way society expects them to. In this less-glamorizing novel, representatives of the late twentieth century have "worn themselves out" and "contorted themselves" trying to adjust their lives to a "new egalitarian culture" which omits servants and includes working wives.

The hero concludes that the "new bright classless enterprising future" has produced no new styles or images to release it from the old system which no longer prevails. He grew up as a clergyman's son, but when he uses the term "God," it is automatically taken to be a "code word" for some local crook. His version of the "greed" which Frances Wingate uses to enlarge her life is to struggle among various life patterns suggested either by the present or the past. He buys a country house which nobody can afford any more, but when he tries to live there, it turns into a rest home instead of a gentleman's estate. He launches a professional career because of values which make him an anachronism, but he also embroils himself in land speculation which makes him a man of the future.

The failure of society to develop any new "system" confuses him, since he would like to know what he ought to feel. On the other hand, society's inability to make or enforce demands leaves him free to become aware of his private values and emotions. He finds he genuinely does like his country house, in spite of his modern distrust of traditional class feelings about it. He is relieved that his mother does not compare him unfavorably with his boringly professional brothers because he is in business.

Regardless of such clear responses to scattered specific situations, he is still bewildered about what it is all "worth." He wants some "grandiose" way of explaining his life to himself. While he is restricted to his country estate by the threat of bankruptcy, he amuses himself by calling himself a "weed on the tide of history." He stops thinking of himself as a weed when he is imprisoned in an East European country. The work camp where he is assigned is physically similar to his country estate, and the parallel helps him begin to figure out what he "deserves." His sentence is a kind of indirect substitute for that of the young woman who would have been his stepdaughter if he had married as he meant to do, and so he is turned into a sort of "English gentleman." He has been convicted of being a spy, but he is known to be innocent and so he is a prisoner.

He decides he is relieved to be in a situation where definite terms are clearly applied. The process is so ambiguous that he can begin to believe that all the various "codes" both do and do not apply. He was a "gentleman" in retrieving his fiancée's daughter, even though he did not intend to sacrifice himself for her. It is true that he carried secret messages for his government, although he did so half unknowingly and the revolution made them useless anyway.

Imprisonment turns out to be a similarly arguable term. His guards are less restricting than the mental confinement of self-image and imagined role which continues to trap his technically free fiancée. His walls are not as confining as the birth defect which shuts his second stepdaughter inside a body incapable of doing what she wants it to.

Exhilarated to discover that prisons are not as restricting as other confinements may be, he is free to think of his actual talents and his real responses. He remembers that he is a musician and uses the talent to make friends. He begins the satisfyingly "grandiose" project of writing a book about "first causes" and "last causes." He has no writing talent, and so, significantly, the book is strictly for himself.

His piecemeal, situation-by-situation response is a low-energy equivalent of Frances Wingate's greed. His experience shows that it is not only the rich and privileged who benefit when old codes lose their relevance and are not replaced. The restrictions of prison are almost exactly the same as those placed on him by his doctor after his heart attack. His awareness of this irony releases him from any restriction less basic than a physical limit or a lack of talent. As a result, he is finally free to experience hope and joy.

Notes

1 "Preface to The Golden Notebook," in her A Small Personal Voice (New York: Random House, 1975), 23-5.

2 (Grand Rapids, Michigan: Eerdmans, 1971).

3 Diana Cooper-Clark, "Margaret Drabble: Cautious Feminist," The Atlantic Monthly, 246 (Nov. 1980), 75.

BIBLIOGRAPHY OF RECOMMENDED WORKS

Bawden, Nina. Afternoon of a Good Woman. London: Macmillan, 1976

———. A Grain of Truth. London: Longmans, 1968

———. Under the Skin. London: Longmans, 1964

———. A Woman of My Age. London: Longmans, 1967

Behn, Aphra. Oroonoko. London: William Canning, 1688

Burnett, Frances Hodgson. A Fair Barbarian. New York: International Association of Newspapers and Authors, 1880

Davis, Rebecca Harding. Doctor Warrick's Daughters. New York: Harper, 1896

Drabble, Margaret. The Ice Age. London: Weidenfeld and Nicolson, 1977

———. The Millstone. London: Weidenfled and Nicolson, 1965

———. Realms of Gold. London: Weidenfeld and Nicolson, 1975

Edgeworth, Maria. The Absentee. London: J. Johnson, 1812

———. Castle Rackrent. Dublin: P. Wogan, 1800

Eliot, George. Daniel Deronda. London: William Blackwood, 1876

———. Felix Holt. London: William Blackwood, 1866

Fielding, Sarah. The Adventures of David Simple. London: A. Millar, 1744

Fitzgerald, Zelda. Save Me the Waltz. New York: Scribner's, 1932

Gaskell, Elizabeth. Cousin Phillis. London: Smith, Elder and Co. 1865

———. Cranford. London: Chapman and Hall, 1853

_____. Mary Barton. London: Chapman and Hall, 1848

_____. Ruth. London: Chapman and Hall, 1853

_____. Wives and Daughters. London: Smith, Elder and Co., 1866

Glasgow, Ellen. Barren Ground. New York: Harcourt, Brace, 1925

Gundy, Elizabeth. Bliss. New York: Viking, 1977

_____. Cat on a Leash. New York: Viking, 1978

Guy Rosa. Edith Jackson. New York: Viking, 1978

Hailey, Elizabeth. A Woman of Independent Means. New York: Viking, 1978

Haring, Firth. A Perfect Stranger. New York: Simon & Schuster, 1973

Howard, Elizabeth Jane. Odd Girl Out. London: Cape, 1972

Jewett, Sarah Orne. A Country Doctor. Boston: Houghton Mifflin, 1884

Jewsbury, Geraldine. Constance Herbert. London: Chapman and Hall, 1855

_____. The Half Sisters. London: Chapman and Hall, 1845

_____. Marian Withers. London: Coburn, 1851

_____. Zoe. London: Chapman and Hall, 1845

Johnson, Diane. Burning. New York: Harcourt Brace Jovanovich, 1971

_____. Loving Hands at Home. New York: Harcourt, Brace and World, 1968

_____. The Shadow Knows. New York: Knopf, 1974

Kotker, Zane. Bodies in Motion. New York: Knopf, 1972

Larsen, Nella. Passing. New York: Knopf, 1929

_____. Quicksand. New York: Knopf, 1928

Lennox, Charlotte. The Female Quixote. London: A. Millar, 1752

Lessing, Doris. The Golden Notebook. London: Michael Joseph, 1962

_____. "Our Friend Judith," in A Man and Two Women. London: Macmillan, 1958

_____. The Summer Before the Dark. London: Cape, 1973

Macaulay, Dame Rose. The World My Wilderness. London: Collins, 1950

Morrison, Toni. Sula. New York: Knopf, 1973

Porter, Katherine Anne. "Old Mortality," in Pale Horse, Pale Rider. New York: Harcourt Brace Jovanovich 1937

Pym, Barbara. A Few Green Leaves. London: Macmillan, 1980

_____. A Glass of Blessings. London: Cape, 1977

Richardson, Henry Handel. The Fortunes of Richard Mahony. London: W. Heinemann, 1930.

Rinehart, Mary Roberts. Miss Pinkerton. New York: Farrar and Rinehart, 1932

Rossner, Judith. Any Minute I Can Split. New York: McGraw-Hill, 1972

Rule, Jane. The Young in One Another's Arms. New York: Doubleday, 1977

Sackville-West, Hon. Victoria Mary. All Passion Spent. London: L. and V. Woolf, 1931

Sayers, Dorothy L. Gaudy Night. London: V. Gollancz, 1935

Shelley, Mary. Frankenstein. London: Lackington, Hughes, Harding, Mavor and Jones, 1818

Smith, Charlotte. The Old Manor House. London; J. Bell, 1793

Spark, Muriel. The Prime of Miss Jean Brodie. London: Macmillan, 1961

Trollope, Frances. The Life and Adventures of Michael Armstrong. London: H. Colburn, 1840

Walker, Margaret. Jubilee. Boston: Houghton Mifflin, 1966

Ward, Elizabeth Stuart Phelps. Dr. Zay. Boston: Houghton Mifflin, 1882

———. *The Silent Partner.* Boston: J. R. Osgood, 1871

Warner, Sylvia Townsend. *Lolly Willowes.* London: Chatto and Windus, 1926

Wharton, Edith. *Age of Innocence.* New York: Appleton, 1920

Wilson, Ethel. *Love and Salt Water.* Toronto: Macmillan, 1956

Woolson, Constance. *For the Major.* New York: Harper, 1883

CHRONOLOGY OF RECOMMENDED WORKS

1688   Behn, Aphra. *Oroonoko.* London: William Canning.

1744   Fielding, Sarah. *The Adventures of David Simple.* London: A. Millar.

1752   Lennox, Charlotte. *The Female Quixote.* London: A. Millar.

1793   Smith, Charlotte. *The Old Manor House.* London: J. Bell.

1800   Edgeworth, Maria *Castle Rackrent.* Dublin: P. Wogan.

1812   Edgeworth, Maria. *The Absentee.* London: J. Johnson.

1818   Shelley, Mary. *Frankenstein.* London: Lackington, Hughes, Harding, Mavor and Jones.

1840   Trollope, Frances. *The Life and Adventures of Michael Armstrong.* London: H. Colburn.

1845   Jewsbury, Geraldine. *The Half Sisters.* London: Chapman and Hall.

1845   Jewsbury, Geraldine. *Zoe.* London: Chapman and Hall.

1848   Gaskell, Elizabeth. *Mary Barton.* London: Chapman and Hall.

1851   Jewsbury, Geraldine. *Marian Withers.* London: Coburn.

1853   Gaskell, Elizabeth. *Cranford.* London: Chapman and Hall.

1853   Gaskell, Elizabeth. *Ruth.* London: Chapman and Hall.

1855   Jewsbury, Geraldine. *Constance Herbert.* London: Chapman and Hall.

1865	Gaskell, Elizabeth. Cousin Phillis. London: Smith, Elder and Co.	
1866	Eliot, George. Felix Holt. London: William Blackwood.	
1866	Gaskell, Elizabeth. Wives and Daughters. London: Smith, Elder and Co.	
1871	Ward, Elizabeth Stuart Phelps. The Silent Partner. Boston: J. R. Osgood.	
1876	Eliot, George. Daniel Deronda. London: William Blackwood.	
1880	Burnett, Frances Hodgson. A Fair Barbarian. New York: International Association of Newspapers and Authors.	
1882	Ward, Elizabeth Stuart Phelps. Dr. Zay. Boston: Houghton Mifflin.	
1883	Woolson, Constance. For the Major. New York: Harper.	
1884	Jewett, Sarah Orne. A Country Doctor. Boston: Houghton Mifflin.	
1896	Davis, Rebecca Harding. Dr. Warrick's Daughters. New York: Harper.	
1920	Wharton, Edith. Age of Innocence. New York: Appleton.	
1925	Glasgow, Ellen. Barren Ground. New York: Harcourt, Brace.	
1926	Warner, Sylvia Townsend. Lolly Willowes. London: Chatto and Windus.	
1928	Larsen, Nella. Quicksand. New York: Knopf.	
1929	Larsen, Nella. Passing. New York: Knopf.	
1930	Richardson, Henry Handel. The Fortunes of Richard Mahony. London: W. Heinemann.	
1931	Sackville-West, Hon. Victoria Mary. All Passion Spent. London: L. and V. Woolf.	
1932	Fitzgerald, Zelda. Save Me the Waltz. New York: Scribner's.	
1932	Rinehart, Mary Roberts. Miss Pinkerton. New York: Farrar and Rinehart.	
1935	Sayers, Dorothy L. Gaudy Night. London: V. Gollancz.	

1937   Porter, Katherine Anne. "Old Mortality," in <u>Pale Horse, Pale Rider</u>. New York: Harcourt Brace Jovanovich.

1950   Macaulay, Dame Rose. <u>The World My Wilderness</u>. London: Collins.

1956   Wilson, Ethel. <u>Love and Salt Water</u>. London: Macmillan.

1958   Lessing, Doris. "Our Friend Judith," in <u>A Man and Two Women</u>. London: Macmillan.

1961   Spark, Muriel. <u>The Prime of Miss Jean Brodie</u>. London: Macmillan.

1962   Lessing, Doris. <u>The Golden Notebook</u>. London: Michael Joseph.

1964   Bawden, Nina. <u>Under the Skin</u>. London: Longmans.

1965   Drabble, Margaret. <u>The Millstone</u>. London: Weidenfeld and Nicolson.

1966   Walker, Margaret, <u>Jubilee</u>. Boston: Houghton Mifflin.

1967   Bawden, Nina. <u>A Woman of My Age</u>. London: Longmans.

1968   Bawden, Nina. <u>A Grain of Truth</u>. London: Longmans.

1968   Johnson, Diane. <u>Loving Hands at Home</u>. New York: Harcourt, Brace and World.

1971   Johnson, Diane. <u>Burning</u>. New York: Harcourt Brace Jovanovich.

1972   Howard, Elizabeth Jane. <u>Odd Girl Out</u>. London: Cape.

1972   Kotker, Zane. <u>Bodies in Motion</u>. New York: Knopf.

1972   Rossner, Judith. <u>Any Minute I Can Split</u>. New York: McGraw-Hill.

1973   Haring, Firth. <u>A Perfect Stranger</u>. New York: Simon & Schuster.

1973   Lessing, Doris. <u>The Summer Before the Dark</u>. London: Cape.

1973   Morrison, Toni. <u>Sula</u>. New York: Knopf.

1974   Johnson, Diane. <u>The Shadow Knows</u>. New York: Knopf.

1975   Drabble, Margaret. <u>Realms of Gold</u>. London: Weidenfeld and Nicolson.

1976	Bawden, Nina.	Afternoon of a Good Woman. London: Macmillan.
1977	Drabble, Margaret.	The Ice Age. London: Weidenfeld and Nicolson.
1977	Gundy, Elizabeth.	Bliss. New York: Viking.
1977	Pym, Barbara.	A Glass of Blessings. London: Cape.
1977	Rule, Jane.	The Young in One Another's Arms. New York: Doubleday.
1978	Gundy, Elizabeth.	Cat on a Leash. New York: Viking.
1978	Hailey, Elizabeth.	A Woman of Independent Means. New York: Viking.
1978	Guy, Rosa.	Edith Jackson. New York: Viking.
1980	Pym, Barbara.	A Few Green Leaves. London: Macmillan.

INDEX

Absentee, The, 90
Afternoon of a Good Woman, The, 238
Age of Innocence, The, 5, 79 ff.
All Passion Spent, 239
Any Minute I Can Split, 45 ff.
"Are Women Human?," 258
Bawden, Nina, 6, 102 ff., 238, 278
Behn, Aphra, 2, 93 ff.
Bliss, 201 ff.
Bodies in Motion, 239
Burnett, Frances Hodgson, 89-90
Burning, 237
Castle Rackrent, 60 ff., 92
Cat on a Leash, 237
Constance Herbert, 56
Country Doctor, A, 209
Cousin Phillis, 210
Cranford, 2, 5, 34 ff., 56
Daniel Deronda, 8, 182 ff.
David Simple, 5, 15 ff., 24, 34, 56, 101, 120
Davis, Rebecca Harding, 176-7
Defoe, Daniel, 93
Dr. Warrick's Daughters, 176-7
Dr. Zay, 210
Drabble, Margaret, 10, 177, 268 ff., 278, 279 ff.
Edgeworth, Maria, 60 ff., 90, 92
Edith Jackson, 132
Eliot, George, 8, 56, 182 ff.
Fair Barbarian, A, 89
Felix Holt, 56
Female Quixote, The, 210
Few Green Leaves, A, 9, 222 ff.
Fielding, Sarah, 5, 14 ff., 24
Fitzgerald, Zelda, 209
For the Major, 178
Fortune of Richard Mahony, The, 214 ff.

Frankenstein, 177-8
Gaskell, Elizabeth, 2, 5, 8, 11, 34 ff., 147 ff., 191 ff., 210
Gaudy Night, 10, 57, 259 ff.
Glass of Blessings, A, 278
Golden Notebook, The, 10, 250 ff.
Grain of Truth, A, 278
Gundy, Elizabeth, 201 ff., 237
Guy, Rosa, 132
Hailey, Elizabeth, 238
Haring, Firth, 239
Howard, Elizabeth Jane, 238
Ice Age, The, 279 ff.
Jewett, Sarah Orne, 209
Jewsbury, Geraldine, 5, 56, 67 ff., 177, 214
Johnson, Diane, 9, 210, 229 ff., 237
Jubilee, 7, 120 ff.
Kotker, Zane, 239
Larsen, Nella, 6, 113 ff., 132
Lennox, Charlotte, 210
Lessing, Doris, 10, 239, 250 ff., 277
Life and Adventures of Michael Armstrong, The, 24 ff., 56
Lolly Willowes, 3-4
Love and Salt Water, 237-8
Loving Hands at Home, 210
Macaulay, Dame Rose, 241 ff.
Marian Withers, 177
Mary Barton, 148
Michael Armstrong, 24 ff., 56, 101
Middlemarch, 182
Millstone, The, 177

Morrison, Toni, 7, 166 ff.
Odd Girl Out, 238
Old Manor House, The, 2, 8, 135 ff.
"Old Mortality," 176
Oroonoko, 2, 93 ff., 103, 119
"Our Friend Judith," 277
Passing, 132
Perfect Stranger, A, 239
Porter, Katherine Anne, 176
Prime of Miss Jean Brodie, The, 210
Pym, Barbara, 9, 222 ff., 278
Quicksand, 6, 113 ff., 132
Realms of Gold, The, 10, 268 ff., 279
Richardson, Henry Handel, 214 ff.
Robinson Crusoe, 93
Rossner, Judith, 45 ff.
Rule, Jane, 57, 90
Ruth, 11, 147 ff.
Sackville-West, Victoria Mary, 239
Save Me the Waltz, 209
Sayers, Dorothy L., 10, 57, 241, 258 ff.
Shadow Knows, The, 9, 229 ff.
Shelley, Mary, 177-8

Silent Partner, The, 7, 156 ff., 177
Smith, Charlotte, 2, 8, 135 ff.
Spark, Muriel, 210
Sula, 7, 166 ff.
Summer Before the Dark, The, 239
Trollope, Frances, 24 ff., 78, 157
Under the Skin, 6, 102 ff.
Walker, Margaret, 7, 120 ff.
Ward, Elizabeth Stuart Phelps, 7, 156 ff., 177, 210
Warner, Sylvia Townsend, 3-4
Wharton, Edith, 5, 79 ff.
Wilson, Elizabeth, 237-8
Wives and Daughters, 8, 11, 148, 191 ff.
Woman of Independent Means, A, 238
Woman of My Age, A, 278
Woolf, Virginia, 1, 2
Woolson, Constance, 178
World My Wilderness, The, 242 ff.
Young in One Another's Arms, The, 57, 90,
Zoe, 5, 68 ff., 214